AID FOR TRADE IN ASIA AND THE PACIFIC

LEVERAGING TRADE AND DIGITAL AGREEMENTS FOR SUSTAINABLE DEVELOPMENT

JULY 2022

ASIAN DEVELOPMENT BANK

ADB

Contents

Tables, Figures, and Boxes

Tables

Figures

Boxes

Forewords

The Hon Pat Conroy MP
Minister for International Development
   and the Pacific
Government of Australia

Senator the Hon Don Farrell
Minister for Trade and Tourism
Government of Australia

Australia is pleased to support the Asian Development Bank's 2022 report on *Aid for Trade in Asia and the Pacific—Leveraging Trade and Digital Agreements for Sustainable Development*. It will make an important contribution to the eighth Global Aid for Trade Review, focused on the theme of Empowering Connected, Sustainable Trade.

The Government of Australia is steadfastly committed to a stable, peaceful, prosperous, and secure Indo-Pacific, where trade is a key part of Australia's engagement. The potential for growth and economic complementarity throughout the Indo-Pacific is significant. It is vital that we work together to secure a sustainable future for all.

Australia's aid for trade initiatives support partner countries across the region seeking to capture the benefits of a more open trading environment and rules-based trading system. We will do this by targeting our aid for trade assistance to help address the contemporary challenges faced by developing and least developed countries (LDCs) in our region while promoting inclusive and sustainable development.

This report underlines the critical role of trade in promoting economic resilience in developing countries and LDCs, especially in the coronavirus disease (COVID-19) context. In particular, the report highlights the benefits of trade and digital agreements in facilitating regional trade and recovery.

The report demonstrates the need for updated approaches to aid for trade in the region to support effective participation in such agreements, undertake reforms, and promote access to digitalization in ways that promote inclusive development and deliver the 2030 Agenda for Sustainable Development.

Australia supports targeted, needs-based aid for trade initiatives to help our Indo-Pacific partners tackle the challenges of effective participation in the digital economy. For example, through the Pacific Digital Economy Programme and Pacific Regional E-Commerce Strategy and Roadmap we are actively supporting regional approaches to address infrastructure and digital connectivity, e-commerce policy, and regulations and digital literacy.

To fully realize the benefits of trade liberalization and the digital economy, access must be available to all. This means promoting policies and programs that analyze and prioritize inclusivity to benefit women; young people; and micro, small and medium-sized enterprises (MSMEs), all of which have been disproportionately affected by the COVID-19 pandemic. This is the right thing to do, and it is essential to economic recovery and ongoing prosperity. Societies and economies prosper when women and girls can participate equally.

Australia actively promotes women's economic empowerment and MSMEs throughout its aid program. Our recently concluded A$5.6 million E-commerce Aid for Trade Fund had a particular focus on addressing barriers to e-commerce faced by women, MSMEs, and other marginalized groups in Southeast Asia and the Pacific.

We commend this year's report as a useful contribution to understanding the contemporary trade challenges and opportunities in our region, which demonstrate the important role aid for trade can play in sustainable and inclusive economic growth in the Indo-Pacific.

Albert Park
Chief Economist and Director General
Economic Research and Regional Cooperation Department
Asian Development Bank

The 2022 Global Aid for Trade Review discusses how global trade is recovering from the coronavirus disease (COVID-19) pandemic, and how to deal with the weaknesses it exposed within the international trading system. With trade central to development and economic prosperity, the disruptions in global supply chains contributed to reversing recent gains in poverty reduction and exacerbated inequality. For example, inflation from rising energy and food costs clearly hurts the poor more than those better off.

Recovery remains uneven across the Asia and the Pacific region. This report, *Aid for Trade in Asia and the Pacific—Leveraging Trade and Digital Agreements for Sustainable Development*, examines the catalytic role aid for trade can play in helping the least developed, lower-middle-income, and small island developing countries build or enhance their trade links with the global economy. It discusses how the Aid for Trade Initiative can mobilize resources effectively to accelerate integration into international markets, address supply-side constraints, and overcome other trade barriers.

Asia and the Pacific has long benefited from trade liberalization. As trade agreements proliferated, they helped the region integrate with new markets and deepen relationships with existing ones. As the pandemic showed, trade under regional agreements was more consistent and efficient than trade outside. There remains much room for improvement, and regional trade agreements present many opportunities as well as challenges.

The two current "mega-regional" agreements—the Regional Comprehensive Economic Partnership and the Comprehensive and Progressive Agreement for Trans-Pacific Partnership—require countries and businesses to better understand what the agreements provide, how they relate with existing agreements, and how best they can be used. As global value chains become increasingly complex, so do the challenges of international cooperation. Negotiating with many partners on technical policy instruments that promote comparative advantage while defending specific interests requires advanced legal skills and trade expertise. Specifically, economies graduating from the least developed countries category require assistance when evaluating policy options and avoiding, for example, preference erosion.

The global trade landscape continues to evolve rapidly. Aside from new trade agreements, there is growing complexity, depth, and rationalization of global supply chain structures, along with the wider, more extensive use of the digital economy. COVID-19 continues to accelerate this digital transformation. Yet, just 0.4% of aid for trade focuses on digitalization. Authorities must carefully review the digital regulatory landscape to help businesses join and maximize gains from a more inclusive—yet increasingly secure—digital economy. The Aid for Trade Initiative, therefore, should refocus on programs that narrow the digital divide and navigate the emerging trade rules in digital agreements, making trade more inclusive, resilient, and sustainable.

The 2022 World Trade Organization ministerial conference emphasized that trade should raise standards of living, ensure full employment, and pursue sustainable development for all. Aid for trade can help developing countries meet the challenges of efficiency, effectiveness, and inclusiveness. Assistance on trade policy and regulations can help countries quantify the costs and benefits of trade and digital agreements; ensure regulatory convergence and coherence; and bring more micro, small, and medium-sized enterprises the benefits of trade and digital trade. I hope this report adds to our understanding of how the Aid for Trade Initiative can help all economies meet these objectives.

Acknowledgments

This report was prepared by the Regional Cooperation and Integration Division (ERCI) in the Asian Development Bank (ADB) Economic Research and Regional Cooperation Department under RETA-6704: Aid for Trade for Inclusive Growth, 2020–2022 (Subproject 2) financed by ADB's Technical Assistance Special Fund and by the Department of Foreign Affairs and Trade (DFAT), Government of Australia.

Cyn-Young Park, ERCI Director, provided overall direction and supervision of the report.

Pramila Crivelli and Shawn W. Tan conducted the groundwork and coordinated the production of this report with support from Paulo Rodelio Halili. Fauzya Moore synthesized diverse contributions and wrote parts of the report. Pia Asuncion Tenchavez provided administrative support.

The main contributors of this report are Francesco Abbate, Stephanie Honey, Pramila Crivelli, and Shawn W. Tan. Background papers or box articles were contributed by Anirudh Shingal, Prachi Agarwal, Jeremy Marand, Pramila Crivelli, Jules Hugot, and Sabrina Varma.

John Eric van Zant edited the manuscript. Mike Cortes created the cover design and did the layout and typesetting. Cherry Lynn Zafaralla performed proofreading, while Marjorie Celis did the page proof checking, with support from Paulo Rodelio Halili, Carol Ongchangco, and Gerald Pascua. Support for printing and publishing this report was provided by the Printing Services Unit of ADB's Corporate Services Department and by the publishing team of the Department of Communications.

The report benefited greatly from comments and inputs by Michael Roberts (World Trade Organization); and Sabrina Varma, Dylan Roux, Matthew Busch, Kerry Sillcock, Stephen Dietz, Brendan Peace, Lydia Trotter, Katy Rengel, and Shannon White (DFAT).

The publication also benefited from valuable insights from the Office of the Chief Economist and Director General, and ADB regional departments during the review process. We are most grateful for their feedback and advice.

Abbreviations

ADB	–	Asian Development Bank
AfT	–	aid for trade
APEC	–	Asia-Pacific Economic Cooperation
ASEAN	–	Association of Southeast Asian Nations
ASYCUDA	–	UNCTAD Automated System for Customs Data
BACI	–	Base pour l'Analyse du Commerce International
COVID-19	–	coronavirus disease
CPTPP	–	Comprehensive and Progressive Agreement for Trans-Pacific Partnership
DEA	–	digital economy agreement
DEPA	–	Digital Economy Partnership Agreement
EU	–	European Union
FTA	–	free trade agreement
G20	–	Group of Twenty
G7	–	Group of Seven
GDP	–	gross domestic product
GSP	–	Generalized System of Preferences
GVC	–	global value chain
HCGm	–	highly concentrated import
HCGx	–	highly concentrated export
HHI	–	Herfindahl-Hirschman Index
HS	–	Harmonized System
ICT	–	information and communication technology
IMF	–	International Monetary Fund
Lao PDR	–	Lao People's Democratic Republic
LDC	–	least developed country
MFN	–	most-favored nation
MSMEs	–	micro, small, and medium-sized enterprises
NTMs	–	nontariff measures
ODA	–	official development assistance
OECD	–	Organisation for Economic Co-operation and Development
PACER Plus	–	Pacific Agreement on Closer Economic Relations Plus
PPML	–	Poisson pseudo maximum likelihood
PRC	–	People's Republic of China
RCEP	–	Regional Comprehensive Economic Partnership
RTA	–	regional trade agreement
SDG	–	Sustainable Development Goal
SMEs	–	small and medium-sized enterprises
UNCTAD	–	United Nations Conference on Trade and Development
UK	–	United Kingdom
US	–	United States
WITS	–	World Integrated Trade Solution
WTO	–	World Trade Organization

Highlights

As the coronavirus disease (COVID-19) pandemic swept through Asia and the Pacific in 2020, it slashed economic growth and gave rise to new trade challenges that need addressing to ensure inclusive and sustainable recovery. The Aid for Trade initiative of the World Trade Organization (WTO) has an important role to play.

Recovery has begun, but it is fragile and uneven. AfT can help establish firmer, trade-led economic growth that reduces inequalities worsened by the pandemic, and it can help ensure that new digital technologies benefit everyone. However, aid for trade, particularly category 1, trade policy and regulations, requires reform and refocusing to be effective in these circumstances. More emphasis could be placed on adjustment assistance and digitalization.

This report explores the promise of aid for trade in economic recovery and the need for reorienting it for maximum benefit.

In 2017–2019, the Asia and Pacific region received 35% of average global aid for trade flows. In 2019, aid for trade inflows to the region totaled $16.4 billion. This made the Asia and the Pacific the second-highest recipient of AfT disbursements in the world after Africa. Within the region, South Asia received 53%, the largest share; Southeast Asia 29.6%; and Central Asia 10.3%. The Pacific received about 4% of total inflows. Least developed countries (LDCs) in Asia and the Pacific accounted for 36.1% of total inflows in 2020 with substantial increases to Bangladesh, Myanmar, and Solomon Islands, and a substantial decrease to Afghanistan[a] in the last 5 years.

Since 2009, regional support for aid for trade outpaced contributions by nonregional donors. In 2020, the Asian Development Bank, Germany, Japan, and the World Bank contributed about three-quarters of AfT disbursements to Asia and the Pacific. Contributions have been highly sector-specific. Between 2002 and 2019, the services sector grew fastest among all sectors, with strong growth in transport and storage. Energy investments made up the second-largest share of aid for trade. Agriculture ranked third, and banking and financial services fifth. Disbursements to the primary sector and industry declined; the two sectors grew much slower than other sectors.

Toward an Inclusive and Sustainable Recovery: The Role of Aid for Trade

Aid for trade can support recovery in Asia and the Pacific, particularly lower-middle-income countries and least developed countries. Aid for trade can help by enabling regional trade agreements to deliver on economic growth, providing adjustment assistance, and importantly, enabling the growth of the digital economy. The region's recovery is advancing, with merchandise trade rebounding 19.7% in 2021 after

[a] ADB placed on hold its assistance in Afghanistan effective 15 August 2021. ADB Statement on Afghanistan | Asian Development Bank (published on 10 November 2021). Manila. This report was prepared based on the information available for Afghanistan as of 31 July.

falling 7%–8% in 2019–2020. However, the services sector has not yet recovered from the steep decline of 21.2% that followed global pandemic control measures. These measures proved catastrophic for tourism and transport services. Foreign direct investment in the region increased during the pandemic, with inflows outpacing growth in North and South America.

Overall recovery in the region hinges on effective trade policy making, recovery of severely affected sectors, and the strategic growth of the digital economy. Digital technologies supported economic growth during the pandemic, and the pandemic accelerated the emergence of the digital economy. Recovery will require greater focus on addressing inequality in the region, including digital inequality.

Recovery is highly uneven among and within countries. Substantial increases in pandemic-related debt are a problem for many lower-middle-income and least developed countries. Growth in transport and tourism lags almost everywhere, Asia and the Pacific must also overcome challenges in lingering supply chain disruptions, shortages of key production inputs, spillover from the February 2022 Russian invasion of Ukraine, global inflationary pressures, the rising costs of energy and food, and debt.

COVID-19 exacerbated inequalities within countries. White-collar workers were able to sustain incomes by shifting to work-from-home as social distancing measures took over. But low-paid, low-skilled, blue-collar workers faced redundancy as factories, manufacturing plants, and offices closed. Worse still, frontline workers saw working conditions grow more dangerous from infection and faced rising redundancies. Even as the pandemic accelerated the shift to the digital economy, more than 2 billion adults in Asia still had no access to the internet and 1 billion had no access to financial services. As countries struggle to recover, poor access to the digital economy and lack of education on how to use it risk worsening inequality between and within countries.

Many of the most severely affected manufacturing and services sectors were staffed by women. These included textiles, apparel, footwear, tourism, travel, telecommunications, and health care. In prepandemic Bangladesh, 80% of the workforce in the readymade garment sector were women. In the first quarter of 2020, orders declined 45.8% compared to 2019, reaching an 81% contraction in April 2020 alone. Order cancellations hurt women's employment in Cambodia, Viet Nam, and several other countries in the region. Women were also disproportionately harmed by the collapse of hospitality and tourism during the pandemic, since they made up a large share of the workforce in those service subsectors.

Aid for trade should address inequality within the region. Globalization, trade liberalization, and financial deregulation have created considerable inequality in Asia and the Pacific, exacerbated by COVID-19. To benefit from trade liberalization, countries must be able to identify vulnerable sectors and respond by upgrading skills, retraining workforces, and providing adjustment assistance. Trade liberalization needs to be accompanied by policies and programs that promote inclusivity. Aid for trade should provide much more analysis of inequality and the means to overcome it.

Aid for trade can support trade liberalization and access to digitalization and provide adjustment assistance to affected sectors. These three areas are key to future growth in the region. Aid for trade, particularly category 1, trade policy and regulations and category 4, adjustment assistance need to be reconfigured and increased to support recovery. Aid for trade expenditures on the digital economy could be increased and applied to enabling universal access.

Aid for trade can help deepen intraregional trade. Exports from the Asia and Pacific region are still concentrated on the United States and the People's Republic of China. Considerably more work is needed in raising living standards to grow and diversify regional markets, through creating value-added products, high-quality jobs, and skills training in digitalization. More work is needed on creating an enabling environment for global value chain investment, liberalization of trade in intermediate goods, and regulatory clarity and coherence in the emerging digital economy. Aid for trade can help countries build capacity to meet these challenges.

Aid for Trade and Trade Agreements

Trade agreements played a key role in maintaining economic activity during the pandemic and will continue to do so in the future. The region is home to mega-regional trade agreements—the Comprehensive and Progressive Agreement for Trans-Pacific Partnership and the Regional Comprehensive Economic Partnership—along with many bilateral and regional trade agreements. Twelve new agreements entered into force during COVID-19. Five other agreements were signed or concluded negotiations. Trade under trade agreements was more resilient than trade not under trade agreements. The potential for economic growth under trade agreements is enormous if countries are able to (i) benefit from them, (ii) negotiate access on favorable terms, and (iii) enhance regulatory convergence.

Aid for trade is needed to help identify the costs and benefits of trade agreements. Amid stalemate at the World Trade Organization (WTO), many countries now lack a benchmark from which to assess the costs and benefits of the new agreements. In many regions, regional trade agreements infamously offer a "noodle bowl" of overlapping rules and regulations. Some agreements liberalize trade rules, others less so; the difference is often in the fine print of the agreements on rules of origin, cumulation, nontariff measures, and a host of other regulatory issues.

Aid for trade can help regional trade grow and develop by using better-evidenced approaches to the design, negotiation, and implementation of trade agreements. Countries enter into trade agreements hoping to participate in the most effective trade regimes. However, new agreements do not always bring additional market access over the existing ones, resulting in low preference uptake. Regulatory convergence, a key element in attracting investment and building digital capacity, is even more opaque, and much more work is needed to determine which agreements improve convergence and coherence and which do not.

Aid for trade should help make trade agreements transparent. Trade agreements should be quantified and assessed for their contribution to growth and development, and their impact on inequality and sustainability. Governments need to have a better idea of best practices in negotiating and implementing trade agreements. Small, medium-sized, and even micro enterprises, so important to Asia and the Pacific, need user-friendly information to take advantage of regional trade agreements. Aid for trade could shift from explaining trade liberalization and trade agreements to a more rigorous, research-based approach. Engaging experts, aid for trade could support activities to (i) quantify and assess costs and benefits of existing and new agreements and their potential for economic growth, (ii) estimate preference utilization, and (iii) assess degrees of regulatory convergence..

Aid for trade could support developing economies overcome graduation and preference erosion. Least developed country graduation is an overarching objective of the international community. Graduation means that countries are growing economically and are making progress in meeting the Sustainable Development Goals (SDGs). Market access in the form of unilateral and/or nonreciprocal preferential tariff treatment for products originating in LDCs is one of the most utilized special and differential treatment provisions in the WTO. Graduating countries will eventually lose highly preferential access, which is a key, and in some cases the main driver of economic growth. Preference erosion is also driven by the proliferation of regional trade agreements (RTAs) in Asia and the Pacific. Aid for trade can help graduating LDCs and developing countries explore policy options and identify new market access opportunities through regional cooperation and RTAs.

Aid for trade could level the playing field between small countries negotiating with larger countries or clarify the issues for small countries negotiating with each other. To do so, it could provide well-researched and quantified evidence of costs and benefits—that is, what agreements will deliver and what countries may lose. This shift to a win-win approach to trade negotiations and trade agreements is in the interest of all countries; the failed Doha Round ended because some countries simply had too much to lose from the outcome. A more evidence-based approach can help all countries maximize benefits.

Aid for Trade and Digitalization

Only 0.4% of aid for trade goes to digital economy issues—yet more digitalization means more trade. The WTO rules in the General Agreement on Trade in Services do not address the new challenges of the digital economy. From 2005 to 2019, trade in services in the region almost tripled, and trade in digitally deliverable services expanded from $403.4 billion in 2005 to $1.4 trillion in 2019. Digital services trade holds substantial promise for developing Asia and the Pacific. Countries with better digital connectivity have greater trade openness and sell more products to more markets. Digitally deliverable services trade proved more robust and resilient during the pandemic.

Aid for trade can help developing countries, particularly the least developed, engage in the digital economy. Countries that lack the infrastructure, human capital, and regulatory environment to trade digitally may suffer a "digital divide" that erodes their resilience to future shocks. Many countries in the region need aid for trade to support them in meeting challenges including digital connectivity, infrastructure, access to technologies, and digital literacy and skills.

Aid for trade can help identify regulatory heterogeneity and ways to promote cooperation and coherence. Digitalization can offer specific advantages for small enterprises and women entrepreneurs. However, regulatory heterogeneity can add to the costs of exporting, with small businesses least able to absorb the high fixed trade costs. Regulatory barriers are emerging in many countries. Micro, small, and medium-sized enterprises (MSMEs) make up 97% of regional businesses and employ 69% of the workforce in Asia. Regulatory barriers pose a serious risk to growth and employment in MSMEs. Digitally delivered services face a range of barriers in international markets, and services exporters can struggle if regulatory settings at home or in foreign markets are diverse, opaque, and costly.

Policy Reform for Aid for Trade

Aid for trade could support the design and implementation of trade and digital agreements by developing international, regional, and national capacities to analyze and assess trade and digital agreements, disseminate useable information on them, and enhance the capacity of governments to negotiate in their best interests. How aid for trade might be deployed to ensure that trade and digital agreements are effective in promoting both trade and inclusive economic growth are the subjects of the first four chapters of this report.

Chapter 5 then proposes revised directions in aid for trade along the following lines:

- Building technical tools and knowledge to support policy dialogue and awareness raising
- Country-specific technical assistance and capacity building
- Trade adjustment assistance
- Reorienting aid for trade from "hard infrastructure" toward supporting effective policy development and regulatory coherence, and promoting regional or subregional approaches for cross-border related issues

The report highlights the importance of the Aid for Trade Initiative for development in Asia and the Pacific and recommends ways to refocus and modernize it. By supporting trade and investment, aid for trade can reduce vulnerability, strengthen resilience, foster economic growth, and help developing Asia meet its SDGs. The initiative needs refocusing and modernizing. It dates back to 2005, and must now better reflect new economic and trade realities. For this purpose, multilateral, regional and bilateral cooperation is needed among donors and recipient countries, thus ensuring sustainable and inclusive development for all.

PART I
AID FOR TRADE LANDSCAPE

1. Aid for Trade in the Context of COVID-19

The coronavirus disease (COVID-19) pandemic revealed weaknesses in the international trading system. Trade performance was severely impacted by supply chains disruption and labor shortages. There were production delays and economic woes across the world. The pandemic also exposed structural issues related to aid for trade support programs as fiscal policies and the traditional aid for trade assistance proved to be insufficient to support trade recovery. In the last 2 decades, most of aid for trade has been directed toward economic infrastructure. Yet, the global trade landscape has changed: bilateral, regional, and plurilateral trade agreements have increased in number and scope, countries have relied on trade policy measures to respond to crisis, and the growing importance of the digital economy creates new challenges. These changes highlight an overdue need to refocus the aid for trade program. Developing countries need support in "soft" infrastructure to be provided with the necessary policy and regulatory tools to effectively reap the benefits of international trade.

1.1   COVID-19 Trade and Fiscal Policy Responses

1.1.1   Trends and Impact of COVID-19 on Merchandise and Services Trade

Introduction

Economic growth in developing Asia rebounded strongly to 7.1% in 2021 from 0.9% in 2020, and may grow to 5.1% in 2022, boosted by increasing domestic demand and healthy exports. However, Asia and the Pacific now faces renewed challenges in its recovery from COVID-19 with lingering supply chain disruptions, spillovers from the Russian invasion of Ukraine in February 2022, and global inflationary pressures. Recovery from the pandemic is particularly uneven among countries in the region. Increasing trade-led growth and trade openness will be an important part of the recovery.

Trade performance

Asia and the Pacific's share of global trade grew markedly from 2005 to 2020 (Figures 1.1 and 1.2). In the period before and during the COVID-19 crisis, 2018–2020, the region's share of world merchandise exports rose just 2.6 percentage points, slower than in previous years. Its share of global merchandise imports stabilized around 34% in that period. However, during 2019–2020, the value of global merchandise trade dropped sharply, by around 7%–8%. And in 2020, the region's share of global imports of services dropped to its lowest level in 7 years while its share of services exports remained stable around 25% (Figure 1.2). The values of exports and imports of services declined 20%–23% during 2019–2020, a decline similar to the total global decline in services trade during the same period. The contraction in trade notwithstanding, Asia and the Pacific was the world's most resilient region during the pandemic, experiencing the slowest decline of exports and imports by value.

Figure 1.1: Share of Asia and the Pacific in Global Merchandise Trade
(%)

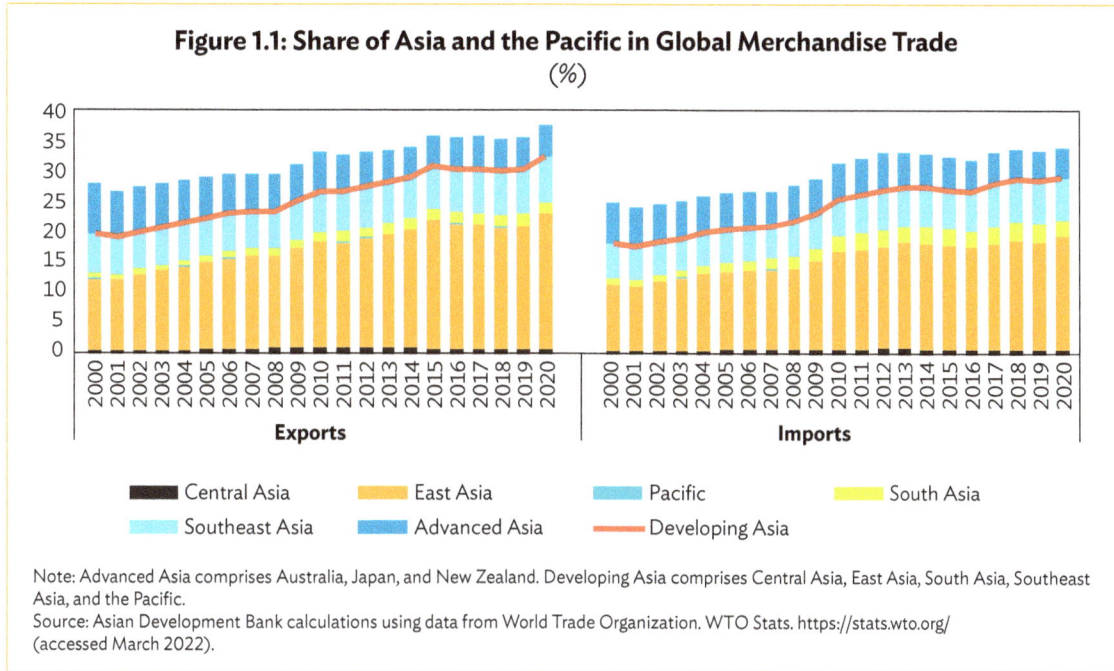

Exports   **Imports**

Central Asia   East Asia   Pacific   South Asia
Southeast Asia   Advanced Asia   Developing Asia

Note: Advanced Asia comprises Australia, Japan, and New Zealand. Developing Asia comprises Central Asia, East Asia, South Asia, Southeast Asia, and the Pacific.
Source: Asian Development Bank calculations using data from World Trade Organization. WTO Stats. https://stats.wto.org/ (accessed March 2022).

Figure 1.2: Share of Asia and the Pacific in Global Services Trade
(%)

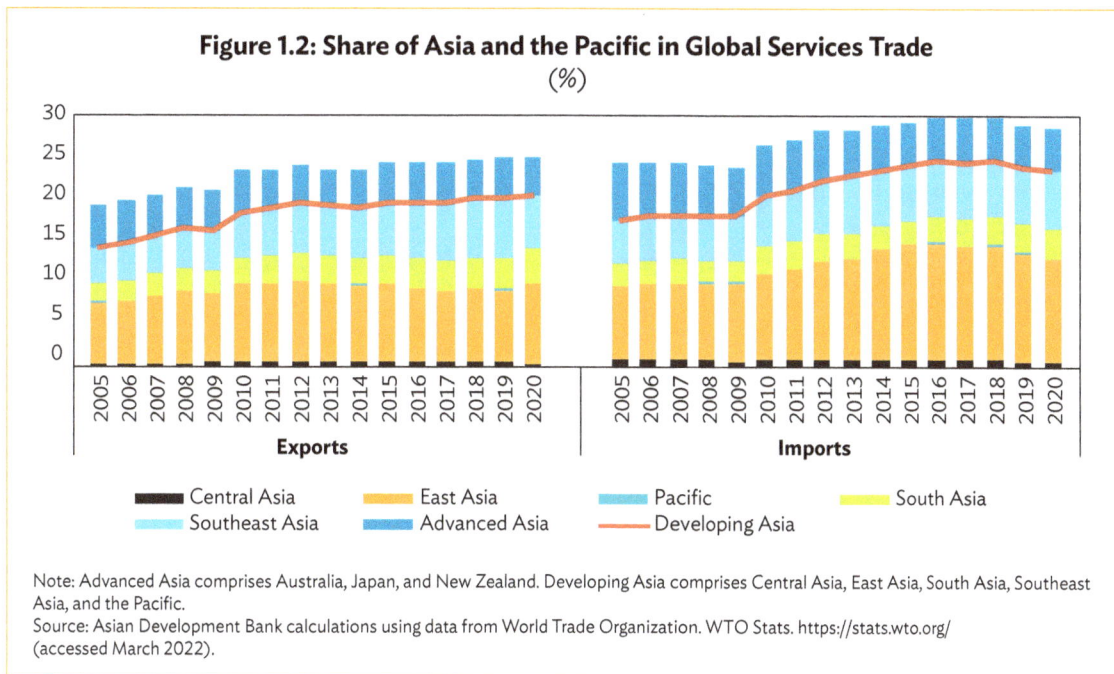

Exports   **Imports**

Central Asia   East Asia   Pacific   South Asia
Southeast Asia   Advanced Asia   Developing Asia

Note: Advanced Asia comprises Australia, Japan, and New Zealand. Developing Asia comprises Central Asia, East Asia, South Asia, Southeast Asia, and the Pacific.
Source: Asian Development Bank calculations using data from World Trade Organization. WTO Stats. https://stats.wto.org/ (accessed March 2022).

Wide disparities in trade performance existed within Asia and the Pacific during 2019–2020. Trade in all subregions contracted during the pandemic, with sharper declines in services trade (Figure 1.3). Among the subregions, the reduction in trade at the onset of the pandemic was sharpest in the Pacific developing member countries: merchandise imports declined 27.3% and exports 18.7%, and the value of services exports fell 64.3% during 2019–2020. Central Asia was the second-hardest-hit subregion: merchandise exports declined 18.1% and services exports 37.4% in the same period.

Figure 1.3: Merchandise and Services Trade Value, 2019–2020
(constant 2019 $, annual change %)

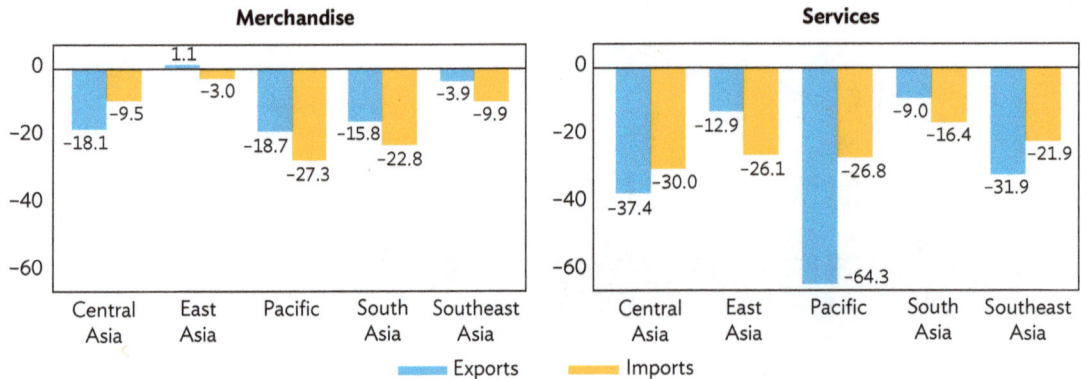

Merchandise

Services

Source: Asian Development Bank calculations using data from World Trade Organization. WTO Stats. https://stats.wto.org/ (accessed March 2022).

Exports for all merchandise subsectors declined during 2019–2020, with the exception of textiles, machinery, and transport equipment, which grew marginally. Trade in fuels and mining products, which represented more than two-thirds of trade in primary products in 2019, decreased by approximately 20%. Conversely, machinery and transport equipment, which accounted for more than half of trade in manufactures, grew in current value. Trade in manufactures did not decline as sharply as trade in raw materials and services.

As a result of cross-border restrictions during the pandemic, trade in travel services, the services subsector with the second-highest value in 2019 (25.5% of exports and 30.0% of imports), fell by more than half during 2019–2020 (Figure 1.4). Within trade in travel services, business, and personal services fell more than 70%, and the value of tourism-related services in travel and passenger transport fell more than 99%.

Figure 1.4: Annual Change in Trade Value by Subsector, 2019–2020
(%, constant 2019 $)

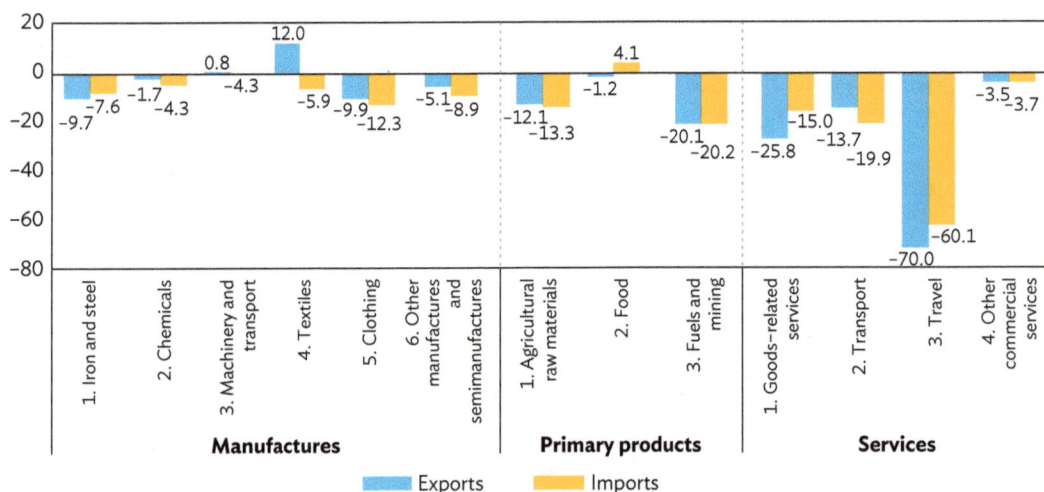

Source: Asian Development Bank calculations using data from World Trade Organization. WTO Stats. https://stats.wto.org/ (accessed March 2022).

Merchandise trade

Manufacturing has dominated Asia trade since 2005. Machinery and transport equipment represent the bulk of manufacturing trade (59.2% in 2020); within this subsector, the share of integrated circuits and electronic components increased continuously from 2012 (+9.8 percentage points) to reach 30.1% of manufacturing trade in 2020. The manufacturing sector, which accounted for about two-thirds of total trade in 2005, declined steadily to 60.2% of total trade in 2019. The share of services trade grew during the same period. During 2019–2020, the share of manufactures rose 4.3 percentage points while the share of services fell 3.1 percentage points. The total value of manufacturing trade contracted more slowly (–0.7%) than trade in services (–21.2%) during the pandemic.

Exports from all merchandise subsectors declined during 2019–2020, with the exception of textiles, machinery, and transport equipment. Trade in fuels and mining products, which represented more than two-thirds of trade in primary products in 2019, decreased about 20%. Conversely, machinery and transport equipment, which accounted for more than half of trade in manufactures, grew in current value. As a result, trade in manufactures did not decline as sharply as trade in raw materials and services.

Services

Services trade varied considerably. Trade in transport and tourism declined sharply, with negative implications for tourism-dependent economies and Pacific island countries. Digitally delivered services increased rapidly.

In 2020, at the height of the pandemic, Asia and the Pacific's share of global service imports dropped to its lowest level in 7 years, while its share in services exports remained stable at around 25%. With cross-border restrictions during the pandemic, trade in travel services (25.5% of exports and 30.0% of services imports) declined more than half during 2019–2020. Trade in travel, business, and personal services fell more than 70% while the value of tourism-related services in travel and passenger transport fell by more than 99%. Conversely, trade in digitally delivered services increased possibly by as much as a decade's worth of growth in 2 years.

Between 2019 and 2020, the countries most affected by the downturn in services trade included nine small Pacific island countries (Fiji, Kiribati, the Marshall Islands, Niue, Palau, Papua New Guinea, Samoa, Solomon Islands, and Tonga); Maldives in the Indian Ocean; and three landlocked developing countries in Central Asia (Azerbaijan, Kazakhstan, and Turkmenistan).

Trade openness

Trade openness in all subregions contracted during the pandemic, with sharper declines in the services trade. Since 2018, the costs and time to trade associated with inspection procedures, customs clearance, and documentary compliance with rules of the destination, proof of origin, and transit countries, declined markedly in Asia and the Pacific. Since 2018, average export costs declined 7.8% and import cost 6.2%. Services trade barriers also declined, but more slowly.

South Asia recorded the highest combined reduction in time to trade (Figure 1.5). During 2018–2020, the average combined time to export and import fell 21.4%. By contrast, the reduction was smallest in the Pacific (–4.5%), followed by Central Asia (–12.5%). The Pacific was the only subregion where trade costs in current United States (US) dollars rose during 2019–2020 (+0.6% for exports and +2.1% for imports). In Asia and the Pacific, average export costs declined 7.8% and import costs 6.2%.

Figure 1.5: Average Time and Cost to Trade by Subregion, Documentary, and Border Compliance, 2015–2020

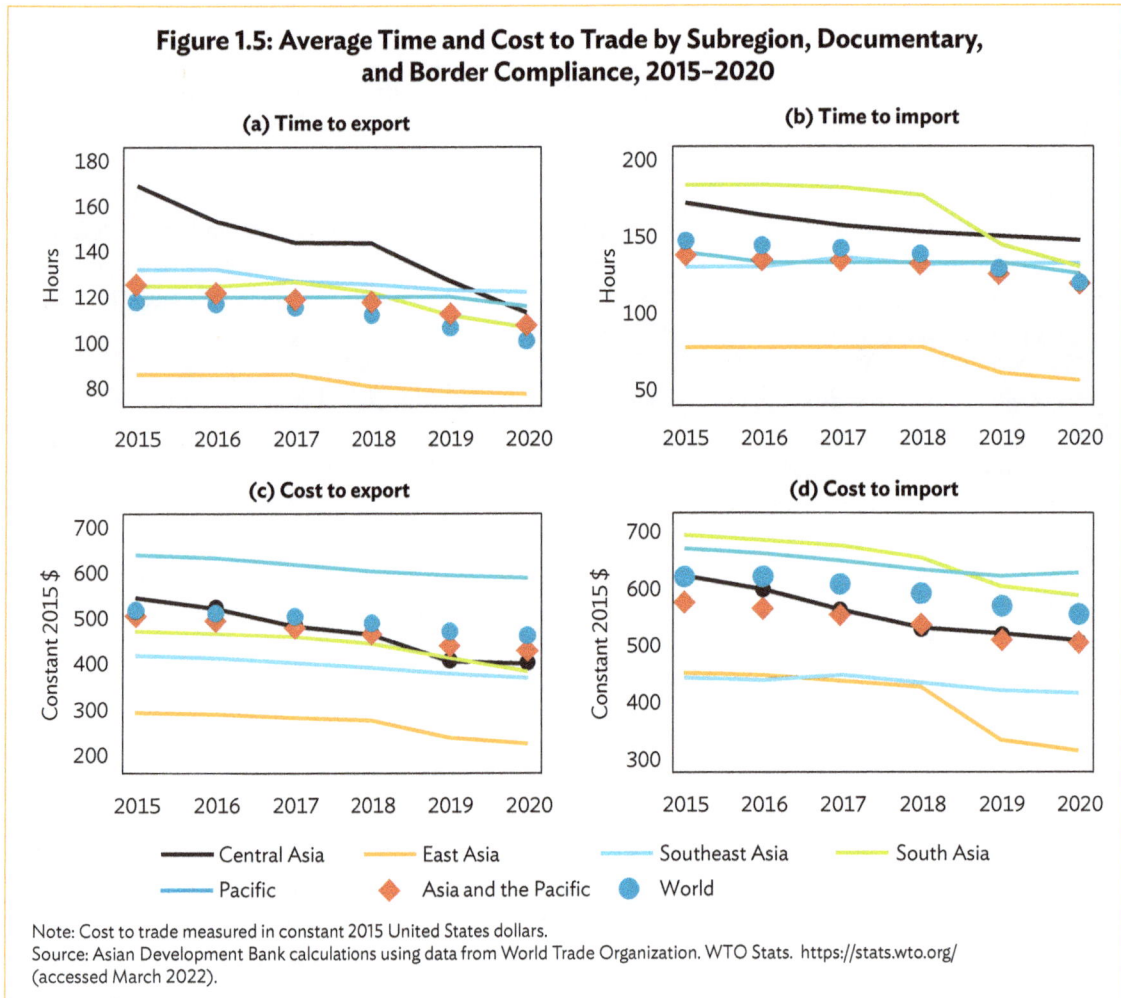

Note: Cost to trade measured in constant 2015 United States dollars.
Source: Asian Development Bank calculations using data from World Trade Organization. WTO Stats. https://stats.wto.org/ (accessed March 2022).

However, data from the Organisation for Economic Co-operation and Development (OECD) Services Trade Restrictiveness Index show that removal of trade barriers declined during the pandemic. Restrictions on trade in services fell for the vast majority of categories during 2014–2021. Openness in 13 out of 22 categories also declined during 2018–2021. In particular, trade openness declined in 80% of the categories listed in the transport and distribution supply group: notably, the air transport index declined by 0.015 from 0.474 to 0.459 from 2014 to 2017 but remained stable between 2018 and 2021.

While WTO rules permit use of trade restrictions in public emergencies, they require these to be temporary, lasting only for the duration of the crisis. Export controls can lead to negative spillovers, including constraining the ability of firms to ramp up production. This, in turn, results in increased prices and impedes the ability of other countries to import supplies. Trade restrictions may impede the flow of trade without necessarily meeting their objective of increasing domestic consumption or consumer protection, as discussed in the next section.

1.1.2 Trade Impact of COVID-19 Trade Policy Measures on Food and Medical Products

During emergencies, open trade can be pivotal in ensuring the supply of essential goods get to where they are needed, such as medical supplies and food. In response to the COVID-19 pandemic, countries implemented temporary trade liberalizing and trade-restricting measures on essential items, particularly medical products and food. Countries imposed most trade policy measures, multilateral and bilateral, during the first peak of the pandemic, March 2020, and/or in months immediately following (Figure 1.6). However, the introduction of new trade policy measures has slowed significantly since 2020. Many countries reverted to the precrisis status quo in trade policy measures by 2021 as their ability to manage the pandemic progressed.

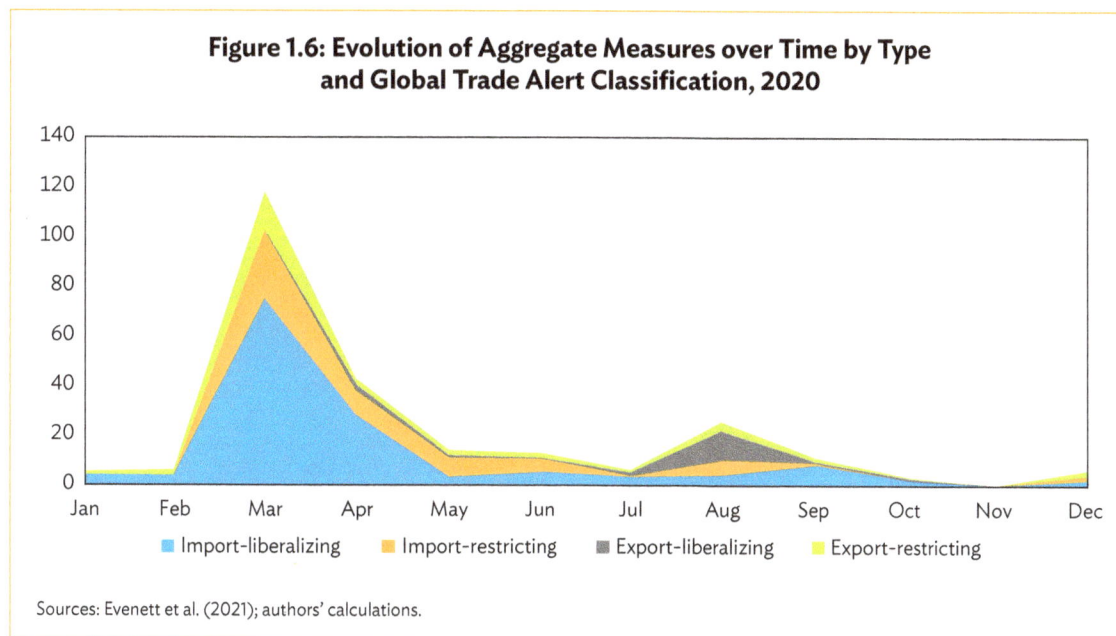

Figure 1.6: Evolution of Aggregate Measures over Time by Type and Global Trade Alert Classification, 2020

Sources: Evenett et al. (2021); authors' calculations.

Countries with the highest number of COVID-19 cases instituted a greater number of trade liberalizing and trade-restricting, both multilateral and bilateral. Some heavily affected countries chose to control trade in food products to meet domestic needs and protect local producers. Medical goods attracted a greater proportion of liberalizing policy measures (68%) aimed at facilitating essential imports and to meet the surge in both domestic and international demand.

Authorities implemented many policy measures to liberalize exports and imports of food and medical goods. Many measures restricting trade in medical goods in 2020 were no longer in force by 2021; conversely, about half of measures imposed to restrict trade in food products in 2020 remained in force in 2021.

Developing Asia introduced most multilateral measures, restrictive and liberalizing, while developed Asia instituted bilateral trade-liberalizing measures. Developing Asia implemented about twice as many multilateral trade liberalizing measures as trade-restricting measures, although bilateral trade policy measures demonstrated a more varied profile. Countries either liberalized bilateral imports or restricted exports to meet increased domestic demand during the peak of the crisis. Over time, the number of export restrictions declined drastically.

A comparison of the number of COVID-19 cases in each of the Asian Development Bank (ADB) members (Figure 1.7), found a positive relationship between the higher number of import-liberalizing measures and a high incidence of infections. The People's Republic of China (PRC), India, and Indonesia had the highest number of cases and of trade-restricting measures. The number of trade-liberalizing measures also increased as the number of cases dropped.

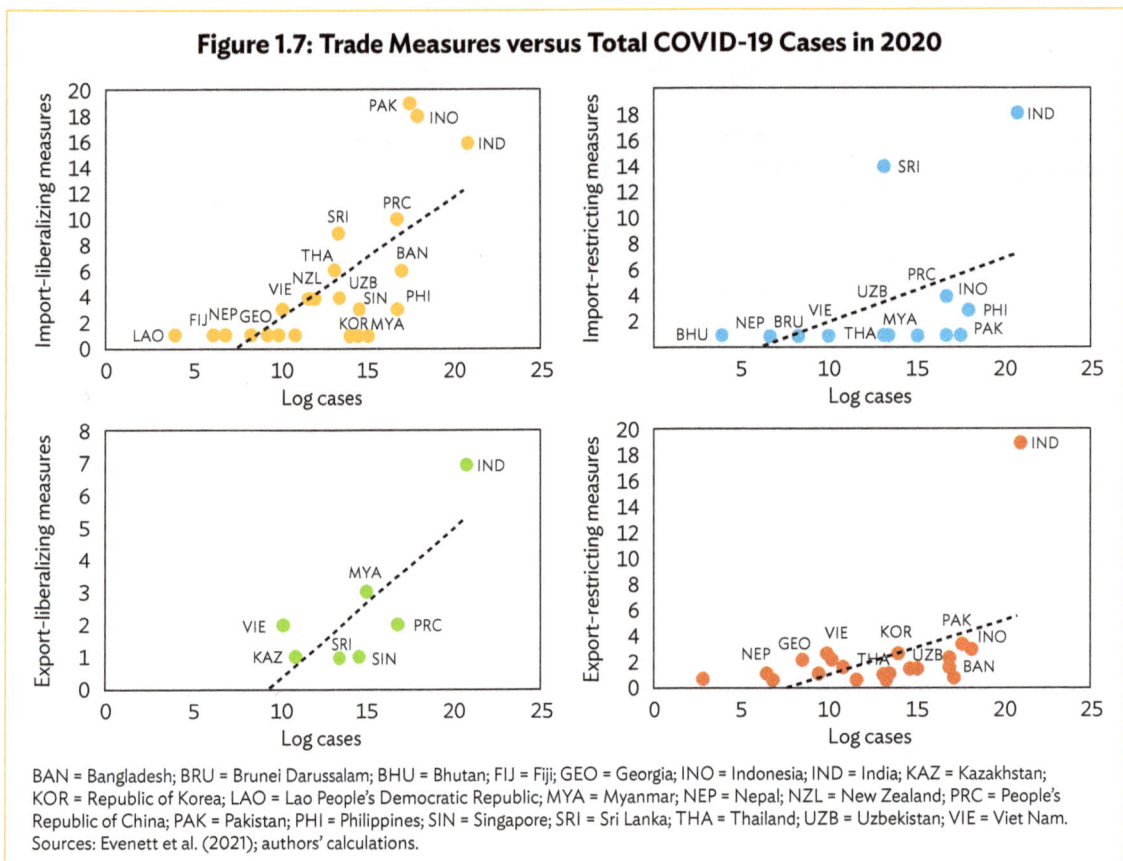

Figure 1.7: Trade Measures versus Total COVID-19 Cases in 2020

BAN = Bangladesh; BRU = Brunei Darussalam; BHU = Bhutan; FIJ = Fiji; GEO = Georgia; INO = Indonesia; IND = India; KAZ = Kazakhstan; KOR = Republic of Korea; LAO = Lao People's Democratic Republic; MYA = Myanmar; NEP = Nepal; NZL = New Zealand; PRC = People's Republic of China; PAK = Pakistan; PHI = Philippines; SIN = Singapore; SRI = Sri Lanka; THA = Thailand; UZB = Uzbekistan; VIE = Viet Nam.
Sources: Evenett et al. (2021); authors' calculations.

Trade-restrictive and liberalizing measures included 112 import policy reforms implemented across 22 jurisdictions. Many liberalized imports of drugs and medicines (including vaccines), medical consumables, and medical equipment. There were also 23 export controls aimed at restricting exports of these medical products. Among ADB developing member countries (DMCs), Bangladesh, Indonesia, the PRC, and Thailand displayed the most policy activity, closely followed by India and Uzbekistan (Figure 1.8a). For food products, 13 DMCs imposed 44 import policy reforms to restrict imports, and 37 policy reforms to liberalize food imports. Only 11 export control measures were imposed, 50% of which restricted food exports. In South Asia, Pakistan and Sri Lanka implemented a number of policy measures, 18 and 13 measures, respectively. While Pakistan mainly liberalized import of food products, Sri Lanka tended to restrict such imports (Figure 1.8b).

In all countries, measures varied across the 12 months of the year. As expected, authorities imposed most import measures on medical products in March 2020 and in the months that followed to meet growing demand for medical goods around the world during the first peak of the pandemic. In March, 73 import policy measures were applied on medical consumables, medicines, and drugs and medical equipment. On the export side, measures to liberalize exports of medical products surged in March and August to ensure global demand was met for essential items, central to containing the spread of the disease. For food products, the number of import measures outweighed the number of export measures throughout the year. This was especially true during March–August, when authorities imposed over 85% of the import policy measures, with the highest spike in March, with 31 measures applied across 13 jurisdictions. Authorities also implemented a large majority of export measures on food products during the same period, making it the most active period for trade policy activity in response to the pandemic.

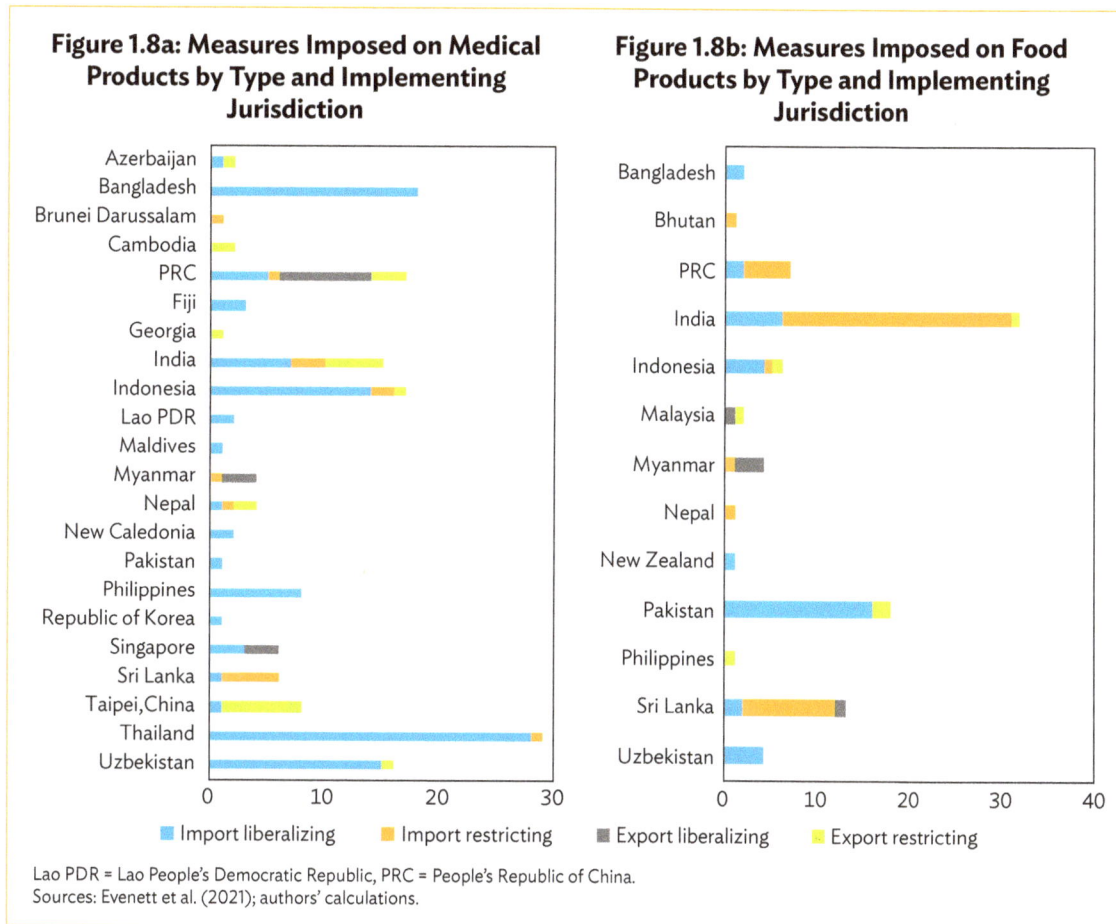

Figure 1.8a: Measures Imposed on Medical Products by Type and Implementing Jurisdiction

Figure 1.8b: Measures Imposed on Food Products by Type and Implementing Jurisdiction

Lao PDR = Lao People's Democratic Republic, PRC = People's Republic of China.
Sources: Evenett et al. (2021); authors' calculations.

Impact

During the pandemic, governments imposed export control measures and requisitioned domestic supplies of essential goods. Such policies tended to exacerbate rather than facilitate provision of vital equipment to health care workers by increasing prices and market volatility, and distorting investment decisions. A structural gravity model analyzing the passthrough between trade policy and trade suggests that they may not have yielded expected outcomes. Appendix 1 discusses the methodology applied and detailed regression results.

In summary, among bilateral measures, import liberalization increased bilateral exports by 8.4%; bilateral exports of medical products by 11.0%; and of medical consumables by 5.4%. Counterintuitively, however, bilateral import restrictions increased bilateral imports of food products and raised bilateral imports and medical exports; all results were estimated at the 1% level of statistical significance. Bilateral export liberalization undertaken during 2020 reduced medical equipment exports in the following months, though the result is only weakly significant.

Exports of drugs and medicines and imports of food products did not necessarily respond to policy measures along expected lines (food imports were more consistent with traditional theory), suggesting that other, short-term or political economy factors likely determined the trade policy passthrough to trade flows. Targeting aid for trade (AfT) at trade policies and regulation may not be optimal for these products; more direct aid interventions aimed at building productive capacity or improving the social and economic infrastructure may be more appropriate to attain desired outcomes.

While DMCs made use of multilateral and bilateral policy measures to ensure supply of essential products during the pandemic, these efforts may not have always yielded the desired outcome. This has implications for DMCs that are particularly reliant on trade policy as an instrument, and for AfT donors in the context of aid design and implementation.

1.1.3 COVID-19 Responses and Impact of Economic Stimulus Packages

Accommodating policy support and prospects for recovery buoyed financial conditions in the first half of 2021. However, financial uncertainties have emerged as inflation concerns in advanced economies have signaled early monetary policy normalization. This scenario may lead to tighter liquidity, lower capital inflows, and weaker regional currencies. Higher interest rates, coupled with growing debt from governments and corporations, may also lead to higher borrowing costs and payment difficulties.

Many governments reacted to the sharp economic decline precipitated by the pandemic by providing support to households and businesses. The support package generally comprised wage support for workers, tax relief for companies, and direct income to households. By March 2021, the Asian member economies of the Asia-Pacific Economic Cooperation (APEC) forum had announced policy packages of $3.29 trillion, or 17.2% of regional gross domestic product (GDP), according to the ADB COVID-19 Policy Database. Much of this support focused on providing direct income support to households and firms.

Developed economies in Asia and the Pacific had the fiscal resources to provide these support packages; many developing economies did not. According to the International Monetary Fund Fiscal Monitor,[1] average additional spending and foregone income among G20 advanced economies was 12.9% of GDP from January 2020 to June 2021.[2] In contrast, the corresponding figures for emerging economies is 4.3% of GDP and 3.2% for low-income economies.

The additional spending has reduced the fiscal space of countries, which was exacerbated by the reduction in tax revenues from slower economic activity. According to the World Bank and International Monetary Fund's joint Debt Sustainability Framework for Low-Income Countries, many such countries were already at high risk of debt distress, including DMCs such as the Lao People's Democratic Republic (Lao PDR), the Marshall Islands, Papua New Guinea, Samoa, Tajikistan, and Tuvalu. The COVID-19 support packages have increased government indebtedness and may reduce financial resources to implement other government priorities.

---

[1]   Source: See International Monetary Fund Fiscal Monitor Database of Country Fiscal Measures in Response to the COVID-19 Pandemic. https://www.imf.org/en/Topics/imf-and-covid19/Fiscal-Policies-Database-in-Response-to-COVID-19 (accessed May 2022).

[2]   The G20 advanced economies are Australia, Canada, the European Union, France, Germany, Italy, Japan, the Republic of Korea, Spain, the United Kingdom, and the United States. The average number includes spending on the health sector (2%) and nonhealth sector (10.9%).

These responses are straining governments' fiscal positions. Sharply slower economic growth and fiscal stimulus are raising public debt ratios. The COVID-19 pandemic sharply lowered short-term growth forecasts across the region. Falling fiscal revenue coupled with unplanned spending and countercyclical policies used to stem the crisis will sharply widen primary deficits. The average public debt ratio among APEC's Asian member economies is projected to reach 47.8% of GDP by 2021, up sizably from 40.6% of GDP in 2019.

Inward foreign direct investment suffered during the pandemic. A silver lining has been investments into digital services sectors—such as telecommunications and information services, financial services, and other business services that proved more resilient than manufacturing and nondigital services sectors. Regional cooperation will be essential to facilitate investment into these sectors and to balance investment openness with regulatory measures.

The tight fiscal space among the developed economies will have implications for future AfT flows. Governments may reduce their development assistance, exacerbating already insufficient financing for developing countries. Governments may also pivot their AfT program or prioritize certain countries and topics due to constrained budgets. For example, Australia has provided significant budget support toward keeping core services (such as healthcare) going in the Pacific in response to the COVID-19 pandemic.[3]

Even prior to 2020, the amount of domestic and external financing for developing countries was inadequate to support spending on the Sustainable Development Goals. If the OECD/Development Assistance Committee members maintain their 2019 official development assistance (ODA) as a share of gross national income, total ODA may decline by $11–$14 billion (OECD 2020). The 2009 financial crisis offers insight into how economic recessions can affect AfT to developing Asia. During that time (2008–2009), the commitments by committee members to all recipient countries fell by 6% from $157.87 billion in 2008 to $148.48 in 2009. The commitments remained stagnant around 2009 levels during 2010–2013, and only surpassing 2008 commitment levels in 2015.

1.2 Evolution of Aid for Trade

1.2.1 Direction and Growth of Aid for Trade in the Context of COVID-19

Aid for Trade is important for developing countries to tackle the changing trade environment, including the lingering COVID-19 pandemic, which has raised inequalities, disrupted supply chains, and accelerated movement toward the digital economy. It is essential for AfT to help countries and regions adjust as efficiently as possible and benefit from the rules, regulations, and requirements of the global value chain trade landscape and the new digital economy. Aid for Trade in trade and digital agreements is required to build resilience and robustness in the most vulnerable economies and fulfill the requirements of specific SDG targets. These include:[4]

- SDG target 17.11 aiming to "significantly increase the exports of developing countries, in particular with a view to doubling the least developed countries' share of global exports by 2020."
- SDG target 17.12, which requires "the timely implementation of duty-free and quota-free market access on a lasting basis for all least developed countries, consistent with World Trade Organization decisions, including by ensuring that preferential rules of origin applicable to

[3] In October 2020, Australia approved a large package to the Pacific in response to COVID–19 with A$100 million for 2020–2021, A$304.7 million for 2021–2022 and A$525 million for 2022–2023.
[4] The list is not exhaustive. Trade and digital agreements contribute to a wide range of SDGs, particularly 8, 9, 10, and 17.

imports from least developed countries are transparent and simple, and contribute to facilitating market access."

- SDG target 17.7 to "promote the development, transfer, dissemination, and diffusion of environmentally sound technologies to developing countries on favorable terms, including on concessional and preferential terms."

From 2002 to 2019, AfT flows to Asia and the Pacific almost tripled to $16 billion in 2019,[5] but then declined 5% during 2019–2020. The region was the second-highest recipient of AfT disbursements in the world after Africa (Figure 1.9). While the region's average share in total AfT inflows was 40.8% during 2002–2004, that number declined to 32.2% in 2011–2013 (Figure 1.10). Subsequently, this share increased slightly to 35.3% in 2017–2019. However, 2020 marked a trend reversal, as the region's share reverted to its 2011–2013 level.

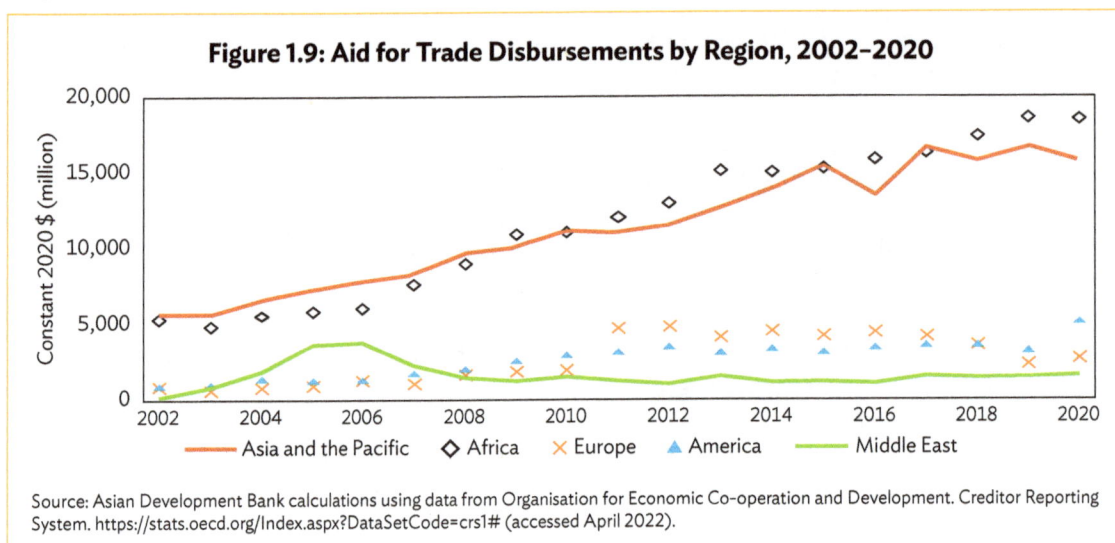

Figure 1.9: Aid for Trade Disbursements by Region, 2002–2020

Source: Asian Development Bank calculations using data from Organisation for Economic Co-operation and Development. Creditor Reporting System. https://stats.oecd.org/Index.aspx?DataSetCode=crs1# (accessed April 2022).

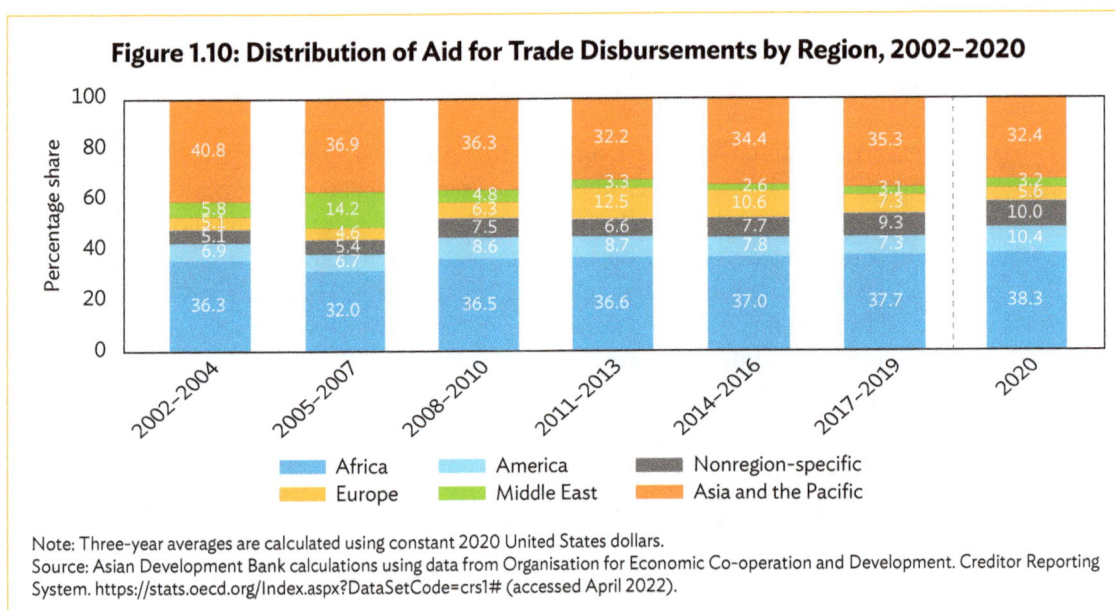

Figure 1.10: Distribution of Aid for Trade Disbursements by Region, 2002–2020

Note: Three-year averages are calculated using constant 2020 United States dollars.
Source: Asian Development Bank calculations using data from Organisation for Economic Co-operation and Development. Creditor Reporting System. https://stats.oecd.org/Index.aspx?DataSetCode=crs1# (accessed April 2022).

---

[5] Calculations in this section only include developing economies. Economies not receiving aid are therefore excluded, namely, Brunei Darussalam; Hong Kong, China; the Republic of Korea; Singapore; and Taipei,China.

Aid for trade is unevenly distributed within Asia and the Pacific

The volume of aid for trade to South Asia increased substantially (230%) during 2002–2019, but the region also had the second-largest decrease during 2019–2020 (10.3%) after the Pacific (17.9%) among all subregions (Figure 1.11). Between 2006 and 2019, per capita AfT inflows tripled in Central Asia and the Pacific, and more than doubled in South Asia. However, per capita AfT flows in the Pacific also dropped most during 2019–2020 (19.3%), followed by South Asia (11.3%) and Southeast Asia (1.0%), while the ratio increased in Central Asia and East Asia.

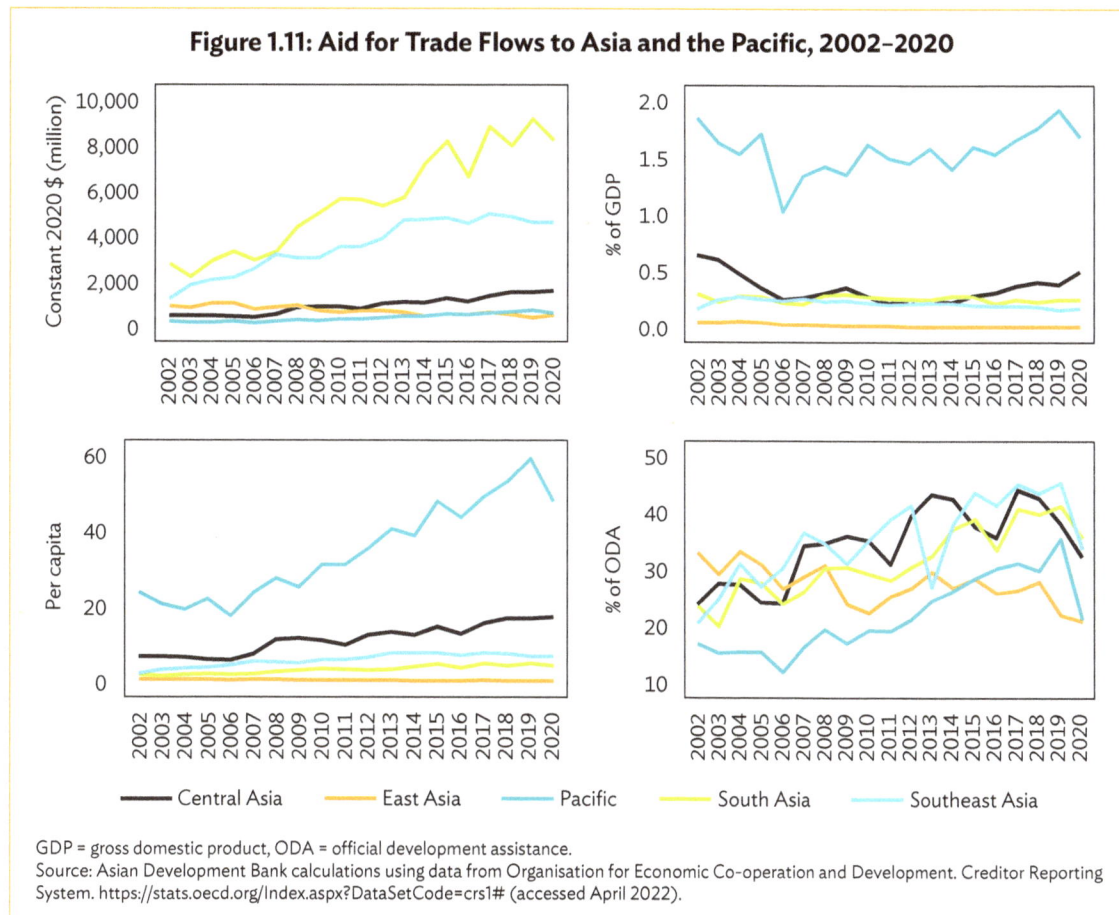

Figure 1.11: Aid for Trade Flows to Asia and the Pacific, 2002–2020

GDP = gross domestic product, ODA = official development assistance.
Source: Asian Development Bank calculations using data from Organisation for Economic Co-operation and Development. Creditor Reporting System. https://stats.oecd.org/Index.aspx?DataSetCode=crs1# (accessed April 2022).

Following the COVID-19 crisis, the Pacific and South Asia were the only two subregions in which aid for trade declined as a percentage of GDP, because GDP declined slower than AfT flows in both subregions. From 2002 to 2019, the share of aid for trade in total ODA disbursements increased in four of the five subregions. The value of AfT disbursements increased 74.0% and the sector's share in total ODA rose by 11.2 percentage points from 2009 to 2019 in these four subregions combined.[6] East Asia is the exception, as the sector's share in the region declined 5.1 percentage points from 2002

---

[6] Simultaneously, disbursements to social infrastructure and services—which include aid directed to health, education, water supply and sanitation, government, and civil society—stabilized at around $14–$16 billion. The sector's share dropped 7.8 percentage points from 2009 to 2019. As a result, aid for trade became the first category in ODA disbursements in 2019 instead of social infrastructure and services, which prevailed from 2009 to 2018.

to 2018.[7] The year 2020 marks a turning point, as the share of AfT in total ODA disbursements dropped in all five subregions. The decline was sharpest in the Pacific (14.1 percentage points), followed by Southeast Asia (11.6 percentage points), Central Asia (5.8 percentage points), and South Asia (5.6 percentage points). These declines are due to the dramatic growth in total ODA in most regions during 2019–2020. Total ODA increased by more than 20% in Central Asia, East Asia, the Pacific, and Southeast Asia, mostly driven by social infrastructure and services.[8] For South Asia, ODA increased about 4%, but, as shown above, AfT flows declined 10.3%. The COVID-19 pandemic most likely precipitated the decline in AfT flows into Asia and the Pacific, restricting the supply of aid (as donors diverted aid flows to combatting the pandemic) and disbursement flows (as recipients struggled to implement projects amid social restrictions and the competing health crisis).

In 2020, South Asia received the bulk of AfT directed to Asia and the Pacific (53%), followed by Southeast Asia (29.6%), and Central Asia (10.3%) (Figure 1.12). During 2005–2009 to 2015–2019, South Asia rose 7.5 percentage points, the Pacific 1.2 percentage points, and Central Asia 1 percentage point. Southeast and East Asia's shares in total AfT regional disbursements continuously dropped during the same period. Changes in 2020 exacerbated this trend, as the share of Central Asia and South Asia further increased while East Asia and Southeast Asia both declined. The Pacific's share almost remained equivalent to its 5-year average for 2015–2019.

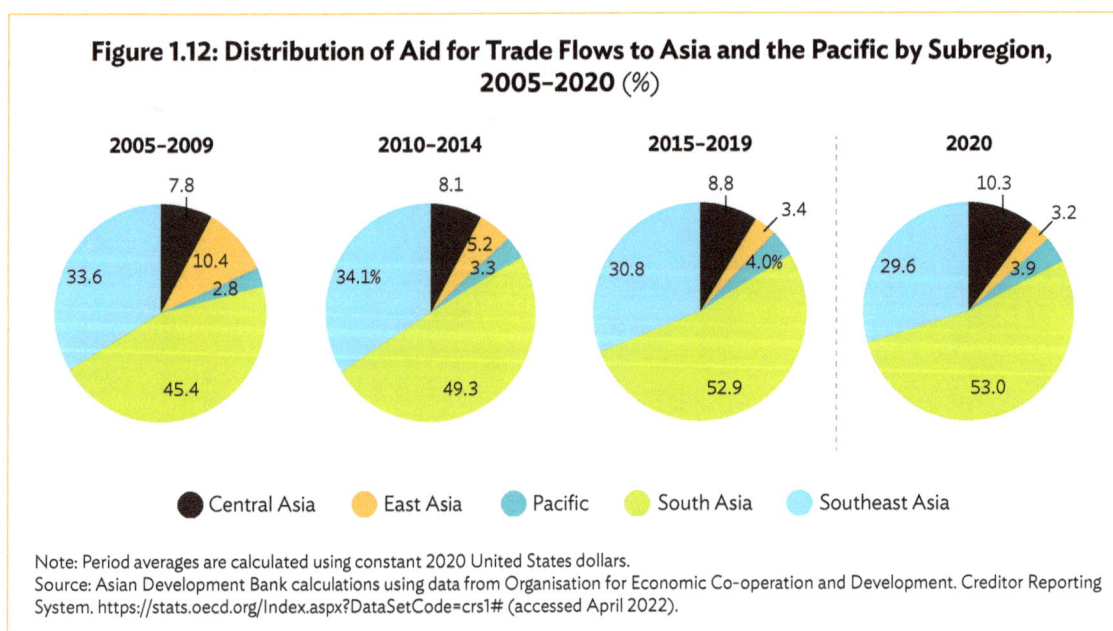

Figure 1.12: Distribution of Aid for Trade Flows to Asia and the Pacific by Subregion, 2005–2020 (%)

Note: Period averages are calculated using constant 2020 United States dollars.
Source: Asian Development Bank calculations using data from Organisation for Economic Co-operation and Development. Creditor Reporting System. https://stats.oecd.org/Index.aspx?DataSetCode=crs1# (accessed April 2022).

At a more granular level, Table 1.1 shows that countries located in South and Southeast Asia are the major regional recipients of AfT flows. Nine of the top 10 recipient countries during 2017–2020 were located in these two subregions, while 7 of the bottom 10 were in the Pacific.

---

[7]   While AfT disbursements declined in East Asia from 2002 to 2019, disbursements to the first category in volume, namely, social infrastructure and services, remained around $1.0–$1.5 billion. As a consequence, the share of AfT in total ODA dropped.

[8]   Social infrastructure and services increased about one-third in Central Asia and the Pacific, 11% in East Asia, 14% in South Asia, and 46% in Southeast Asia from 2019 to 2020.

Table 1.1: Top 10 and Bottom 10, Selected Aid for Trade Indicators, 2017–2020
(annual averages)

Total AfT ($ million)		Per Capita ($)		% of GDP		% of ODA	
Top 10		**Top 10**		**Top 10**		**Top 10**	
India	3,532.1 (−29.0)	Niue	2,823.5 (−27.4)	Tuvalu	25.511 (−0.04)	Thailand	61.5 (−9.1)
Bangladesh	2,169.7 (+25.0)	Nauru	1,621.8 (−80.4)	Niue	18.965[a]	India	58.7 (−11.6)
Viet Nam	1,393.5 (+14.1)	Tuvalu	995.6 (−0.5)	Nauru	14.528 (−26.4)	Uzbekistan	58.2 (−12.2)
Pakistan	1,110.2 (−20.3)	Palau	705.2 (+138.6)	Kiribati	12.825 (−7.1)	Viet Nam	48.5 (+3.7)
Indonesia	1,073.1 (+16.9)	Tonga	409.7 (−52.4)	Tonga	8.470 (−6.0)	Maldives	44.5 (−17.4)
Myanmar	784.9 (+20.4)	Cook Islands	297.2*	Samoa	6.442 (−5.4)	Tajikistan	43.7 (−20.4)
Afghanistan	779.3 (−4.0)	Samoa	279.6 (−72.5)	Vanuatu	5.836 (−0.3)	Philippines	41.9 (−37.1)
Uzbekistan	661.9 (−3.4)	Kiribati	218.9 (−57.7)	Micronesia, FS	5.723 (−3.5)	Nauru	41.7 (−45.0)
Philippines	600.1 (−41.2)	Micronesia, FS	206.8 (−49.0)	Palau	4.619 (+5.7)	Bhutan	41.0 (−6.2)
Nepal	474.7 (+0.9)	Vanuatu	181.3 (−15.4)	Solomon Islands	4.345 (−2.9)	Indonesia	40.8 (−21.4)
Bottom 10		**Bottom 10**		**Bottom 10**		**Bottom 10**	
Micronesia, FS	23.4 (−48.4)	Azerbaijan	8.1 (+67.2)	Sri Lanka	0.368 (+0.02)	Kyrgyz Republic	25.6 (−9.6)
Nauru	17.4 (−80.3)	Philippines	5.6 (−42.0)	Azerbaijan	0.181 (+0.15)	PRC	23.0 (+2.6)
Palau	12.7 (+139.8)	Pakistan	5.2 (−21.9)	Philippines	0.162 (−0.1)	Micronesia, FS	21.5 (−22.7)
Tuvalu	11.5 (+0.7)	Thailand	4.2 (−19.7)	India	0.126 (−0.02)	Fiji	20.9 (+7.9)
Marshall Islands	9.9 (+22.1)	Indonesia	4.0 (+15.7)	Indonesia	0.099 (+0.02)	Cook Islands	19.3*
Kazakhstan	9.7 (−17.6)	India	2.6 (−29.7)	Thailand	0.056 (−0.005)	Turkmenistan	18.8 (+29.3)
Malaysia	9.6 (−19.9)	Turkmenistan	1.1 (+1071.0)	Turkmenistan	0.010*	Afghanistan	18.7 (+0.2)
Turkmenistan	6.3 (+1088.6)	Kazakhstan	0.5 (−18.6)	Kazakhstan	0.005 (−0.001)	Marshall Islands	11.0 (−9.7)
Cook Islands	5.7*	Malaysia	0.3 (−20.9)	Malaysia	0.003 (−0.0002)	Malaysia	10.1 (+0.5)
Niue	5.2 (−26.4)	PRC	0.2 (+20.3)	PRC	0.002 (+0.0004)	Kazakhstan	8.4 (−3.0)

AfT = aid for trade, FS = Federated States, GDP = gross domestic product, ODA = official development assistance, PRC = People's Republic of China,
[a] Annual average is for 2017–2019 instead of 2017–2020 due to missing data for 2020.
Notes: Four-year averages calculated using 2020 constant United States dollars. Numbers in parentheses are percentage changes for total aid for trade ($) and per capita ($) and the percentage-point change for % of GDP and % of ODA during 2019–2020.
Sources: Asian Development Bank calculations using data from Organisation for Economic Co-operation and Development. Creditor Reporting System. https://stats.oecd.org/Index.aspx?DataSetCode=crs1# (accessed April 2022); World Bank. World Development Indicators, https://databank.worldbank.org/ (accessed April 2022); for Cook Islands' population and GDP: ADB. Key Indicators for Asia and the Pacific 2021. https://www.adb.org/publications/keyindicators-asia-and-pacific-2021 (accessed April 2022).

However, accounting for population size and GDP, a more nuanced picture emerges. Pacific countries represented all of the top 10 countries with the highest per capita AfT inflows and AfT inflows as a percentage of GDP. Aid for trade in all these countries, except Palau, declined significantly during 2019–2020. India, ranked first in total AfT inflows in 2020, was among the last countries on aid for trade per capita and relative to GDP. Indonesia and the Philippines also ranked in the bottom 10 for these two indicators, while the two countries were among the major recipients of total AfT disbursements.

Aid for trade represented more than half of total ODA disbursements received by Thailand, India, and Uzbekistan in order of disbursements. By contrast, three Central Asian countries (the Kyrgyz Republic, Turkmenistan, and Kazakhstan) and four Pacific countries (Micronesia, Fiji, Cook Islands, and the Marshall Islands) were classified among the bottom 10 of this category. Aid for trade accounted for less than 26% of total ODA in these economies.[9]

Turkmenistan and Kazakhstan, two Central Asian countries classified as landlocked developing countries, as well as Malaysia, were among the bottom 10 of all four categories. Almost all indicators in Malaysia and Kazakhstan declined significantly during 2019–2020.

Most aid for trade is directed to economic infrastructure while flows targeting trade policies and regulations remain limited

The portion of ODA going to AfT in Asia and the Pacific rose to 40% in 2019. However, this share dropped considerably following the COVID-19 crisis, and the magnitude of this decline was larger for Asia and the Pacific countries (7.5 percentage points) compared with all developing economies taken together (2.3 percentage points). The 6% decline in total AfT in Asia and the Pacific during 2019–2020 is entirely attributable to the decrease in disbursements directed to the economic infrastructure category (13.1%). By contrast, disbursements targeting the building productive capacity category increased 13.6% (Figure 1.13). Disbursements to the trade policies and regulations category also rose during the same period (30.9%) but it did not recover to its 2018 levels.

Economic infrastructure remains the largest category in cumulative AfT disbursements. In 2020, official donors disbursed more than $10 billion to support economic infrastructure in Asia and the Pacific. The category accounted for 71.4% of the regional AfT disbursements over 2017–2019 (Figure 1.14), which was about 16 percentage points above the corresponding share for all developing economies.

On average, building productive capacity accounted for a significantly smaller share of total AfT disbursements in Asia and the Pacific (30.9%) compared to all developing economies taken together as a group (43.1%) during 2010–2020. As Figure 1.14, the category's share dropped from 2002–2004 to 2017–2019 (-16.9 percentage points) in Asia and the Pacific as average disbursements directed to building productive capacity grew at the slower rate (67.2%)[10] than those targeting economic infrastructure (250%) between the two periods.

---

9   Low shares indicate that aid and assistance is needed beyond trade-related issues. In 6 of these bottom 10 economies in AfT as a percentage of ODA, social infrastructure and services accounted for 58%–74% of total ODA in 2019. By contrast, the countries in the top 10 may receive a larger share of aid targeting trade due to the importance of trade in their economies or the potential for trade to support development.

10   Average disbursements to building productive capacity more than doubled for all developing economies taken as a group between the same two periods (+160%).

Figure 1.13: Aid for Trade and as a Share of Official Development Assistance, 2002–2020
(constant 2020 $, %)

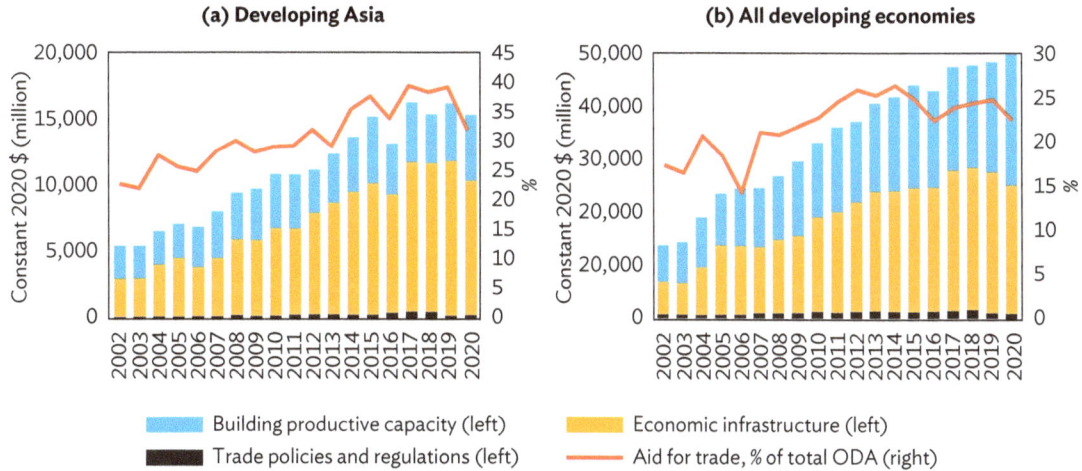

(a) Developing Asia

(b) All developing economies

- Building productive capacity (left)
- Trade policies and regulations (left)
- Economic infrastructure (left)
- Aid for trade, % of total ODA (right)

ODA = official development assistance.
Note: Total aid for trade is the sum of aid for infrastructure, aid for building productive capacity, and trade policy and regulations, and trade-related adjustment.
Source: Asian Development Bank calculations using data from Organisation for Economic Co-operation and Development. Creditor Reporting System. https://stats.oecd.org/Index.aspx?DataSetCode=crs1# (accessed April 2022).

Figure 1.14: Distribution of Aid for Trade Inflows to Asia and the Pacific by Category
(3-year averages)

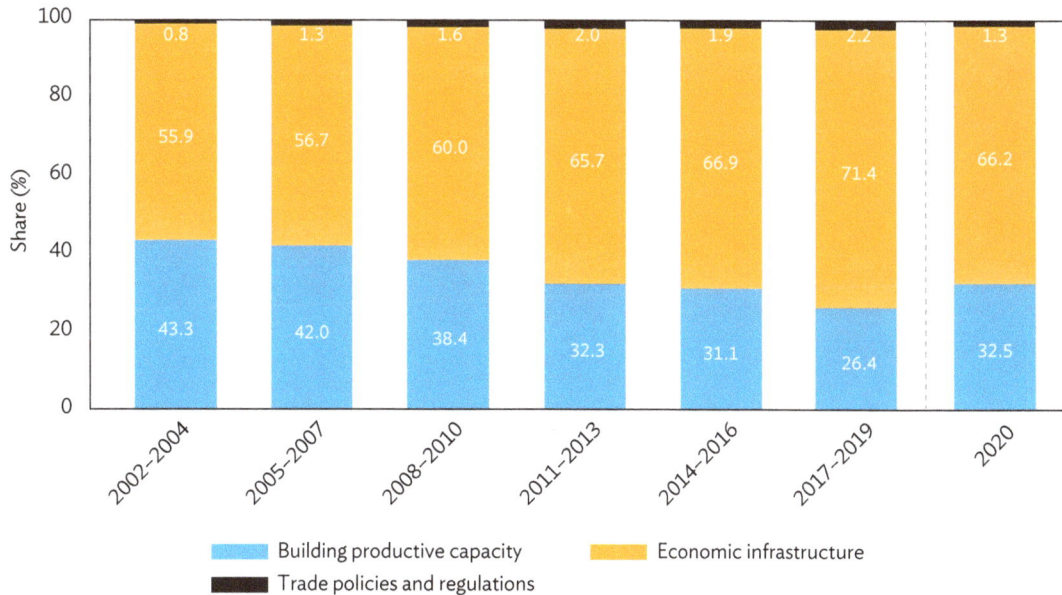

	2002–2004	2005–2007	2008–2010	2011–2013	2014–2016	2017–2019	2020
Trade policies and regulations	0.8	1.3	1.6	2.0	1.9	2.2	1.3
Economic infrastructure	55.9	56.7	60.0	65.7	66.9	71.4	66.2
Building productive capacity	43.3	42.0	38.4	32.3	31.1	26.4	32.5

- Building productive capacity
- Economic infrastructure
- Trade policies and regulations

Note: Three-year averages are calculated using constant 2020 United States dollars.
Source: Asian Development Bank calculations using data from the Organisation for Economic Co-operation and Development. Creditor Reporting System. https://stats.oecd.org/Index.aspx?DataSetCode=CRS1 (accessed April 2022).

Disbursements to trade policies and regulations more than halved in Asia and the Pacific from 2018 to 2020. While its 3-year average increased 1.4 percentage points from 2002–2004 to 2017–2019, the share of trade policies and regulations fell to 1.3% in 2020.

Transport and storage and energy are the top sectors supported through aid for trade

As Figure 1.15 shows, the share of transport and storage markedly increased from 2005–2009 to 2015–2019 (6.9 percentage points) but its value in 2020 was 1.1 percentage points lower than its 5-year average for 2015–2019. Energy, which made up the second-largest share (25.2%) in 2020, followed a very similar trend, with a continuous rise from 2005–2009 to 2015–2019 and a decline (1.7 percentage points) in 2020. The shares of agriculture (ranked third in size) and banking and financial services (ranked fifth) declined between 2005–2009 and 2015–2019 but grew in 2020 (0.6 and 2.3 percentage points, respectively).

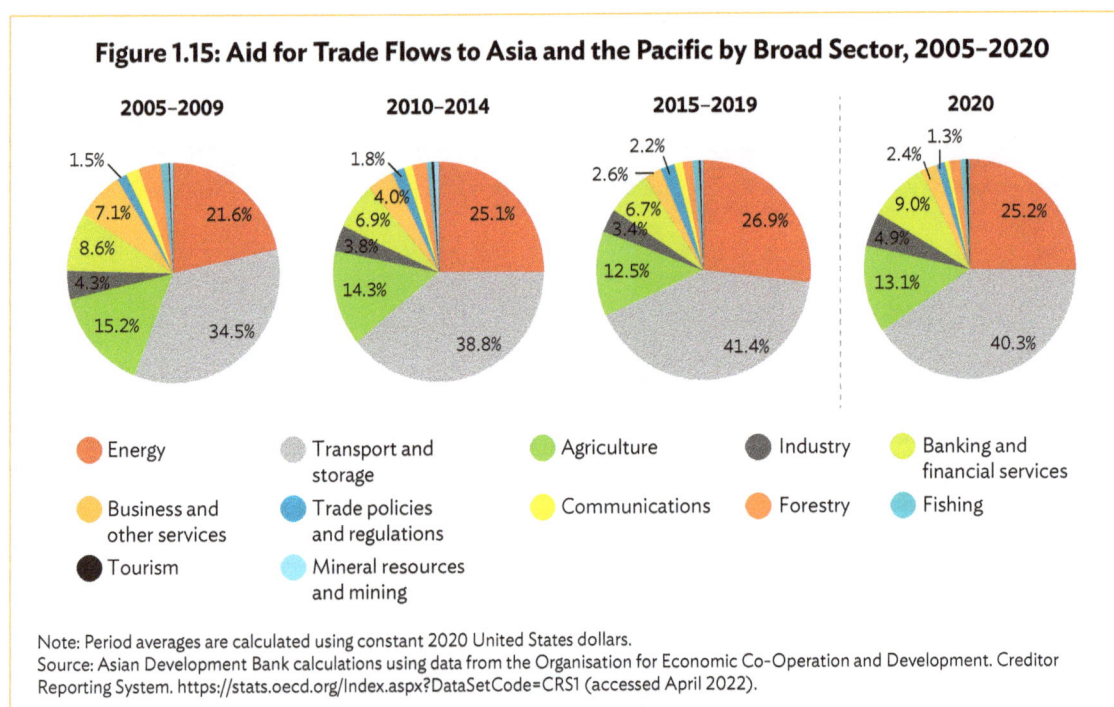

Figure 1.15: Aid for Trade Flows to Asia and the Pacific by Broad Sector, 2005–2020

Note: Period averages are calculated using constant 2020 United States dollars.
Source: Asian Development Bank calculations using data from the Organisation for Economic Co-Operation and Development. Creditor Reporting System. https://stats.oecd.org/Index.aspx?DataSetCode=CRS1 (accessed April 2022).

Within economic infrastructure, the value of AfT disbursements grew in all broad sectors from 2005–2009 to 2015–2019 (Figure 1.16, panel A). The share of transport and storage remained stable around 59%, the share of energy increased by 1.5 percentage points, while the share of communications decreased 1.7 percentage points (panel B). However, from 2019 to 2020, disbursements targeting communications halved, while those targeting transport and storage decreased by 17%. Energy declined least (-3%) among the three broad sectors.

Agriculture, banking, and finance, as well as industry, are the dominant broad sectors within the building productive capacity category (panels C and D). Together, they accounted for approximately 80% of disbursements in 2015–2019. The average shares of agriculture, banking, and finance and industry increased from 2005–2009 to 2015–2019, while business and other services declined. In contrast with economic infrastructure, the building productive capacity category grew from 2019 to 2020 (Figure 1.13).

Figure 1.16: Aid for Trade Flows to Asia and the Pacific for Aid Categories by Sector 2005–2020

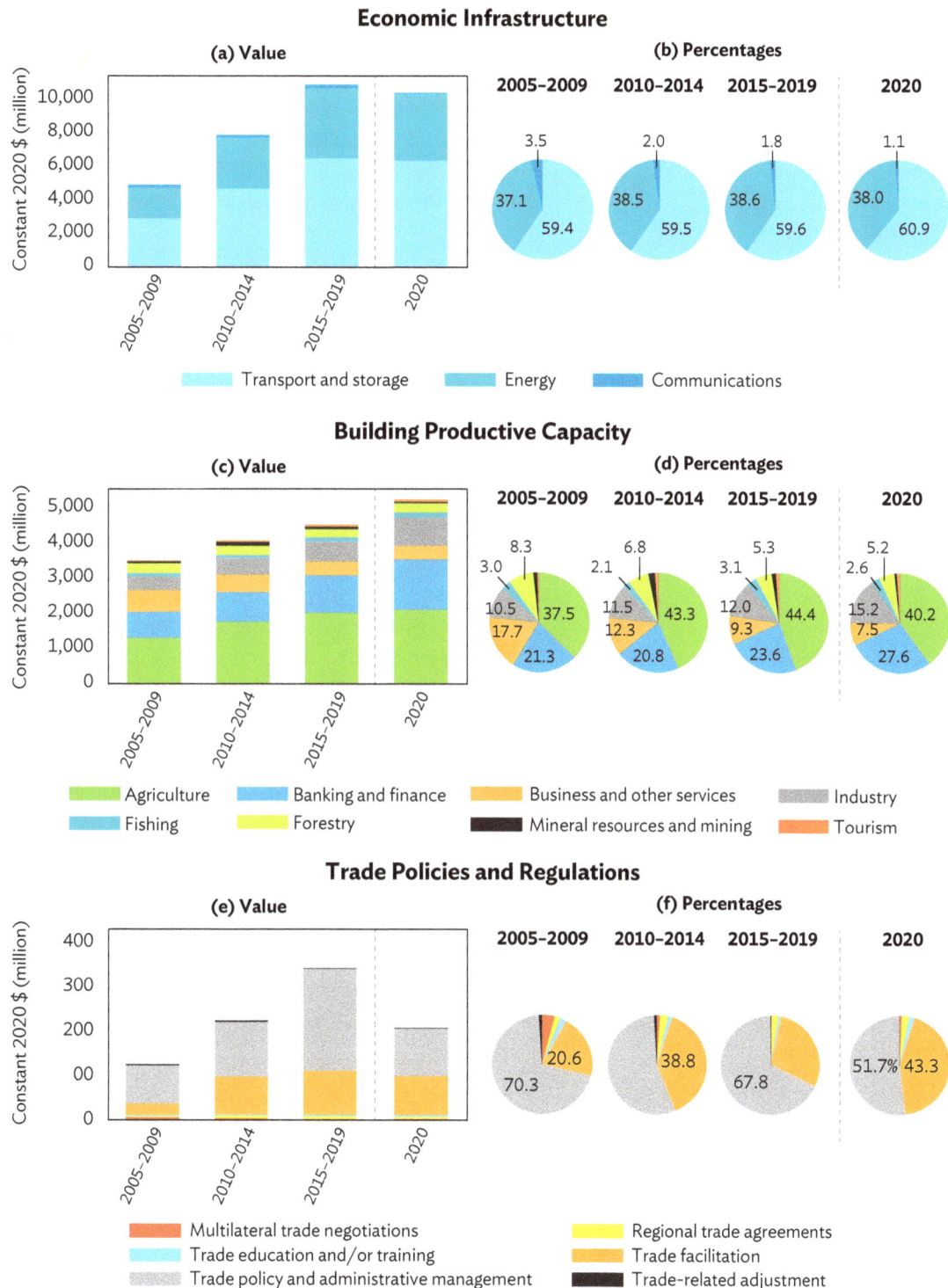

Economic Infrastructure

(a) Value

Constant 2020 $ (million)

10,000
8,000
6,000
4,000
2,000
0

2005–2009 2010–2014 2015–2019 2020

(b) Percentages

2005–2009   2010–2014   2015–2019   2020

3.5   2.0   1.8   1.1
37.1 59.4   38.5 59.5   38.6 59.6   38.0 60.9

Legend: Transport and storage | Energy | Communications

Building Productive Capacity

(c) Value

Constant 2020 $ (million)

5,000
4,000
3,000
2,000
1,000
0

2005–2009 2010–2014 2015–2019 2020

(d) Percentages

2005–2009   2010–2014   2015–2019   2020

8.3   6.8   5.3   5.2
3.0   2.1   3.1   2.6
10.5 37.5   11.5 43.3   12.0 44.4   15.2 40.2
17.7   12.3   9.3   7.5
21.3   20.8   23.6   27.6

Legend: Agriculture | Banking and finance | Business and other services | Industry | Fishing | Forestry | Mineral resources and mining | Tourism

Trade Policies and Regulations

(e) Value

Constant 2020 $ (million)

400
300
200
00
0

2005–2009 2010–2014 2015–2019 2020

(f) Percentages

2005–2009   2010–2014   2015–2019   2020

20.6   38.8   51.7% 43.3
70.3   67.8

Legend: Multilateral trade negotiations | Regional trade agreements | Trade education and/or training | Trade facilitation | Trade policy and administrative management | Trade-related adjustment

Note: Calculated using constant 2020 United States dollars.
Source: Asian Development Bank calculations using data from the Organisation for Economic Co-operation and Development. Creditor Reporting System. https://stats.oecd.org/Index.aspx?DataSetCode=CRS1 (accessed April 2022).

Among the broad sectors, banking and finance experienced the most marked growth as disbursements almost doubled. The share of agriculture declined relative to its average for the period 2015–2019 (-4.2 percentage points). In addition, disbursements targeting tourism decreased by 18% from 2019 to 2020.

Trade policy and administrative management, as well as trade facilitation, dominate the trade policies and regulations category (panels E and F). Together, these two components accounted for 95% of disbursements targeting the category in 2020. The share of trade policy and administrative management decreased between 2005–2009 and 2010–2014 before growing sizably from 2010–2014 to 2015–2019 (+12 percentage points). By contrast, trade facilitation declined 10 percentage points from 2010–2014 to 2015–2019.

Aid for trade targeted at regional trade cooperation and integration policies remains limited. Looking at period averages, aid to support regional trade agreements,[11] which represented 2.4% of total disbursements directed to the category in 2020, increased threefold from 2005–2009 to 2015–2019. However, between 2015 and 2020, disbursements to the regional trade agreements subcategory more than halved. Overall, from 2018 to 2020, the value of disbursements directed to the trade policies and regulations category dropped considerably (Figure 1.13). Most of this decline was due to disbursements for trade policy and administrative management, which decreased more than 70%, while trade facilitation increased 16%. Consequently, the share of trade facilitation grew to reach 43.3% in 2020 and the share of trade policy and administrative management declined to 51.7%.

As Figure 1.17 shows, AfT flows targeting the trade policies and regulations category are mostly directed to individual countries. For example, country-specific disbursements accounted for 97% and 76% of total AfT flows to the multilateral trade negotiations and trade facilitation subcategories in 2020. The regional trade agreements subcategory is an exception as the bulk of aid is provided at the regional and subregional levels. In general, subregional and regional aid dropped considerably in 2020 relative to the averages for 2015–2019. For regional trade agreements, regional aid halved, subregional aid decreased by 42% while country-specific aid declined 24%. Regional aid directed to trade facilitation declined almost two-thirds.

---

[11]   The subcategory also includes support to work on technical barriers, sanitary and phytosanitary measures, inclusion of special and differential treatments, and elaboration of rules of origin.

Figure 1.17: Aid for Trade Flows to Trade Policies and Regulations by Subcategory, 2005–2020 (constant 2020 $, million)

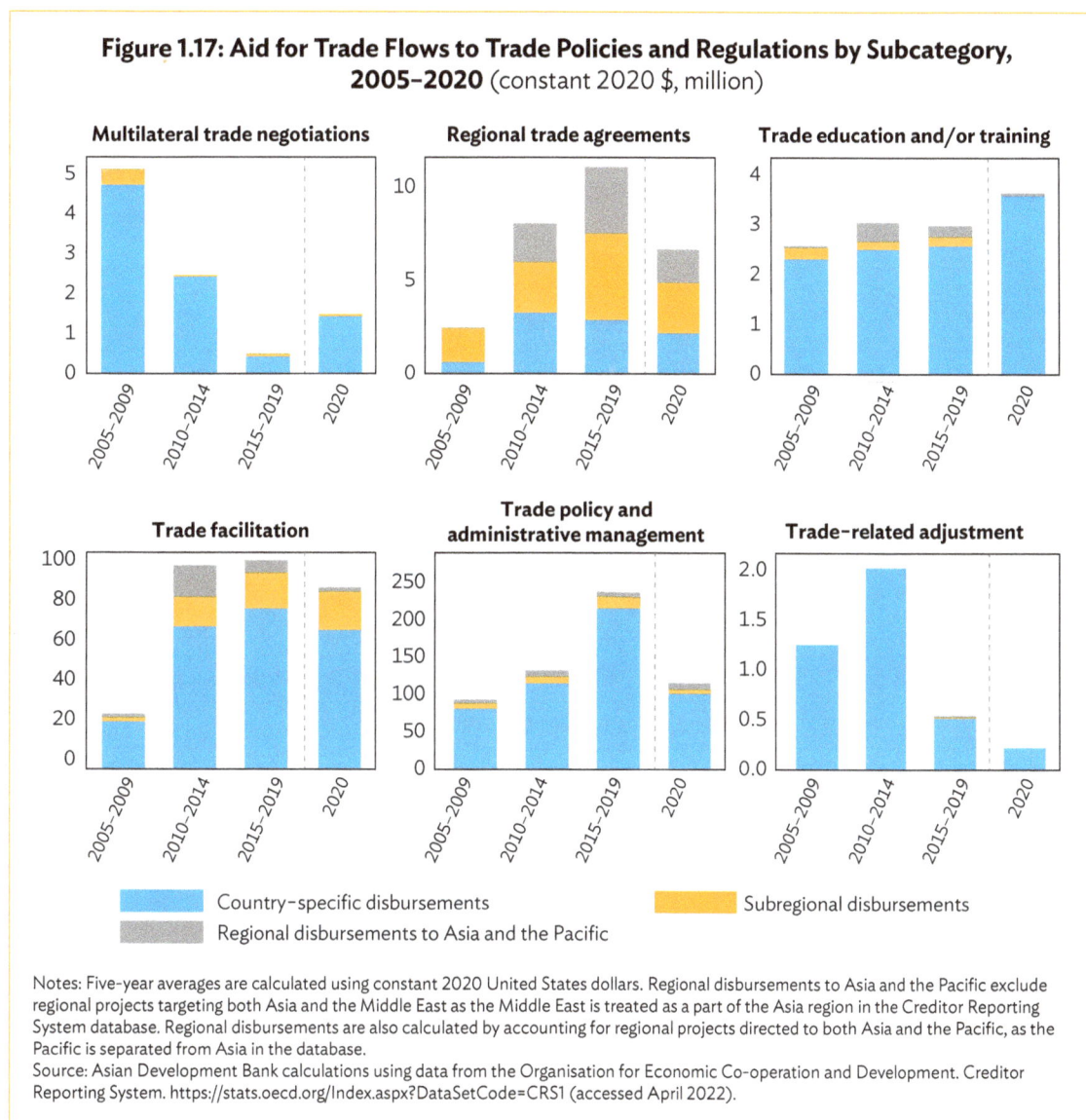

Notes: Five-year averages are calculated using constant 2020 United States dollars. Regional disbursements to Asia and the Pacific exclude regional projects targeting both Asia and the Middle East as the Middle East is treated as a part of the Asia region in the Creditor Reporting System database. Regional disbursements are also calculated by accounting for regional projects directed to both Asia and the Pacific, as the Pacific is separated from Asia in the database.
Source: Asian Development Bank calculations using data from the Organisation for Economic Co-operation and Development. Creditor Reporting System. https://stats.oecd.org/Index.aspx?DataSetCode=CRS1 (accessed April 2022).

Disbursements from multilateral organizations on the rise

The amount of aid for trade from donor countries located in Asia and the Pacific considerably increased from 2002 to 2020 (Figure 1.18). Asia and Pacific donor countries were the fastest-growing group, as disbursements made by these countries increased fivefold from 2002 to 2019, but contracted about 15% from 2019 to 2020.

After initial growth from 2006 to 2015, disbursements from multilateral providers stabilized around $5 billion between 2017 and 2019 and grew 9.6% during 2019–2020.

The year 2009 marks a turning point in the distribution of donors. The share of AfT disbursements from donor countries not located in Asia and the Pacific decreased from 41.4% to 19.6% (-21.8 percentage points) between 2009 and 2020. By contrast, the share of AfT disbursements from multilateral providers (including ADB) increased 15.8 percentage points during the same period.

Figure 1.18: Aid for Trade Disbursements to Asia and the Pacific by Type of Donors, 2002–2020

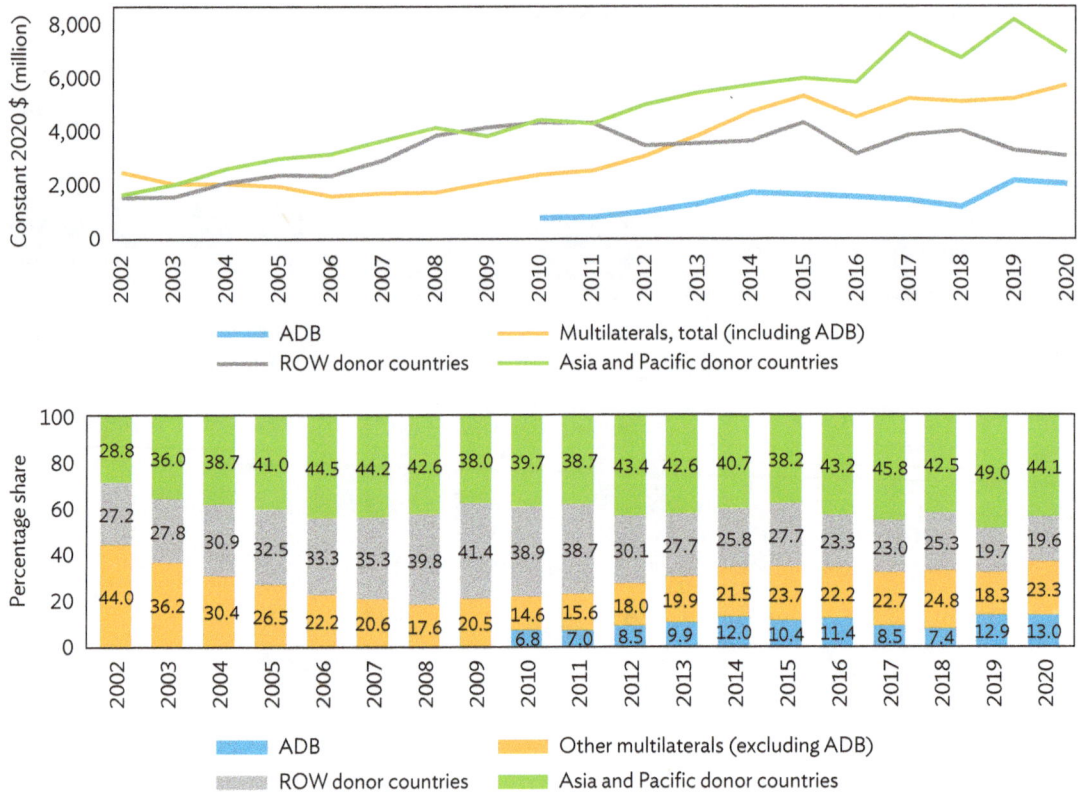

ADB = Asian Development Bank, ROW = rest of world.
Note: "Other multilaterals" include European Union institutions, Islamic Development Bank, United Nations organizations, and the World Bank Group.
Source: Asian Development Bank calculations using data from the Organisation for Economic Co-operation and Development. Creditor Reporting System. https://stats.oecd.org/Index.aspx?DataSetCode=crs1# (accessed April 2022).

A few countries and multilateral organizations account for most of regional disbursements. Germany, Japan, the World Bank, and ADB represented about three-quarters of AfT disbursements to Asia and the Pacific in 2020.

A Deeper Dive: Least Developed Countries in Asia and the Pacific

Asia is home to 11 of the 46 least developed countries (LDCs) as defined by the United Nations. Of the 11, four are in South Asia (Afghanistan, Bangladesh, Bhutan, and Nepal); three in Southeast Asia (Cambodia, the Lao PDR, and Myanmar); and four in the Pacific (Kiribati, Solomon Islands, Timor-Leste, and Tuvalu). Maldives, Samoa, and Vanuatu[12] transitioned out of LDC status in 2011, 2014, and 2020, respectively; Bangladesh, Bhutan, the Lao PDR, Nepal, and Solomon Islands are scheduled to graduate before 2026.[13]

---

[12]   Maldives, Samoa, and Vanuatu are not included in the calculations and the figures as the three countries graduated during the period of analysis.

[13]   For more information, please see the graduation eligibility, process and timeline here: United Nations. Graduation from the LDC Category. https://www.un.org/development/desa/dpad/least-developed-country-category/ldc-graduation.html.

The global community has been supporting the LDCs through AfT, among a variety of development programs. From 2010 to 2020, over $43 billion[14] were directed to LDCs in the Asia and Pacific region to build trade capacity and infrastructure.

After a decline from 2011–2013 to 2014–2016, the share of LDCs in AfT disbursements targeting Asia and the Pacific increased 7 percentage points to 30.3% in 2017–2019. The share increased a further 5.8 percentage points in 2020 compared with the average for 2017–2019 (Figure 1.19). As shown in Table 1, 4 of the 10 top regional AfT recipients were classified as LDCs: Afghanistan, Bangladesh, Myanmar, and Nepal. Inflows to LDCs as a percentage of GDP declined from 2008–2010 to 2014–2016 (-0.52 percentage points), but subsequently increased 0.14 percentage points from 2014–2016 to 2017–2019. The share slightly increased in 2020 compared with the 3-year average for 2017–2019 (panel C).

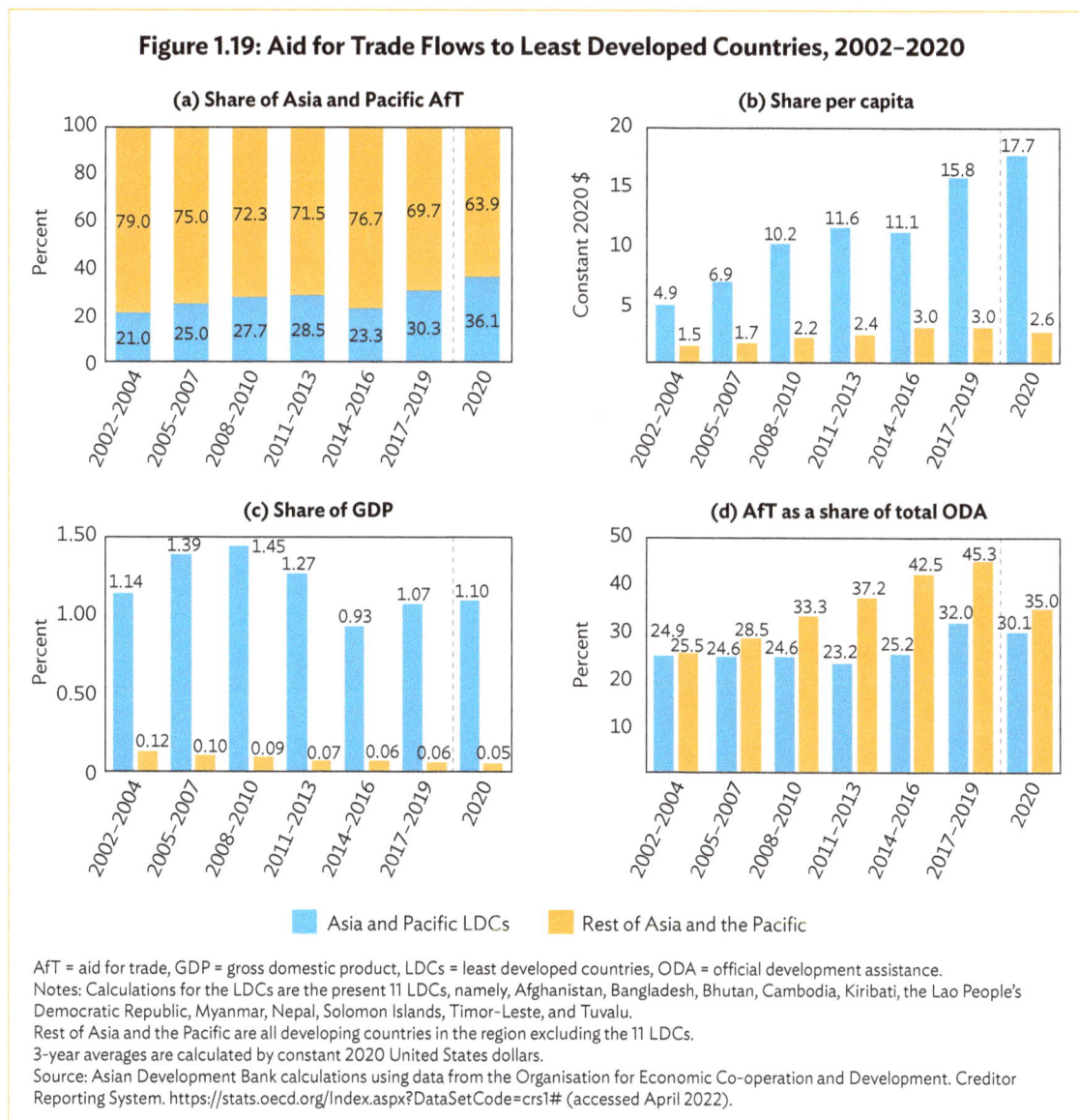

Figure 1.19: Aid for Trade Flows to Least Developed Countries, 2002–2020

AfT = aid for trade, GDP = gross domestic product, LDCs = least developed countries, ODA = official development assistance.
Notes: Calculations for the LDCs are the present 11 LDCs, namely, Afghanistan, Bangladesh, Bhutan, Cambodia, Kiribati, the Lao People's Democratic Republic, Myanmar, Nepal, Solomon Islands, Timor-Leste, and Tuvalu.
Rest of Asia and the Pacific are all developing countries in the region excluding the 11 LDCs.
3-year averages are calculated by constant 2020 United States dollars.
Source: Asian Development Bank calculations using data from the Organisation for Economic Co-operation and Development. Creditor Reporting System. https://stats.oecd.org/Index.aspx?DataSetCode=crs1# (accessed April 2022).

[14] Constant 2020 US dollars.

Inflows on a per capita basis and as a percentage of total ODA increased considerably from 2002–2004 to 2017–2019 (panels B and C). The share of aid for trade in total ODA was consistently lower for LDCs than for non-LDCs over 2002–2004 to 2017–2019 (panel D) because a significantly higher portion of ODA went to social infrastructure,[15] debt-related aid,[16] and humanitarian aid in LDCs relative to other countries in Asia and the Pacific.[17] This reflects that LDCs are more likely to face urgent needs in these areas than other countries. While AfT flows as a percentage of ODA dropped significantly for the rest of Asia and the Pacific in 2020 relative to the average for 2017–2019 (-10.3 percentage points), it dropped 1.9 percentage-point only in least developed countries.

Disparities are widening in the distribution of aid for trade among Asia and Pacific least developed countries

Aid for trade flows grew in all LDCs from 2002 to 2019 (Figure 1.20). The countries with the most substantial increases in aid for trade from 2009 to 2019 included Myanmar (3,165%); Bangladesh (584%); and Solomon Islands (342%). Afghanistan is an exception, as AfT total inflows to the country declined dramatically ($1.1 billion[18]) during the period.

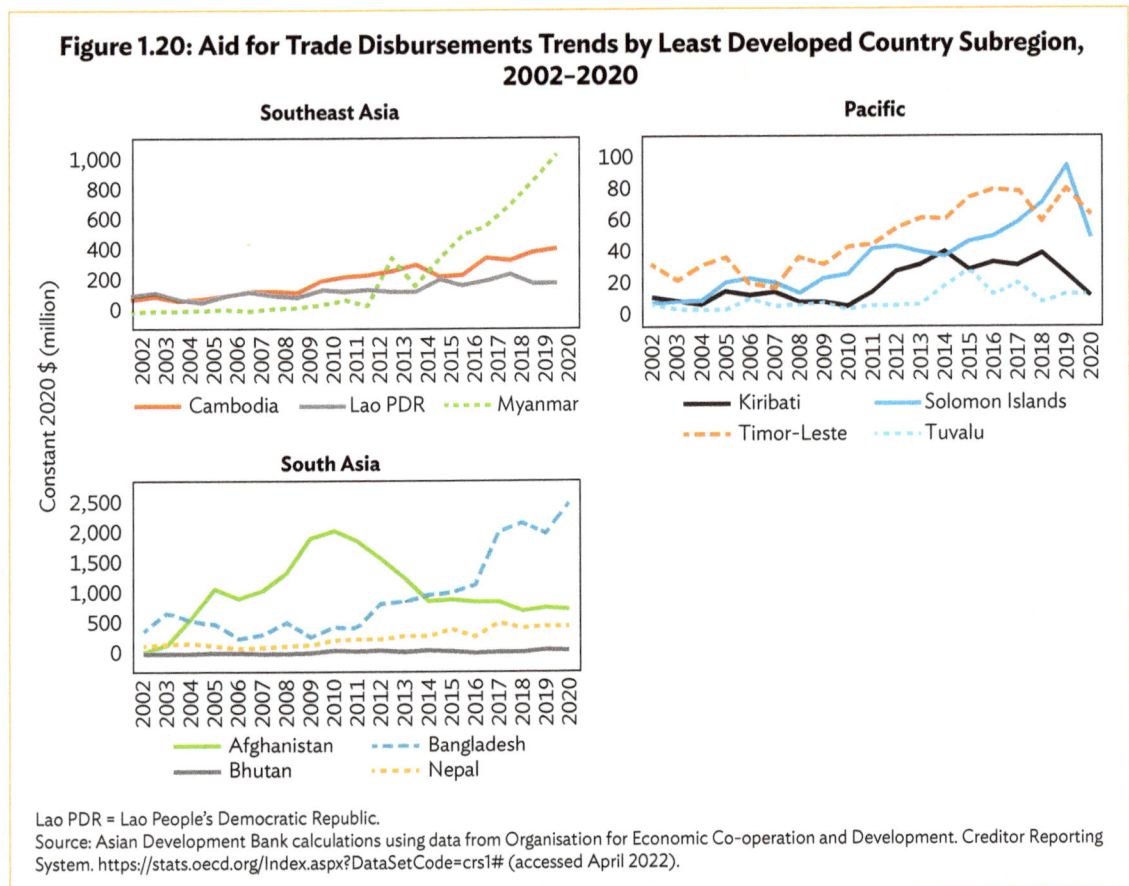

Figure 1.20: Aid for Trade Disbursements Trends by Least Developed Country Subregion, 2002–2020

Lao PDR = Lao People's Democratic Republic.
Source: Asian Development Bank calculations using data from Organisation for Economic Co-operation and Development. Creditor Reporting System. https://stats.oecd.org/Index.aspx?DataSetCode=crs1# (accessed April 2022).

---

[15] This category includes education, health, conflict, peace and security, and aid targeting government and civil society.

[16] This category includes debt forgiveness, debt relief, debt swaps, and buy-back.

[17] On average over 2002–2019, 46.9% of ODA targeted social infrastructure in LDCs in Asia and the Pacific, while this proportion was 38.8% for non-LDCs. 8.8% of ODA was allocated to humanitarian aid in LDCs (4.8% in non-LDCs) and 3.5% went to actions related to debt in LDCs (1.5% to non-LDCs).

[18] Constant 2020 US dollars.

However, AfT inflows declined in more than half of LDCs from 2017 to 2019. The largest declines were in two Pacific countries, Tuvalu (38.9%) and Kiribati (21.1%). In 2020, Kiribati saw the largest reduction (57.1%) among all LDCs, followed by Solomon Islands (50%), and Timor-Leste (21.8%). In contrast with these three, AfT flows increased in six LDCs amid the COVID-19 crisis, with Bangladesh and Myanmar highest (25% and 20.4%, respectively).

Despite these recent downward trends, Kiribati and Tuvalu were still among the first three countries in AfT inflows as a share of GDP and inflows on a per capita basis (Figure 1.21). Aid for trade accounted for 26.4% of GDP in Tuvalu and 15.4% in Kiribati in 2017–2019, well above the average for Asia and Pacific countries (3.7%)[19] (Figure 1.21, panels A and B). However, among all LDCs, declines in the three indicators in 2020 were largest in Kiribati relative to the 3-year average for 2017–2019. Cambodia, Bangladesh, Bhutan, and Myanmar were the only four countries in which AfT flows increased per capita and as a percentage of GDP. Nevertheless, AfT flows as a percentage of total ODA decreased in all least developed countries.[20]

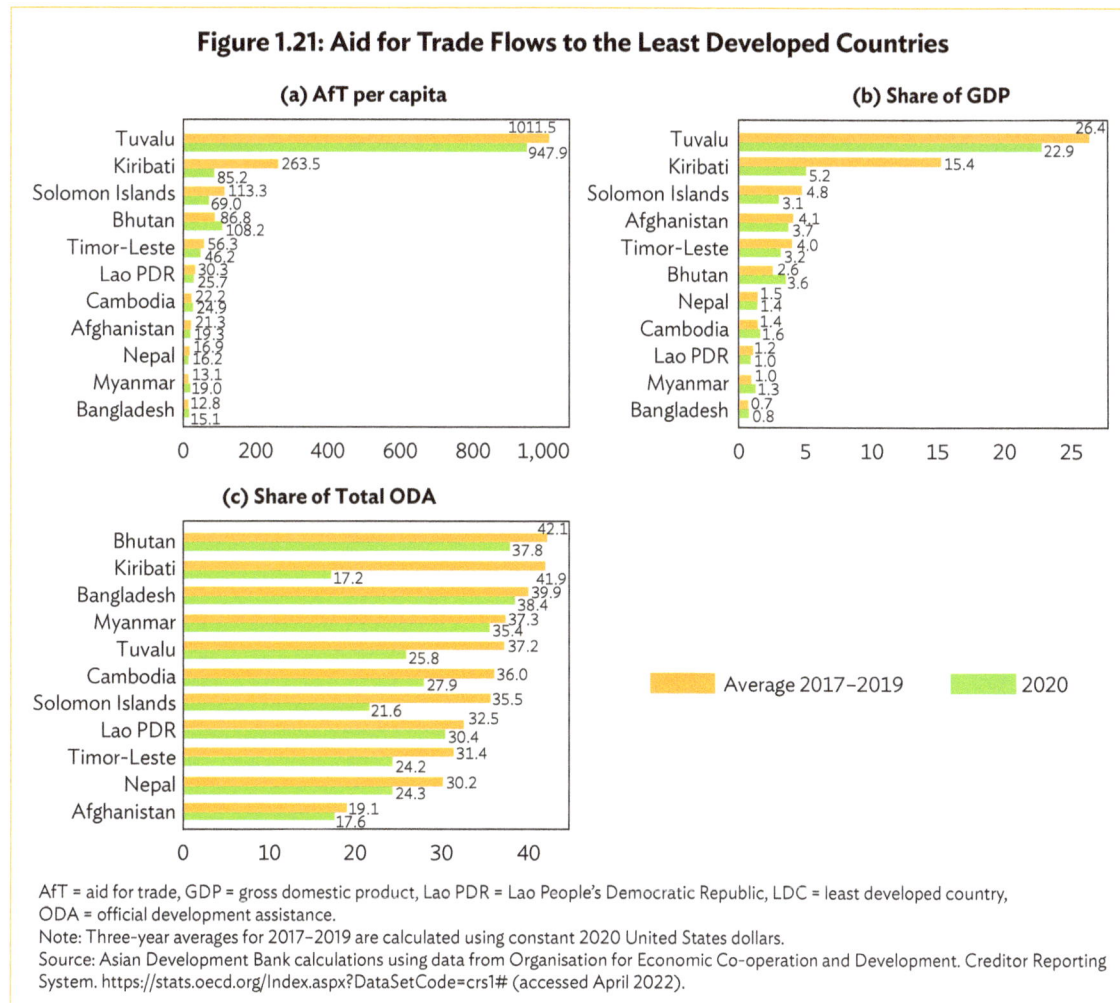

Figure 1.21: Aid for Trade Flows to the Least Developed Countries

AfT = aid for trade, GDP = gross domestic product, Lao PDR = Lao People's Democratic Republic, LDC = least developed country, ODA = official development assistance.
Note: Three-year averages for 2017–2019 are calculated using constant 2020 United States dollars.
Source: Asian Development Bank calculations using data from Organisation for Economic Co-operation and Development. Creditor Reporting System. https://stats.oecd.org/Index.aspx?DataSetCode=crs1# (accessed April 2022).

[19] Unweighted average.
[20] Mostly driven by social infrastructure and services, total ODA increased in all LDCs during 2019–2020, except Afghanistan, the Lao PDR, and Solomon Islands. During the same period, AfT flows either increased but at a slower rate than total ODA (e.g., Cambodia, Myanmar, Nepal, and Tuvalu), or declined (e.g., Bhutan, Kiribati, and Timor-Leste). As a result, AfT flows decreased as a percent of total ODA.

Multilateral and Asia and Pacific providers also account for the bulk of disbursements for least developed countries

Aid for trade disbursements from Asia and Pacific donor countries and multilateral organizations to LDCs had increased tenfold as of 2009 and sixfold by 2020 (Figure 1.22). By contrast, disbursements made by donor countries not located in Asia and the Pacific dropped considerably during the same period (-64.1%). However, this trend is mostly due to Afghanistan and excluding the country from the analysis (panel B) shows that disbursements from rest-of-world countries to LDCs increased from 2009 to 2018. Concomitantly, disbursements to Afghanistan from multilateral providers grew significantly (panel B). These disbursements more than doubled from 2015 to 2020 (+$266 million).

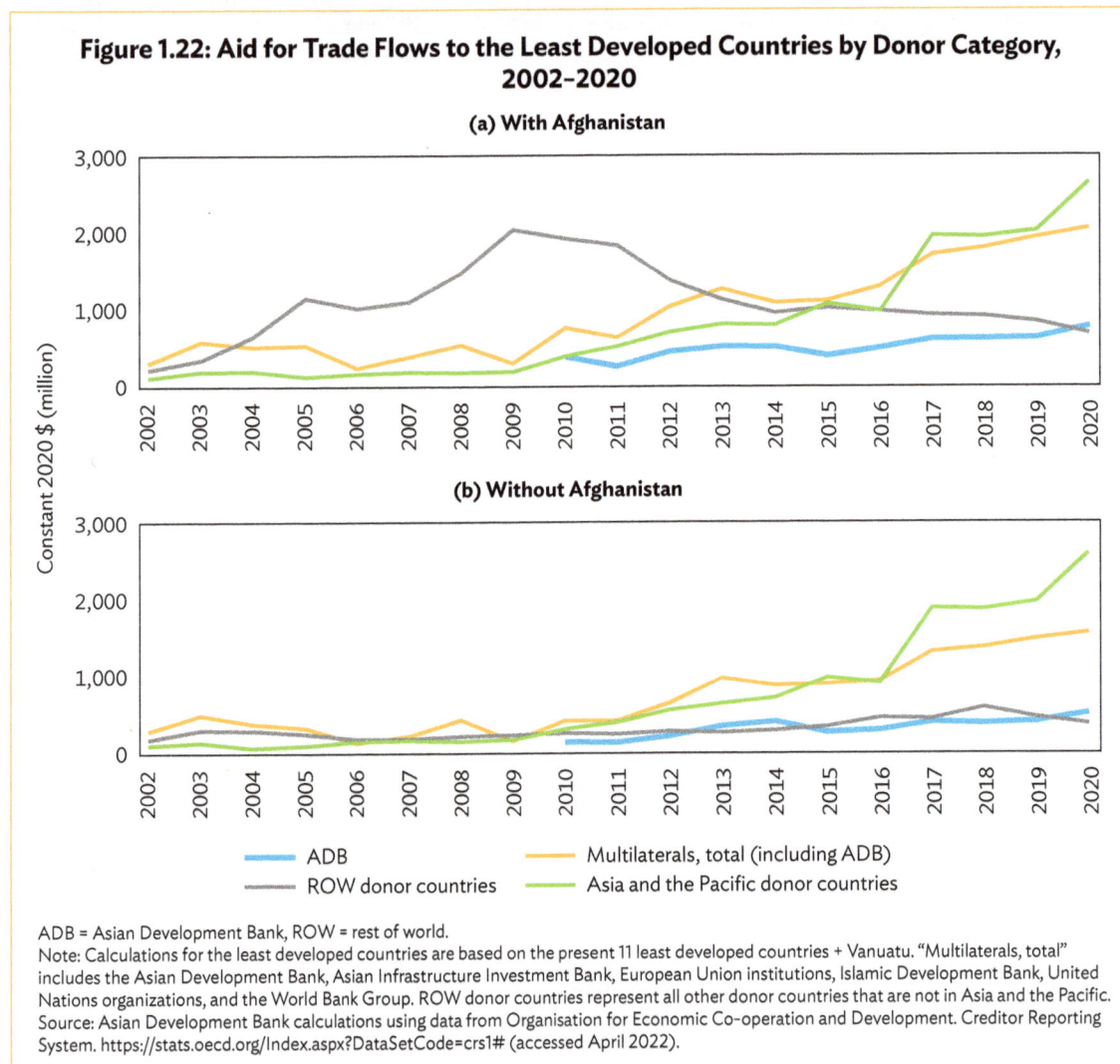

Figure 1.22: Aid for Trade Flows to the Least Developed Countries by Donor Category, 2002–2020

(a) With Afghanistan

(b) Without Afghanistan

ADB = Asian Development Bank, ROW = rest of world.
Note: Calculations for the least developed countries are based on the present 11 least developed countries + Vanuatu. "Multilaterals, total" includes the Asian Development Bank, Asian Infrastructure Investment Bank, European Union institutions, Islamic Development Bank, United Nations organizations, and the World Bank Group. ROW donor countries represent all other donor countries that are not in Asia and the Pacific.
Source: Asian Development Bank calculations using data from Organisation for Economic Co-operation and Development. Creditor Reporting System. https://stats.oecd.org/Index.aspx?DataSetCode=crs1# (accessed April 2022).

However, disbursements made by rest-of-world countries dropped 17% during 2019–2020. By contrast, flows from Asia and the Pacific donors increased 30.6% during the same period.

Only three providers—Japan, the World Bank, and ADB—accounted for about three-quarters of AfT disbursements to LDCs in Asia and the Pacific in 2020.

1.2.2 Implications for Developing Asia

Aid for trade can help developing Asia achieve the Sustainable Development Goals in many ways and support their integration into global markets. However, the Aid for Trade initiative launched in 2005 at the WTO Ministerial Conference in Hong Kong, China will need reform to reflect new trade realities and emerging challenges.

As discussed in this chapter, the region has been active in trade liberalization and disparities are widening among AfT recipients. Least developed countries need particular attention: while AfT flows have increased to LDCs in the last 10 years, there has been some large decreases in the last 3 years, particularly to LDCs in the Pacific. In addition, countries may face challenges of inclusive growth and supply chain reliability as further developed in Chapter 2.

Aid for trade is complex and broadly defined. This chapter shows that the bulk of AfT disbursement goes to economic infrastructure while flows targeting trade policies and regulations remain very limited. The trade landscape has changed: multilateral negotiations at the WTO have stalled and regionalism has become the most common approach to liberalize trade. Supporting developing economies, and in particular LDCs, in assessing the potential gains from regional trade and new digital agreements to negotiate, draft, and implement these agreements should be a priority component of Aid for Trade. More specifically, assistance is needed in leveraging trade agreements to address new challenges of exports diversification, supply chains disruption, and preference erosions, an issue that is particularly important for LDCs. These discussions are further discussed in Chapter 3. The COVID-19 pandemic has also accelerated digitalization among its enterprises and households, raising the importance of understanding digital regulations and digital agreements. This will help to prepare developing Asia for the digital economy in a context of growing international regulatory heterogeneity as discussed in Chapter 4. Chapter 5 presents the policy recommendations on how to support developing Asia to leverage trade and digital agreements for their sustainable development.

Bibliography

Anderson, J. E. 1979. A Theoretical Foundation for the Gravity Equation. *The American Economic Review.* 69 (1): pp. 106–116.

Anderson, J. E., and E. van Wincoop. 2004. Trade Costs. *Journal of Economic Literature* 42 (3): pp. 691–751.

Atkinson, C., C. McCue, E. Prier, and A. Atkinson. 2020. Supply Chain Manipulation, Misrepresentation, and Magical Thinking During the COVID-19 Pandemic. *American Review of Public Administration.* https://doi.org/10.1177/0275074020942055.

Baier, S. L. and J. H. Bergstrand. 2007. Do Free Trade Agreements Actually Increase Members' International Trade? *Journal of international Economics.* 71 (1): pp. 72–95.

Baier, S. L., J. H. Bergstrand, and M. Feng. 2014. Economic Integration Agreements and the Margins of International Trade. *Journal of International Economics.* 93 (2): pp. 339–350.

Baldwin, R., and S. Evenett (eds.) 2020. *COVID-19 and Trade Policy: Why Turning Inward Won't Work.* London: CEPR Press.

Evenett, S. 2020. Sicken Thy Neighbour: The Initial Trade Policy Response to COVID-19. *The World Economy.* 43 (4): pp. 828–839. DOI: 10.1111/twec.12954.

Evenett, S., M. Fiorini, J. Fritz, B. Hoekman, P. Lukaszuk, N. Rocha, M. Ruta, F. Santi, and A. Shingal. 2021. Trade Policy Responses to the COVID-19 Pandemic Crisis: A New Dataset. *The World Economy.* 45 (2): pp. 342–364. https://doi.org/10.1111/twec.13119.

Fiorini, M., B. Hoekman, and A. Yildirim. 2020. COVID-19: Expanding Access to Essential Supplies in a Value Chain World. In R. Baldwin and S. Evenett, eds. *COVID-19 and Trade Policy: Why Turning Inward Won't Work.* London: CEPR Press.

Gereffi, G. 2020. What Does the COVID-19 Pandemic Teach Us about Global Value Chains? The Case of Medical Supplies. *Journal of International Business Policy.* 3 (3): pp. 287–301.

Hale, T., A. Petherick, T. Phillips, and S. Webster. 2020. Variation in Government Responses to COVID-19. *Blavatnik School of Government Working Paper.* 31.

Hoekman, B., M. Fiorini, and A. Yildirim. 2020. COVID-19: Export Controls and International Cooperation. In R. Baldwin and S. Evenett (eds.) *COVID-19 and Trade Policy: Why Turning Inward Won't Work.* London: CEPR Press.

Organisation for Economic Co-Operation and Development (OECD). 2020. The Face Mask Global Value Chain in the COVID-19 Outbreak: Evidence and Policy Lessons. Paris. https://bit.ly/3gtfWqc.

OECD. 2021. Using Trade to Fight COVID-19: Manufacturing and Distributing Vaccines. Paris. https://bit.ly/3HbVZBI.

Piermartini, R. and Y. Yotov. 2016. Estimating Trade Policy Effects with Structural Gravity. *CESifo Working Paper Series.* No. 6009.

Shingal, A., P. Crivelli, and P. Agarwal. 2021. COVID-Era Trade Policy Passthrough to Trade Flows: First Evidence. Forthcoming.

Silva, J. S., and S. Tenreyro . 2006. The Log of Gravity. *The Review of Economics and Statistics* 88 (4): pp. 641–658.

TradeMap. 2021. https://www.trademap.org/Index.aspx.

Appendix 1: Empirical Analysis of Passthrough between Trade Policy and Trade

The regression results from estimation are reported in Table A1.1. Columns 1 and 2 pool food and medical products together. Columns 3 and 4 only include medical products, which are further categorized as medical consumables (columns 5–6), medical equipment (columns 7–8) and drugs and medicines (columns 9–10). Finally, columns 11 and 12 include only food products. Note that the underlying data in columns 1–4 are organized in monthly panels varying at the HS6-digit level; the associated specifications can therefore accommodate importer-product-time and exporter-product-time fixed effects. However, the product variation is missing in the data in columns 5–12; the associated specifications therefore only include time-varying exporter and importer fixed effects. The bilateral fixed effects are included in all specifications.

Among bilateral measures, import liberalization is found to increase bilateral exports by 8.4%[1] in the pooled sample (column 1), bilateral exports of medical products by 11.0% (column 3), and medical consumables by 5.4% (column 5). These results, precisely estimated at 1%, can be easily explained in a world of integrated regional and global value chains, where exports are dependent on imports of intermediate inputs from abroad. These results also provide evidence of a reversal of the Learner's symmetry argument, wherein a tax on imports is equivalent to a tax on exports.

Counterintuitively, however, bilateral import restrictions are found to increase bilateral imports of food products and raise bilateral imports in the pooled sample and medical exports in column (3); all results are precisely estimated at 1%. These findings likely emanate from endogeneity when import restrictions are precisely imposed when the surge in imports (that could have been even more important without the measure) is expected. In contrast, bilateral restrictive subsidy measures seem to have had the expected adverse effect on exports in the pooled sample (column 1) and for food exports (column 11).

Meanwhile, bilateral export policy seems to have had largely counterintuitive effects in these results. Export liberalization undertaken during 2020 is found to have reduced medical equipment exports in the following month (column 7), though the result is only weakly significant. Such measures also seem to have reduced imports of drugs and medicines (column 10) and food imports (column 12). Counterintuitively, again, bilateral export restrictions are found to have increased bilateral exports of all medical goods, and within these, medical consumables and medical equipment in particular (columns 3, 5, and 7, respectively), alluding again to endogeneity or simply suggesting that these policy measures may not have had the desired effect. However, these measures curtailed food exports and imports of drugs and medicines.

Among aggregate measures rendered bilateral by construction, a reporting country's import liberalization had a positive impact on medical imports (column 4) and within those imports of drugs and medicines (column 10) when such measures were accompanied by export liberalization by its trading partner. This combination of measures also increased exports (column 1) in the pooled sample (possibly via the reverse Learner's symmetry effect) though it reduced exports of medical equipment (column 7) and drugs and medicines (column 9).

---

[1] The percentage changes are calculated as [exp(coefficient_estimate)-1]*100.

Table A1.1: Poisson Pseudo Maximum Likelihood Estimates

VARIABLES	(1) Pooled X_{ijkt}	(2) Pooled M_{ijkt}	(3) Medical X_{ijkt}	(4) Medical M_{ijkt}	(5) MC X_{ijkt}	(6) MC M_{ijkt}	(7) ME X_{ijkt}	(8) ME M_{ijkt}	(9) DR X_{ijkt}	(10) DR M_{ijkt}	(11) Food X_{ijkt}	(12) Food M_{ijkt}
m_lib_ijijkt-1	1.364***	-0.041	0.073	0.590**	-0.161	-0.047	-0.820**		-1.066***	1.247*	0.235	0.588
	(0.462)	(0.317)	(0.309)	(0.280)	(0.207)	(0.000)	(0.402)		(0.332)	(0.729)	(0.259)	(0.424)
m_lib_jijkt-1	0.455	0.052	0.265	-0.202	0.214	1.001	2.290***	-0.018	-1.912***	-0.064	0.755*	-0.112
	(0.368)	(0.310)	(0.361)	(0.280)	(0.525)	(0.000)	(0.527)	(0.338)	(0.688)	(0.244)	(0.432)	(0.221)
m_res_ijijkt-1	0.472	0.299	0.384	0.057	0.250	1.086	-0.815**	0.176	0.478	-1.484***	-0.276	0.167
	(0.356)	(0.274)	(0.352)	(0.277)	(0.516)	(0.000)	(0.388)	(0.251)	(0.429)	(0.423)	(0.265)	(0.292)
m_res_jijkt-1	-0.517*	-0.375	-0.186	-0.652***	-1.939***	1.466	-0.841***	-0.152	2.976***	-0.801***	-0.162	0.797***
	(0.297)	(0.304)	(0.317)	(0.167)	(0.539)	(0.000)	(0.127)	(0.113)	(0.792)	(0.251)	(0.490)	(0.266)
m_libijkt-1	0.081***	0.016	0.104***	-0.012	0.053***	-0.005	0.008	0.026	-0.183	-0.184	-0.083	-0.146
	(0.027)	(0.013)	(0.033)	(0.012)	(0.019)	(0.000)	(0.036)	(0.020)	(0.425)	(0.115)	(0.087)	(0.143)
m_resijkt-1	0.013	0.186***	0.066***	0.015	-0.083	-0.007	-0.010	-0.025			0.035	0.165***
	(0.025)	(0.054)	(0.024)	(0.024)	(0.105)	(0.000)	(0.015)	(0.024)			(0.056)	(0.059)
sbsdy_resijkt-1	-0.212***	0.171***	-0.112	0.188**	-0.046	0.319	0.034	-0.039	0.002	-0.226***	-0.159**	0.014
	(0.080)	(0.059)	(0.108)	(0.079)	(0.057)	(0.000)	(0.060)	(0.039)	(0.052)	(0.069)	(0.072)	(0.047)
x_libijkt-1	0.028	-0.084	-0.038	-0.149	0.098	-0.029	-0.756*		-0.080	-1.810***	0.007	-0.116*
	(0.018)	(0.056)	(0.130)	(0.118)	(0.125)	(0.000)	(0.404)		(0.102)	(0.300)	(0.013)	(0.068)
x_resijkt-1	0.100	0.046	0.401***	-0.059	0.217***	-0.046	0.062**	-0.032	-0.074	-0.627**	-0.276***	0.137
	(0.070)	(0.043)	(0.085)	(0.048)	(0.082)	(0.000)	(0.030)	(0.024)	(0.058)	(0.319)	(0.066)	(0.123)
Observations	6,575	6,673	4,859	4,932	1,879	2,015	1,596	1,498	1,317	1,374	1,696	1,723
Exporter-Importer FE	YES	YES	YES	YES	YES	YES	YES	YES	YES	YES	YES	YES
Importer-Product-Month FE	YES	YES	YES	YES	YES	YES	YES	YES	YES	YES	YES	YES
Exporter-Product-Month FE	YES	YES	YES	YES								
Importer-Month FE									YES	YES	YES	YES
Exporter-Month FE									YES	YES	YES	YES
Pseudo R2	0.964	0.962	0.975	0.980	0.991	0.996	0.992	0.991	0.989	0.973	0.979	0.979

DR = drugs and medicines, FE = _____, MC = medical consumables, ME = medical equipment, M_{ijkt} = _____, X_{ijkt} = _____.
Note: Counterintuitive coefficient estimates are color-coded red. Standard errors, clustered by dyad–HS6 product-month, included in parentheses. Levels of significance: *** p<0.01, ** p<0.05, * p<0.1.
Source: Asian Development Bank estimates.

Meanwhile, a reporting country's export liberalization accompanied by its partner's import liberalization enhanced its bilateral exports of medical equipment and food products (albeit only at the 10% level of significance; columns 7 and 11, respectively) but it reduced its exports of drugs and medicines (column 9), which is counterintuitive.

In other results, a reporting country's import restriction had the expected adverse effect on its imports of drugs and medicines (column 10) when such measures were accompanied by export restriction by its partner; this combination of measures also reduced the reporting country's bilateral exports of medical equipment (column 7), which suggests the role of integrated value chains in the production of medical equipment.

2. Trade, Inequality, and Vulnerability— Challenges and Opportunities for a Resilient and Inclusive Recovery

2.1 International Trade and Inequality

2.1.1 Impact of Trade Liberalization

Trade liberalization can increase growth and decrease inequality between countries, but it may also increase inequality within countries. COVID-19 has enhanced existing inequalities, particularly for frontline and blue-collar workers. Digitalization of economic activity driven by COVID-19 means that more capacity building will be needed to address the digital divide, in particular by ensuring that micro, small, and medium-sized enterprises (MSMEs) and working people shift to the digital economy.

International trade theory maintains that trade liberalization has significant and long-term redistributive impacts. Trade liberalization may affect income differently among different social groups, skilled and unskilled workers, women, and men. As an economy becomes more open to trade, domestic relative prices shift, leading to income redistribution and trade gains. Gains and losses among various groups in society are determined by changes in the relative pricing in each group, and the overall socioeconomic characteristics of the group.

Income inequality

Empirical research in Asia and the Pacific and other countries shows that the impact of trade liberalization on inequality is far more varied than is often maintained. Export-oriented industrialization and trade competitiveness can be engines of growth, as the East Asian markets demonstrate, especially the PRC. Conversely, severe import competition may lead to deindustrialization, as in the United Kingdom (UK) in the 1970s.[21] Trade liberalization may force labor reallocation from the manufacturing sector to lower-productivity sectors, reducing wages and exacerbating inequality. Trade liberalization can help significantly reduce inequality between countries, but it may aggravate inequality within countries.

Empirical evidence shows that globalization has led to an increase of in-country income inequality. Studies have found that greater financial openness is linked to higher income inequality. In particular, Pal and Ghosh (2007) argue that trade liberalization can harm the agricultural sector, which employs low-wage workers, while benefitting just a small segment of the manufacturing sector. These disparities lead to rising inequality.

---

[21] See Gregory and Greenhalgh (1987) for a discussion.

Industry- or employer-specific employee skills can widen the gap between trade winners and losers. Workers' difficulty in moving across regions within a country can also affect the distribution of benefits from trade. Both theoretical and empirical studies suggest that income redistribution due to trade liberalization hurts the less fortunate, especially in advanced economies. The disadvantaged are, for the most part, poorer and less skilled or educated employees, and regions already suffering from deindustrialization and job losses.

Governments can compensate by providing social benefits for job losses, but such benefits can sometimes capture a large share of the gains from trade, reducing the net welfare effect of trade. Further, trade liberalization may decrease revenues from tariffs so government has less revenue to finance social programs.

Freer trade may enhance productivity growth within an economy, but even medium- or long-run growth may not always lead to a rise in welfare. Welfare-enhancing growth is most likely when trade increases productivity within sectors, either within firms or by reallocation among firms. This is especially true if import competition forces less-efficient firms to exit the market, while making the rest more efficient.

Gender

Global and local variables—such as resource endowments, labor market institutions, consumer preferences, and government interventions—can influence the impact of trade liberalization and foreign direct investment on gender disparity. If men and women are imperfect substitutes in the production process and in different industries, trade liberalization may positively affect the wages and income of women. But whenever a positive relationship is discovered between the liberalization of trade and demand for female labor, a proviso often exists. Where trade leads to the installation of capital- and skill-intensive technology, both the demand for female labor and women's relative wages may decrease. Studies have found that poor, elderly, or unskilled female laborers are hurt most. However, if trade liberalization is accompanied by an understanding of the barriers and impacts, including data, and greater acquisition of education and skills along with incentives, such as women's legal rights and access to technology, it can lead to gender-responsive actions and thereby increase gender equality.

Empirical evidence

Several authors have explored the relationship between trade liberalization and inequality (Table 2.1). While the review is not exhaustive, the evidence in these studies is mixed. In some countries, trade liberalization has aggravated income inequality among various segments of the worker population, while in others it has been successful in abating wage inequality through wage premium channels.

Table 2.1: Economy-Specific Findings on Impact of Trade Liberalization on Inequality

Reference	Findings from Select Papers
Autor, Dorn, and Hanson (2013)	In the United States (US), exposure of local labor markets to growing Chinese imports led to a decline in the share of manufacturing employment in the US working population. Import shocks triggered a decline in wages primarily outside the manufacturing sector. Reductions in both employment and wage levels led to a decline in the average earnings of households. This resulted in rising transfer payments through multiple federal and state programs.
Mah (2013)	In the People's Republic of China (PRC), several variables were used to measure income inequality and trade liberalization. Regardless of the measure, the empirical evidence showed that trade liberalization had a strong, positive effect on the PRC's income inequality. The higher the ratio of trade openness the higher the resulting income inequality. The evidence of the positive effect of foreign direct investment inflows on income inequality is at most weak. The authors could not find any evidence that the pursuit of decentralization leads to higher income inequality.
Kumar and Mishra (2008)	In India, results pointed to a significant relationship between trade policy and industry wage premiums. In sectors with the largest tariff reductions, wages increased relative to the economy-wide average. Trade liberalization led to decreased wage inequality between skilled and unskilled workers in India. Results show that since tariff reductions were proportionately larger in sectors that employed a larger share of unskilled workers. Unskilled workers benefited relative to skilled workers.
Aldaba (2013)	In the Philippines, openness and trade liberalization led to increases in import competition. This seemed to have lowered the wage skill premium as domestic firms shifted their manufacturing process toward low, value-added activities requiring relatively less skill-intensive production. This, in turn, reduced the wage skill premium within firms. Results suggest the need to transform and upgrade manufacturing in the Philippines and shift toward more diversified and sophisticated export products. Technological upgrading should be an important channel to drive the demand for skilled labor and skill-intensive manufacturing processes.
Amiti and Davis (2012)	The empirical results of a 1991–2000 study on the trade liberalization experience of Indonesia show that firm heterogeneity matters when it comes to trade liberalization. The wages of their workers are also affected by trade liberalization. The modes of globalization of the firms at which they work, i.e., whether liberalization occurs in final or intermediate goods, also have an impact on wages. Cuts in output tariffs reduce wages at firms oriented exclusively to the domestic market but raise wages at firms that export a sufficient share of their output. Cuts in input tariffs raise wages at firms that import inputs while having an insignificant effect on wages of workers at firms that fail to import. In short, liberalization along each dimension raises wages for workers at firms that are most globalized and lowers wages at firms oriented to the domestic economy or which are marginal globalizers.
Anwar and Sun (2012)	Results suggest that trade liberalization has contributed to an increase in the skilled–unskilled wage gap in the PRC and increased market competition has contributed to a decrease in the wage gap. Results also suggests that the impact of firm characteristics like labor productivity positively affects the wage gap and an increase in foreign invested firms contributes to rising wage gap.

continued on next page

Table 2:1 continued

Reference	Findings from Select Papers
Berik et al. (2004)	Competition from foreign trade in concentrated industries is positively associated with wage discrimination against female workers.
	In Taipei,China, greater trade openness in concentrated industries is associated with wider residual wage gaps between men and women. Import competition appears to widen the wage gap by hurting women's relative employment prospects, leading to a loss of bargaining power for them. Women thus appear to be bearing the brunt of employers' competitive cost-cutting efforts. In the Republic of Korea, a slight reduction in export openness appears to be associated with less wage discrimination by gender in concentrated industries.
Tejani and Milberg (2016)	The authors find that the relative employment of women increased in developing countries but decreased in the high-income ones.
	Results show that while Latin American countries continued to experience rising female intensity of employment, most Southeast Asian and Pacific countries experienced a "defeminization" of employment. Evidence suggests that initial low levels of female intensity and slower industrial upgrading explain the increase on female employment participation in manufacturing in Latin America, while initial high levels of female intensity and a dramatic industrial upgrading experienced in Southeast Asia explains the defeminization of manufacturing labor in that region.
Mugan (2020)	In Viet Nam, firms that adopt new technologies and restructure their organization are likely to move part of their activities to more value-added and skill-based. This restructuring increases the wage gap between the skilled and unskilled workers due to the increase in demand for skilled workers. Firms that are part of production networks and value chains are likely to undertake more restructuring and international activities.
Kohpaiboon et al. (2013)	In Thailand, the impacts of engaging in the global production network on the wage skill premium varies among firms and tends to be an increasing function of a number of skilled operation workers. When the mean value of skill share in Thailand is used, evidence shows that participation in networks requires more skilled workers than unskilled ones and slightly widens the wage skill premium within firms. Results also show that output tariffs were important in determining the industry wage skill premium across firms in Thailand. Opening up to the international trade would lead to specialization across countries according to their comparative advantage (in firms where output tariffs are high) and ultimately reduce the wage skill premium. Reduction in input tariff could help reduce the wage skill premium, but only for firms that import their intermediate input.

Source: Compiled by ADB.

2.1.2 Challenges and Opportunities Arising from COVID-19

The pandemic affected advanced and poorer economies differently, with developing countries and LDCs most heavily affected. Since March 2020, workers in developing countries experienced a 43% greater reduction in working hours and incomes than did workers in high-income countries. Governments in advanced countries supported workers through social security nets, unemployment benefits, and relaxation in tax laws. However, governments in emerging and poorer economies did not have access to the required funds to mitigate the impact on affected workers. International trade can help alleviate these disparities. The reduction of inequality between countries requires multilateral cooperation to improve trade options for developing countries. The WTO's Agreement on Trade Facilitation demonstrates that linking trade obligations with development assistance programs is viable: its Aid for Trade initiative is important in encouraging governments and donors to recognize the role that trade can play in development.

COVID-19 also exacerbated inequalities within many countries. Social distancing measures and government mandated lockdowns affected working people differently. High-paid, white-collar workers were able to shift to a work-from-home environment, but low-paid, low-skilled, blue-collar workers were not. They faced redundancies caused by factory, manufacturing plant, and office closures. Some became delivery agents engaged with e-commerce portals (food, medicines, groceries) and household staff (cleaners, refuse removal). Other groups of blue-collar workers engaged in sectors most hurt during the pandemic simply became redundant, such as in hotels, restaurants, tourism services, and factories.

Frontline workers, on the other hand, were engaged in providing essential services during the pandemic: health workers (nurses, hospital staff ambulance drivers), providers of government services, and staff at essential services, pharmacies, and groceries faced dangerous working conditions. These workers were more exposed to the virus and faced redundancies because of infection.

The disparities between both blue-collar and frontline workers and white-collar workers led to a rise in inequality within the working population. Increased out-of-pocket health care expenses also worsened the gap and led to inequality in access to health services. A survey revealed that 64% of households in Indonesia, 50% in Pakistan, and 46% in the Philippines were unable to receive medical attention in the beginning of the pandemic due to lack of financial resources. By October 2020, fiscal stimulus packages announced in developing countries reached only 13% of population impacted by the pandemic. Indonesia, Pakistan, and the Philippines reallocated domestic spending to help scaleup social protection, but it was not enough. Consequently, governments were forced to borrow large amounts from international funding and financial institutions, adding to their growing debt while collecting lower government tax revenues during the pandemic. Because of this, the divide between wealthier and poorer countries widened during the pandemic and may take years to close.

Women make up a larger share of employment in the textiles, apparel, footwear, tourism, travel, and telecommunications sectors. These sectors were severely affected by declines in export activity. For example, in prepandemic Bangladesh, 80% of the workforce in the readymade garment sector were women. That industry witnessed a decline of 45.8% in orders in the first quarter of 2020 and an 81% decline in April 2020 alone. Order cancellations also affected women's employment in Cambodia, Viet Nam, and other Asia and Pacific countries. In other export-oriented industries women constituted about 33.2% of the total work force. About 36.7% of the workforce of firms engaged in global value chains were women.

If international trade is to be sustainable even during pandemics, it needs to be more inclusive. Poorer countries, small businesses and producers, marginalized workers, women, and youth should all be able to benefit. Removing trade barriers and enhancing trade facilitation and finance can increase market access for disadvantaged groups. Improvements in the capacity (such as better education, health systems, and infrastructure) can also enable them to take advantage of these opportunities. In addition, gender-specific programs such as all-women training programs or gender-responsive loan financing programs may be required to overcome sociocultural biases in certain countries. Aid for trade has a role to play in promoting skills upgrading via programs specifically aimed at small businesses and digitalization.

Ramping up export promotion programs is critical for small businesses. These programs should provide small businesses with up-to-date information on market access conditions—tariff preferences, quotas, rules of origin, standards, and the complicated processes associated with regulatory compliance.

Levelling the playing field for small and large firms is important. This includes enabling diversification of markets and portfolios, information and communication technology (ICT) services, and introducing skills development programs. Two programs stand out as examples: Malaysia's MyDigitalWorkforce Work in Tech program rolled out by the Malaysia Digital Economy Corporation and Singapore's SkillsFuture program (Box 2.1).

Box 2.1: Examples of Skills Development Program to Address Globalization Challenges

In 2021, the Malaysia Digital Economy Corporation rolled out the initiative MyDigitalWorkforce Work in technology to incentivize employers to hire Malaysians via digital upskilling and reskilling programs. Through its Digital Business Services program, the initiative aims to increase digital literacy and skills among Malaysians to curb rising unemployment. The Government of Malaysia funds the program and offers a 40% salary subsidy for 6 months and training incentives for in-house and external or third-party training. Anybody unemployed for a minimum of 2 months, retrenched, or a fresh graduate is eligible for this program.

In 2015, the Singapore government rolled out the SkillsFuture program, a national movement to maximize the potential of Singaporeans and to enable them to achieve potential regardless of starting point. The key aim is to empower individuals to take ownership of skills acquisition and to support lifelong learning. The movement encompasses a range of initiatives that target various segments of the population, such as SkillsFuture Credit, SkillsFuture Earn and Learn, SkillsFuture Mid-Career Enhanced Subsidy, and the SkillsFuture Study Awards. The SkillsFuture Credit provides every Singaporean aged 25 and above 500 Singapore dollars to pay for a variety of courses, from cooking to photography. The government also planned to invest $1 billion annually between 2015 and 2020 on a slew of initiatives like student counselling, internships, and midcareer learning.

Source: Asian Development Bank.

As the discussion shows, trade liberalization can lower income inequality between countries and raise it within countries. COVID-19 has exacerbated that latter situation, particularly for blue-collar and frontline workers. Post-COVID-19, many countries in Asia and the Pacific will need to focus on reintegration of marginalized sectors and workers, particularly women, into the mainstream economy, such as through programs that provide trade-related adjustment support. A focus on technical education and training is particularly important. So is ensuring that limitations created by digital inequality are reversed and that all businesses and citizens are able to participate in the digital economy.

2.2 COVID-19 Supply Chains Vulnerability and Resilience

2.2.1 Supply Chains Vulnerability, Resilience, and Robustness

Advances in science and technology coupled with trade liberalization have created a more integrated world economy and increased the number and reach of global value chains (GVCs). As GVCs dominate international trade, ensuring their ability to deliver is a critical part of the COVID-19 response. Global sourcing and outsourcing have not only made supply networks complex, they have increased the risk of supply chain disruptions. Firm failures to manage these risks will disrupt the efficient functioning of supply chains and profits, and the profits of direct and indirect suppliers and customers. There are five distinct types of risks that GVCs face:

(i)   Risks internal to the firm such as low value-added, failure of managerial processes, and supply chain controls.

(ii)   Risks external to the firm but internal to the supply chain network. These include demand or downstream dependency and supply or upstream dependency.

(iii) Risks external to the supply chain network, including environmental, socioeconomic, political, or technological hazards.

(iv)   Demand-side risks from a sudden fall in demand as well as supply-side risks, e.g., a drop in the quality of supply.

(v)   Catastrophic risks external to the supply chain.

Firms often choose between robustness and resilience in addressing these risks.

Robustness is the ability to cope with changes and sustain function and value creation despite disruptions and disturbances. Simply, robustness is the ability to withstand or overcome adverse conditions without disruption. Robustness can be increased, for example, through proper selection of efficient supply chain partners. Static robustness includes ensuring viability of factories and warehouses, the right size of networks, and strong linkages between different operations. Dynamic robustness addresses processes in the supply chain, including efficient delivery systems.

Resilience is the ability of a system to recover quickly from difficulties and return to an original state or move to a new, better state. It is the ability to quickly resume production when interrupted. Resilient approaches require shorter reaction times to absorb negative shocks and a faster recovery period. Resilience often relies on advanced digital tools such as Logistics 4.0 (discussed below), which connects subsystems across all levels of production to logistics networks through ICT.

The choice to invest in building robustness or resilience involves a managerial tradeoff between investment in visible capacity and investment in inventory. Highly complex supply chains will build robustness while firms competing on agility and flexibility will invest in building resilience.

Firms can develop proactive strategies by increasing agility to react to an unpredictable event. Such strategies build greater adaptability to change achieved by following redundancy practices. They include more buffers, inventories, or slack times and capacity, as well as resource pooling or multiple suppliers to manage uncertainty in demand and supply. In contrast, reactive strategies imply that supply chains adjust to contain a negative shock. They are often undertaken by companies with greater flexibility in operations and recovery capacity. "Flexibility" is the ability and agility to reconfigure supply chain operations quickly and effectively.

Supply chain agility can be defined as the ability to respond rapidly to unpredictable changes in demand or supply. It can be further broken down into visibility and velocity. Visibility is the ability to see a supply chain end-to-end with close collaboration with customers and suppliers, and internal integration. This can be facilitated through an increase in speed and quality of information sharing. Visibility also allows firms to mitigate threats and safeguard performance, boosting resilience and robustness. Velocity refers to quicker responses through streamlining and synchronization of processes.

Some of the most effective tools used to manage network-wide risk and improve resilience and robustness of supply chains through collaboration along the network are collaborative planning, forecasting, and replenishment initiatives developed by Ireland and Bruce (2000). Other forms of supply chain management tools can also be used, such as demand management through collaborative designing and merchandising, collaborative transportation management, joint optimization across the supply chain, and real-time collaboration to minimize discrepancies or stoppages that may arise during execution. Supply chain risk management combines these different strategies, focusing on business and process continuity through greater risk control, to support both supply chain resilience and robustness.

The COVID-19 pandemic resulted in supply- and demand-side risks. The supply-side risk emerged from geographical clusters located in the same region. In the worst-case scenario, this risk halted production and caused furloughs and layoffs. The demand-side risk originated from a global recession due to government-initiated lockdowns, restrictions on the movement of people, and erosion of consumer confidence. Because the pandemic was recent, we do not yet have empirical evidence of its impact on supply- and demand-side risks for supply chains.

However, preliminary observations exist. This crisis has created the need to make supply chains more robust to anticipate possible disruptions, including diversification of supplier networks, information sharing, and greater knowledge or visibility of inventory and output levels along the supply chain. Risk assessments and supply chain monitoring are also important. Fostering a long-term relationship with a single supplier or a set of safe suppliers may also help increase resilience but may not be ideal for robustness of supply chains. The pandemic could also accelerate a shift in global production away from the manufacturing hubs in the PRC, a trend that emerged before the US-PRC trade tensions.

Digitalization: The future of supply chain management

During the pandemic, large global supply chains, particularly automobile manufacturing and airline services, were severely affected. High dependence on a few suppliers for imports of automobile components reduced overall demand, and restricted global movements of goods and services. Regionalization of sourcing, real-time information systems, use of digital connectivity, and supply chain automation were the most widely used resilience strategies by automobile manufacturers. Airline companies preferred to use virtual marketplaces and business continuity plans to minimize the impact of the pandemic. The impact of COVID-19 has compelled companies to embrace a digital transformation to increase information processing and streamline supplier selection procedures.

A new concept, Logistics 4.0, has been developed for supply chain management. Logistics 4.0 connects subsystems across all levels of production to logistics networks through ICT. This concept uses the Internet of Things to increase transparency along the chain, in addition to Big Data mining and analysis to facilitate sharing of information, and synchronization of optimization strategies for robust supply chains.

Supply-chain nodes also need to be integrated to assist firms in remobilizing their networks and protecting human capital. There is scope for building partnerships with governments, as well as industries, to ensure logistic continuity and to collaborate on combined resilience and recovery strategies.

Companies across sectors are yet to fully understand the impact of the COVID-19 pandemic on their production, supply, and demand patterns. Although some governments have already announced strategies to reopen their economies, factories continue to have shortages in supply of inputs and demand for their products. COVID-19 is likely to continue affecting the economy and any recovery strategy must include coordinated effort across industries and economies to ensure greater resilience.

2.2.2 Geographical Diversification of Value Chains in Developing Asia

The COVID-19 pandemic reignited discussions about repatriation of value chains, near-shoring, and geographical or supplier diversification. The persistence of COVID-19 and the possibility of new contagions are prompting firms to formulate new international strategies on GVCs under the assumption that this could again disrupt movement of people, goods, and services. Policy debates after COVID-19 focus on reshoring and greater international diversification of GVCs as options, with the latter possibly offering more resilience to macroeconomic shocks.

However, diversification of GVCs—redesigning products to make their components less specific and reorganizing the production chains accordingly—entails significant costs, which in turn discourage diversification.

An analysis is performed to investigate the extent to which ADB countries rely on certain partners as export markets for their GVC-based exports and as sources for their GVC-based imports, and the potential for geographical diversification of GVCs. The analysis uses prepandemic merchandise trade data at the HS 6-digit level. Appendix 2 details methodology and findings.

Several factors determine geographical diversification. These include market size, labor costs, quality of infrastructure and institutions, regulatory framework, such as trade and investment policy, and political and social stability in potential investment destinations. National and international economic policies can also play a vital role in promoting GVC diversification—economic cooperation or provision of economic assistance can contribute to building and improving the quality of soft and hard infrastructure in developing countries and make them attractive destinations.

The empirical results point to countries' vulnerability along multiple dimensions including (i) a rise over time in the number of HS6-digit products that are traded between just a few partners, and (ii) large shares of the highly concentrated goods in the total count of HS6-traded products, for Pacific island states and low-income countries in particular. The top 20 destinations and sources of ADB member countries account for nearly 70% and over 90% of highly concentrated exports and highly concentrated imports, respectively. This concentration highlights another dimension of GVC vulnerability to macroeconomic shocks.

In remaining concentrated in both suppliers and markets, ADB member countries may have become more vulnerable over time. The absolute number of highly concentrated exports (HCGx) and highly concentrated imports (HCGm) increased between 2010–2011 and 2018–2019 (Figure 2.1).

Figure 2.1: Increase in the Absolute Number of Highly Concentrated Exports and Highly Concentrated Imports between 2010–2011 and 2018–2019

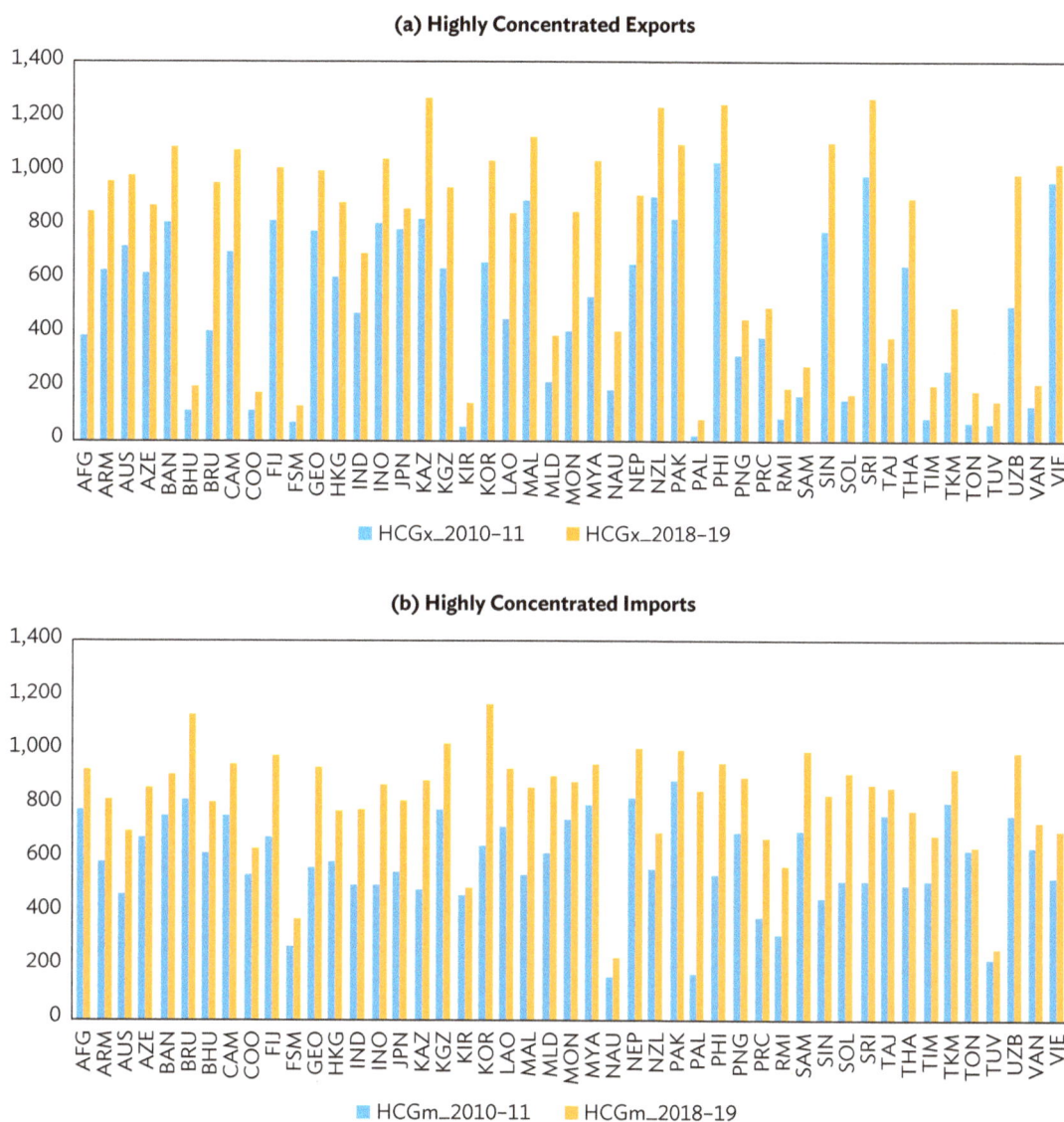

(a) Highly Concentrated Exports

■ HCGx_2010–11   ■ HCGx_2018–19

(b) Highly Concentrated Imports

■ HCGm_2010–11   ■ HCGm_2018–19

AFG = Afghanistan; ARM = Armenia; AUS = Australia; AZE = Azerbaijan; BAN = Bangladesh; BHU = Bhutan; BRU = Brunei Darussalam; CAM = Cambodia; COO = Cook Islands; FIJ = Fiji; FSM = Federated States of Micronesia; GEO = Georgia; HCGM = highly concentrated imports; HCGx = highly concentrated exports; HKG = Hong Kong, China; IND = India; INO = Indonesia; JPN = Japan; KAZ = Kazakhstan; KGZ = Kyrgyz Republic; KIR = Kiribati; KOR = Republic of Korea; LAO = Lao People's Democratic Republic; MAL = Malaysia; MLD = Maldives; MON = Mongolia; MYA = Myanmar; NAU = Nauru; NEP = Nepal; NZL = New Zealand; PAK = Pakistan; PAL = Palau; PHI = Philippines; PNG = Papua New Guinea; PRC = People's Republic of China; RMI = Marshall Islands; SAM = Samoa; SIN = Singapore; SOL = Solomon Islands; SRI = Sri Lanka; THA = Thailand; TAJ = Tajikistan; TKM = Turkmenistan; TIM = Timor-Leste; TON = Tonga; TUV = Tuvalu; UZB = Uzbekistan; VAN = Vanuatu; VIE = Viet Nam.

Source: Asian Development Bank calculations based on Base pour l'Analyse du Commerce International database (accessed May 2022).

The increase in HCGx is found to be inversely related to per capita income levels (Figure 2.1a), suggesting that lower-income ADB countries may have become even more vulnerable over time and underlying the significance of partner diversification in destination markets. In contrast, the increase in HCGm between 2010–2011 and 2018–2019 is positively correlated with per capita income levels, suggesting that lower-income ADB countries may have become less vulnerable along this dimension.

The United States (US) and the PRC remain the top export markets followed in order by the Russian Federation, Japan, and Australia for ADB members' highly concentrated exports in 2018–2019. The US and the PRC were also the top two destinations in 2010–2011 (Table 2). The PRC, India, the US, Türkiye, and New Zealand were among the top five sources of ADB members' highly concentrated imports in 2018–2019; the PRC and India were also the top two sources in 2010–2011 with Australia, Japan, and the US and the next three most important (Table 2.2).

Figure 2.2: Highly Concentrated Exports and Highly Concentrated Imports Increase between 2010–2011 and 2018–2019—Correlation with Per Capita Income

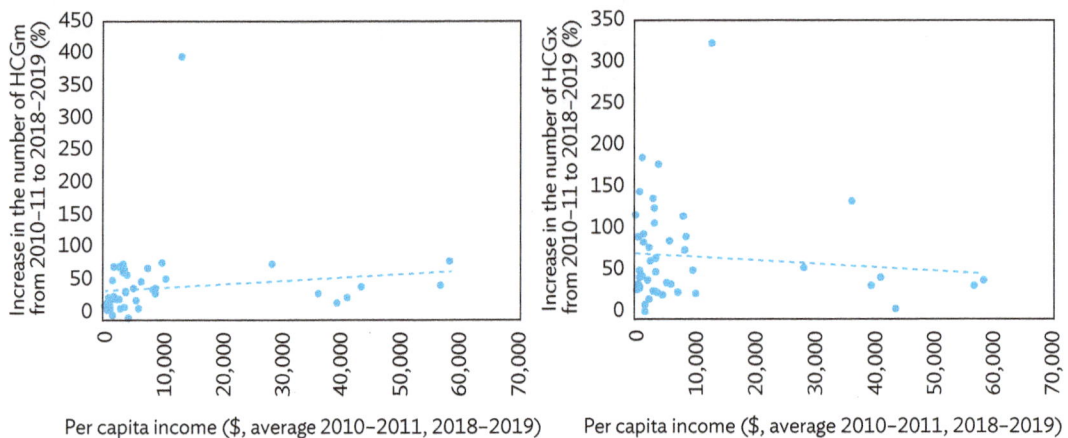

HCGm = highly concentrated imports, HCGx = highly concentrated exports.
Source: Asian Development Bank calculations based on Base pour l'Analyse du Commerce International and World Bank. World Development Indicators. https://databank.worldbank.org/source/world-development-indicators (accessed May 2022).

Table 2.2: Top 20 Destinations and Source Countries of ADB Members' Highly Concentrated Exports and Highly Concentrated Imports Over Time

Highly Concentrated Exports

HCGx Destinations	2010–2011	Share (%)	HCGx Destinations	2018–2019	Share (%)
USA	2,682	11.75	USA	3,902	11.57
PRC	1,233	5.4	PRC	1,963	5.82
AUS	1,175	5.15	RUS	1,739	5.16
RUS	977	4.28	JPN	1,514	4.49
JPN	945	4.14	AUS	1,381	4.1
UKG	895	3.92	SIN	1,304	3.87
IND	854	3.74	GER	1,259	3.73
SIN	802	3.51	UKG	1,207	3.58
GER	794	3.48	HKG	1,031	3.06
HKG	708	3.1	MAL	874	2.59
FRA	524	2.3	FRA	870	2.58
MAL	494	2.16	IND	859	2.55
KOR	475	2.08	THA	842	2.5
NZL	475	2.08	KOR	757	2.25
INO	461	2.02	NZL	650	1.93
THA	429	1.88	INO	617	1.83
VIE	348	1.52	CAN	588	1.74
ITA	347	1.52	ARE	573	1.7
GEO	345	1.51	NET	544	1.61
TUR	332	1.45	VIE	517	1.53
Top 20	15,295	67.0	Top 20	22,991	68.2

Highly Concentrated Imports

HCGm Sources	2010–11	Share (%)	HCGm Sources	2018–19	Share (%)
PRC	8,577	31.48	PRC	14,681	38.52
IND	1,629	5.98	IND	2,480	6.51
AUS	1,418	5.21	USA	1,865	4.89
USA	1,416	5.20	TUR	1,713	4.49
JPN	1,387	5.09	NZL	1,461	3.83
THA	1,320	4.85	AUS	1,397	3.67
TUR	1,267	4.65	THA	1,361	3.57
NZL	1,266	4.65	JPN	1,324	3.47
SIN	1,116	4.10	SIN	1,040	2.73
GER	827	3.04	ITA	933	2.45
ITA	642	2.36	MAL	924	2.42
KOR	603	2.21	GER	831	2.18
HKG	574	2.11	HKG	776	2.04
RUS	522	1.92	RUS	766	2.01
MAL	464	1.70	VIE	749	1.97
IDN	455	1.67	KOR	700	1.84
FIJ	400	1.47	IDN	552	1.45
UKG	373	1.37	ARE	547	1.44
IRN	302	1.11	FIJ	540	1.42
FRA	265	0.97	N/A	348	0.91
Top 20	24,823	91.1	Top 20	34,988	91.8

ARE = United Arab Emirates; AUS = Australia; CAN = Canada; GER = Germany; FIJ = Fiji; FRA = France; GEO = Georgia; HCGm = highly concentrated imports; HCGx = highly concentrated exports; HKG = Hong Kong, China; INO = Indonesia; IND = India; IRN = Iran; ITA = Italy; JPN = Japan; KOR = Republic of Korea; MAL = Malaysia; NET = Netherlands; NZL = New Zealand; PRC = People's Republic of China; RUS = Russian Federation; SIN = Singapore; THA = Thailand; TUR = Türkiye; UKG = United Kingdom; USA = United States; VIE = Viet Nam.
Source: Asian Development Bank calculations based on Base pour l'Analyse du Commerce International database (accessed May 2022).

There is considerable diversity within ADB members, however. Higher-income countries in Asia and the Pacific relied on a larger number of ADB trading partners, both as destinations for their highly concentrated exports and as sources of their highly concentrated imports, and both in 2010–2011 and 2018–2019. Lower income and Pacific countries showed much higher levels of concentration.

Australia, the PRC, the Republic of Korea, and Singapore reported the largest number of destination countries while the PRC, Japan, and the Republic of Korea reported the largest number of source countries (Figure 2.3). This group of higher-income countries may be relatively less vulnerable to macroeconomic shocks as they already trade with a more diversified set of partners even when it comes to highly concentrated GVC-based products.

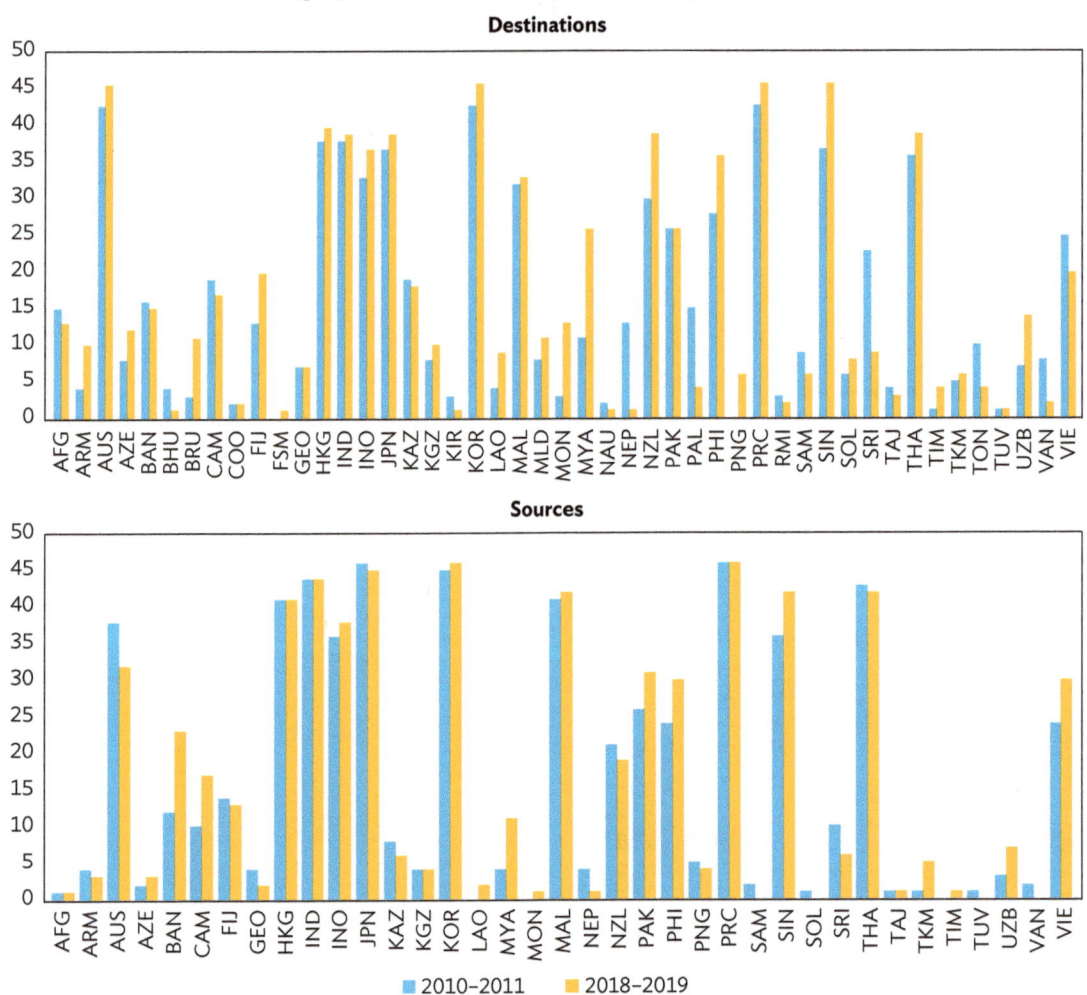

Figure 2.3: Destinations for and Sources of Highly Concentrated Imports and Highly Concentrated Exports Among ADB Members

AFG = Afghanistan; ARM = Armenia; AUS = Australia; AZE = Azerbaijan; BAN = Bangladesh; BHU = Bhutan; BRU = Brunei Darussalam; CAM = Cambodia; COO = Cook Islands; FIJ = Fiji; FSM = Federated States of Micronesia; GEO = Georgia; HKG = Hong Kong, China; IND = India; INO = Indonesia; JPN = Japan; KAZ = Kazakhstan; KGZ = Kyrgyz Republic; KIR = Kiribati; KOR = Republic of Korea; LAO = Lao People's Democratic Republic; MAL = Malaysia; MLD = Maldives; MON = Mongolia; MYA = Myanmar; NAU = Nauru; NEP = Nepal; NZL = New Zealand; PAK = Pakistan; PAL = Palau; PHI = Philippines; PNG = Papua New Guinea; PRC = People's Republic of China; RMI = Marshall Islands; SAM = Samoa; SIN = Singapore; SOL = Solomon Islands; SRI = Sri Lanka; TAJ = Tajikistan; THA = Thailand; TKM = Turkmenistan; TIM = Timor-Leste; TON = Tonga; TUV = Tuvalu; UZB = Uzbekistan; VAN = Vanuatu; VIE = Viet Nam.
Source: Asian Development Bank calculations based on Base pour l'Analyse du Commerce International database (accessed May 2022).

Exports from some low- and middle-income countries and LDCs are highly concentrated in the EU and the US markets. Pacific DMCs and low-income DMCs report among the highest shares of HCGx and HCGm during 2018–2019 in exported and imported products (Figure 2.4). Vulnerability is comparatively higher on the export side, suggesting that a policy priority should be to locate alternative destinations for highly concentrated exports from some of these countries.[22]

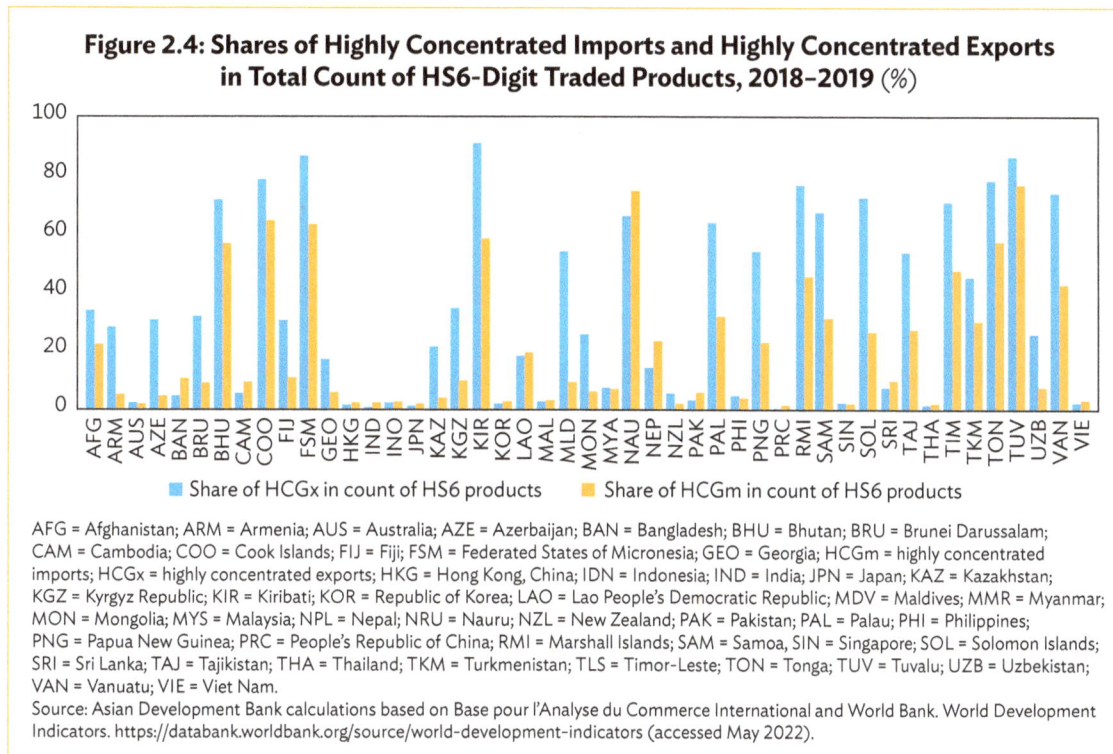

Figure 2.4: Shares of Highly Concentrated Imports and Highly Concentrated Exports in Total Count of HS6-Digit Traded Products, 2018–2019 (%)

AFG = Afghanistan; ARM = Armenia; AUS = Australia; AZE = Azerbaijan; BAN = Bangladesh; BHU = Bhutan; BRU = Brunei Darussalam; CAM = Cambodia; COO = Cook Islands; FIJ = Fiji; FSM = Federated States of Micronesia; GEO = Georgia; HCGm = highly concentrated imports; HCGx = highly concentrated exports; HKG = Hong Kong, China; IDN = Indonesia; IND = India; JPN = Japan; KAZ = Kazakhstan; KGZ = Kyrgyz Republic; KIR = Kiribati; KOR = Republic of Korea; LAO = Lao People's Democratic Republic; MDV = Maldives; MMR = Myanmar; MON = Mongolia; MYS = Malaysia; NPL = Nepal; NRU = Nauru; NZL = New Zealand; PAK = Pakistan; PAL = Palau; PHI = Philippines; PNG = Papua New Guinea; PRC = People's Republic of China; RMI = Marshall Islands; SAM = Samoa, SIN = Singapore; SOL = Solomon Islands; SRI = Sri Lanka; TAJ = Tajikistan; THA = Thailand; TKM = Turkmenistan; TLS = Timor-Leste; TON = Tonga; TUV = Tuvalu; UZB = Uzbekistan; VAN = Vanuatu; VIE = Viet Nam.
Source: Asian Development Bank calculations based on Base pour l'Analyse du Commerce International and World Bank. World Development Indicators. https://databank.worldbank.org/source/world-development-indicators (accessed May 2022).

Other countries can be potential alternative sources and destinations for ADB members' exports and imports. Belgium, Ghana, Italy, Mexico, the Netherlands, South Africa, Spain, Switzerland, and the United Arab Emirates did not appear among the top 20 destinations of ADB members' HCGx but were prominent recipients of HCGx of non-ADB countries, alluding to their potential for diversifying ADB members' partner distribution on the exports side. Similarly, Bangladesh, Belgium, France, Guyana, Mexico, the Netherlands, South Africa, and Switzerland did not appear among the top 20 sources of ADB members' HCGm but these countries were prominent sources of HCGm for non-ADB countries, alluding to their potential for diversifying ADB members' partner distribution on the imports side.

Across sample countries, HCGx and HCGm are concentrated in product codes that are classified for use both as intermediates and final goods in GVCs (Figures 2.5 panel A and 2.6 panel A); moreover, the respective distributions did not change over time. For 20 of the 47 ADB members, more than half of the HCGx were destined to another ADB member in 2010–2011; this number fell marginally to 19 in 2018–2019 (Figure 2.5, panel B). Only 7 ADB members sourced their HCGm from a non-ADB partner in 2010–2011; this number further fell to 6 in 2018–2019 (Figure 2.6, panel B). Thus, there seemed to be far greater reliance on other ADB members for sourcing HCGm compared to exporting HCGx and this reliance may have also intensified over time.

---

[22] A preliminary analysis following the methodology reported in Appendix 2 has been conducted for Kiribati, Micronesia, and Tuvalu on the export side; and the Cook Islands, Nauru, and Tuvalu on the import side. Results are not reported but are available upon request.

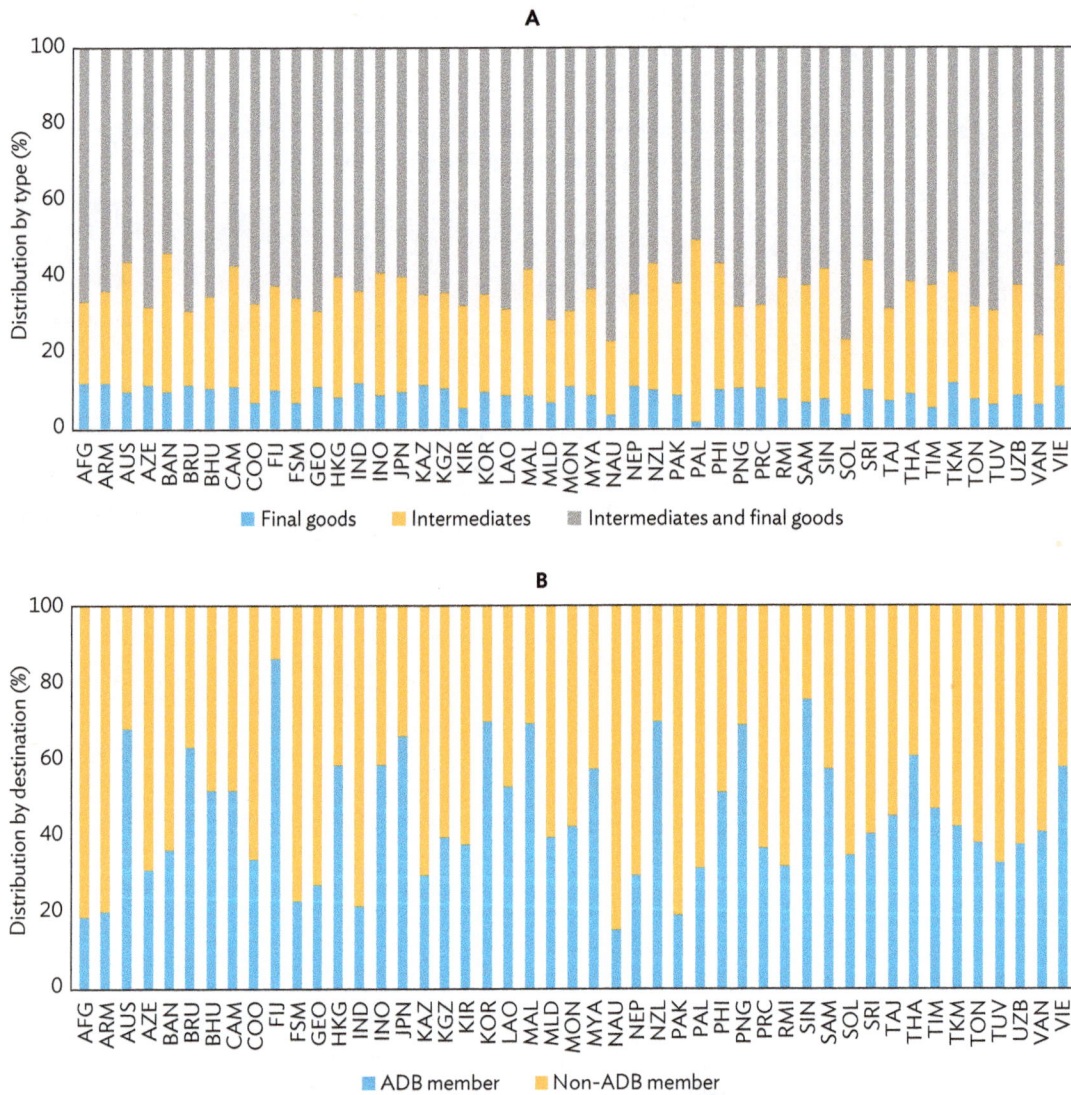

Figure 2.5: Distribution of Highly Concentrated Exports by Product Type (A) and Destination (B), 2018–2019

ADB = Asian Development Bank; AFG = Afghanistan; ARM = Armenia; AUS = Australia; AZE = Azerbaijan; BAN = Bangladesh; BHU = Bhutan; BRU = Brunei Darussalam; CAM = Cambodia; COO = Cook Islands; FIJ = Fiji; FSM = Federated States of Micronesia; GEO = Georgia; HKG = Hong Kong, China; IND = India; INO = Indonesia; JPN = Japan; KAZ = Kazakhstan; KGZ = Kyrgyz Republic; KIR = Kiribati; KOR = Republic of Korea; LAO = Lao People's Democratic Republic; MAL = Malaysia; MLD = Maldives; MON = Mongolia; MYA = Myanmar; NAU = Nauru; NEP = Nepal; NZL = New Zealand; PAK = Pakistan; PAL = Palau; PHI = Philippines; PNG = Papua New Guinea; PRC = People's Republic of China; RMI = Marshall Islands; SAM = Samoa; SIN = Singapore; SOL = Solomon Islands; SRI = Sri Lanka; TAJ = Tajikistan; THA = Thailand; TKM = Turkmenistan; TIM = Timor-Leste; TON = Tonga; TUV = Tuvalu; UZB = Uzbekistan; VAN = Vanuatu; VIE = Viet Nam.
Source: Asian Development Bank calculations based on Base pour l'Analyse du Commerce International database (accessed May 2022).

Figure 2.6: Distribution of Highly Concentrated Imports by Product Type (A) and Source (B), 2018–2019 (%)

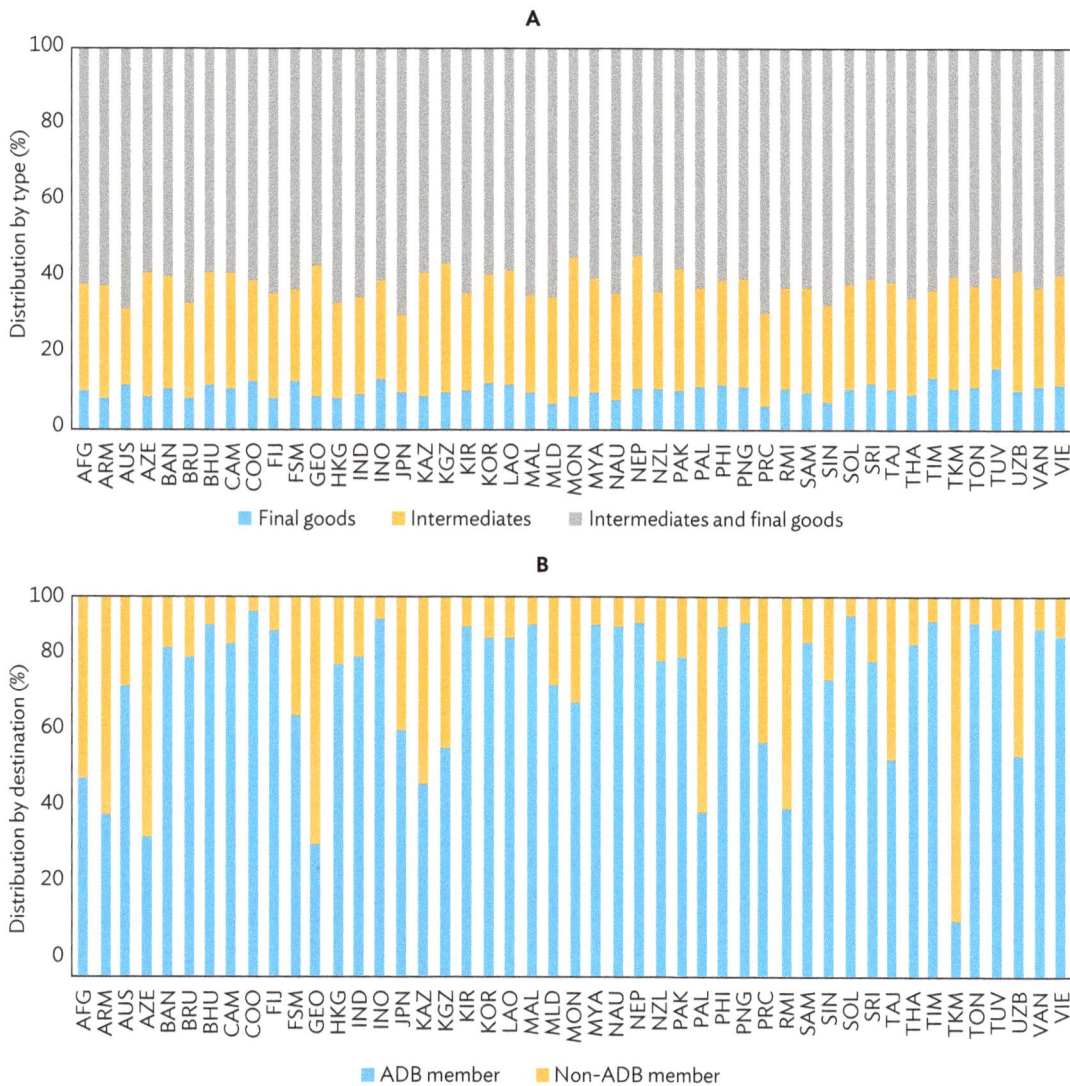

A

Legend: ■ Final goods ■ Intermediates ■ Intermediates and final goods

B

Legend: ■ ADB member ■ Non-ADB member

AFG = Afghanistan; ARM = Armenia; AUS = Australia; AZE = Azerbaijan; BAN = Bangladesh; BHU = Bhutan; BRU = Brunei Darussalam; CAM = Cambodia; COO = Cook Islands; FIJ = Fiji; FSM = Federated States of Micronesia; GEO = Georgia; HKG = Hong Kong, China; IDN = Indonesia; IND = India; JPN = Japan; KAZ = Kazakhstan; KGZ = Kyrgyz Republic; KIR = Kiribati; KOR = Republic of Korea; LAO = Lao People's Democratic Republic; MDV = Maldives; MMR = Myanmar; MON = Mongolia; MYS = Malaysia; NPL = Nepal; NRU = Nauru; NZL = New Zealand; PAK = Pakistan; PAL = Palau; PHI = Philippines; PNG = Papua New Guinea; PRC = People's Republic of China; RMI = Marshall Islands; SAM = Samoa; SIN = Singapore; SOL = Solomon Islands; SRI = Sri Lanka; TAJ = Tajikistan; THA = Thailand; TKM = Turkmenistan; TLS = Timor-Leste; TON = Tonga; TUV = Tuvalu; UZB = Uzbekistan;VAN = Vanuatu; VIE = Viet Nam.
Source: Asian Development Bank calculations based on Base pour l'Analyse du Commerce International database (accessed May 2022).

The distributions of HCGx and HCGm by broad sector may have remained relatively stable over time across ADB member countries, textiles, and apparel accounted for the bulk of HCGx/ HCGm in 2010–2011 and 2018–2019 followed by electrical machinery, other machinery, and transport equipment (Figure 2.7).[23] The absolute number of distinct, highly concentrated goods also increased over time for the ADB sample.

Figure 2.7: Distribution of Highly Concentrated Exports and Highly Concentrated Imports by Broad Sector, 2018–2019

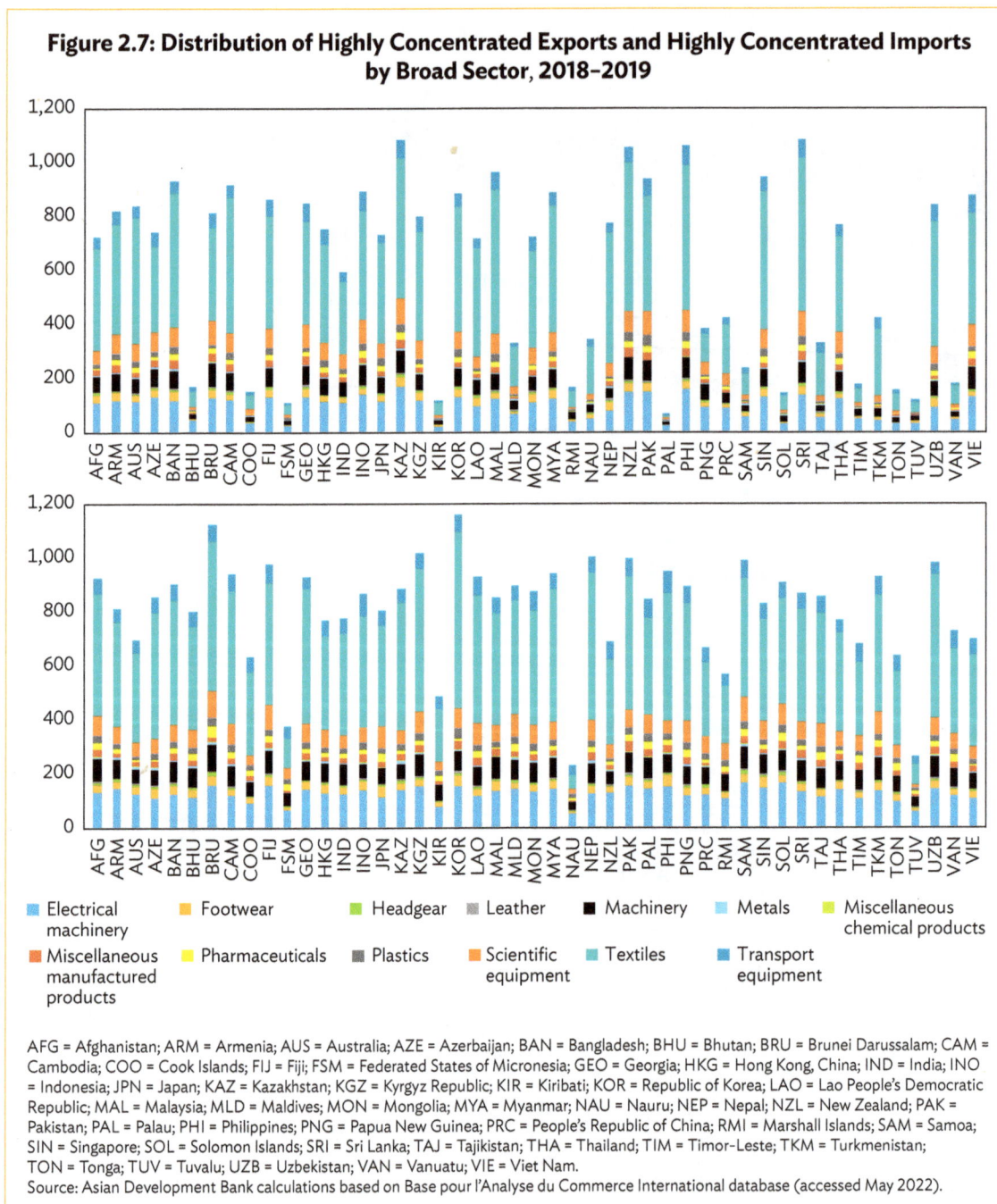

Legend: Electrical machinery; Footwear; Headgear; Leather; Machinery; Metals; Miscellaneous chemical products; Miscellaneous manufactured products; Pharmaceuticals; Plastics; Scientific equipment; Textiles; Transport equipment

AFG = Afghanistan; ARM = Armenia; AUS = Australia; AZE = Azerbaijan; BAN = Bangladesh; BHU = Bhutan; BRU = Brunei Darussalam; CAM = Cambodia; COO = Cook Islands; FIJ = Fiji; FSM = Federated States of Micronesia; GEO = Georgia; HKG = Hong Kong, China; IND = India; INO = Indonesia; JPN = Japan; KAZ = Kazakhstan; KGZ = Kyrgyz Republic; KIR = Kiribati; KOR = Republic of Korea; LAO = Lao People's Democratic Republic; MAL = Malaysia; MLD = Maldives; MON = Mongolia; MYA = Myanmar; NAU = Nauru; NEP = Nepal; NZL = New Zealand; PAK = Pakistan; PAL = Palau; PHI = Philippines; PNG = Papua New Guinea; PRC = People's Republic of China; RMI = Marshall Islands; SAM = Samoa; SIN = Singapore; SOL = Solomon Islands; SRI = Sri Lanka; TAJ = Tajikistan; THA = Thailand; TIM = Timor-Leste; TKM = Turkmenistan; TON = Tonga; TUV = Tuvalu; UZB = Uzbekistan; VAN = Vanuatu; VIE = Viet Nam.
Source: Asian Development Bank calculations based on Base pour l'Analyse du Commerce International database (accessed May 2022).

[23] These broad sectors comprised 1,032 and 1,135 HCGx products at the HS6-digit level in 2010–2011 and 2018–2019, respectively; the corresponding number of HS6-digit HCGm products was 966 and 1,085. The top-20 HS6-digit HCGx and HCGm are reported in Table A2.1 along with the absolute number of highly concentrated goods per HS6-digit code and its share in the total number of highly concentrated goods.

The COVID-19 pandemic has highlighted the vulnerability of countries integrated in GVCs and reignited discussion around repatriation of value chains, near-shoring, and geographical and/or supplier diversification. Many ADB members are vulnerable to overconcentration of exports and imports in multiple ways, including a rise over time in the number of HS6-digit products that are only traded with a few partners. Pacific island countries and low-income countries are particularly vulnerable. An important policy initiative would be to identify options for geographical diversification, both for alternative sources and destination countries for exports and imports of ADB members. Vulnerabilities can be reduced through diversification, and diversification can be achieved both by building productive capacity and ensuring the best possible access to other countries' markets.

2.3 Aid for Trade Implications for Developing Asia

This chapter highlighted the potential downsides of international trade: the deepening of within-country inequalities and supply chain vulnerability. Trade liberalization can generate welfare gains for a country, but the benefits may not be shared equally among workers and enterprises. In addition, openness and participation in GVCs can bring productivity gains and higher value-added, but the COVID-19 pandemic has highlighted the risks of just-in-time supply chain practices and the importance of supply chain resiliency.

Trade liberalization can be an engine for economic growth and development, particularly if accompanied by policies and programs that promote inclusiveness. Aid for trade has a key role to play in ensuring that sustainable and inclusive trade liberalization can benefit poorer economies, small businesses, marginalized workers, women, and youth, while fostering economic diversification. Aid for trade is also crucial in supporting supply chain resiliency, in promoting the productive capacity of enterprises, and improving trade facilitation measures of countries. Supporting the design and implementation of trade and digital agreements by developing the ability to research and assess their effectiveness both as trade instruments and their potential inclusive economic growth are discussed in Chapters 3 and 4.

Bibliography

Acemoglu, D. and A. Tahbaz-Salehi. 2020. Firms, Failures, and Fluctuations: The Macroeconomics of Supply Chain Disruptions. *NBER Working Paper*. No. 27565. Cambridge, MA. http://www.nber.org/papers/w27565.

Aguayo-Tellez, E. 2012. The Impact of Trade Liberalization Policies and FDI on Gender Inequalities: A Literature Review. Washington, DC: World Bank. https://openknowledge.worldbank.org/handle/10986/9220.

Aldaba, R. M. 2013. Impact of Trade Liberalization on Wage Skill Premium in Philippine Manufacturing. *PIDS Discussion Paper Series No. 2013-25*. Manila: Philippine Institute for Development Studies.

Amiti, M. and D. R. Davis. 2012. Trade, Firms, and Wages: Theory and Evidence. *The Review of Economic Studies*. 79 (1). pp. 1–36. https://doi.org/10.1093/restud/rdr016.

Antràs, P. 2020. Conceptual Aspects of Global Value Chains. *The World Bank Economic Review*. Forthcoming.

Antràs, P., A. de Gortari, and O. Itskhoki. 2017. Globalization, Inequality and Welfare. *Journal of International Economics*. 108. pp. 387–412.

Anwar, S., and Sun, S. 2012. Trade Liberalisation, Market Competition and Wage Inequality in China's Manufacturing Sector. *Economic Modelling*. 29 (4). pp. 1268–1277.

Asian Development Bank (ADB). 2003. *Asian Development Outlook 2003: Competitiveness in Developing Asia*. Manila.

Autor, D., D. Dorn, and G. Hanson. 2013. The China Syndrome: Local Labor Market Effects of Import Competition in the United States. *American Economic Review*. 103 (6). pp. 2121–68.

Baldwin, R. and E. Tomiura. 2020. Thinking Ahead About the Trade Impact of COVID-19. In R. Baldwin and B. W. di Mauro, eds. *Economics in the Time of COVID-19*. London: CEPR Press.

Baslevent, C., and O. Onaran. 2004. The Effect of Export-Oriented Growth on Female Labor Market Outcomes in Turkey. *World Development*. 32 (8). pp. 1375–93.

Bamber, P., K. Fernandez-Stark, G. Gereffi, and A. Guinn. 2014. Connecting Local Producers in Developing Countries to Regional and Global Value Chains: Update. *OECD Trade Policy Papers*. No. 160. Paris: OECD Publishing.

Behzadi, G., M. J. O'Sullivan, T. L. Olsen, F. Scrimgeour, and A. Zhang. 2017. Robust and Resilient Strategies for Managing Supply Disruptions in an Agribusiness Supply Chain. *International Journal of Production Economics*. No. 191. pp. 207–220. https://doi.org/10.1016/j.ijpe.2017.06.018.

Berik, G., Y. Van der Meulen Rodgers, and J. E. Zveglich. 2004. International Trade and Gender Wage Discrimination: Evidence from East Asia. Review of Development Economics. 8 (2). pp. 237–254. New Jersey: John Wiley & Sons Ltd.

Brandon-Jones, E., B. Squire, C. W. Autry, and K. J. Petersen. 2014. A Contingent Resource-Based Perspective of Supply Chain Resilience and Robustness. *Journal of Supply Chain Management*. 50 (3). pp. 55–73. https://doi.org/10.1111/jscm.12050.

Bunkley, N. 2011. Japan's Automakers Expect More Delays. *The New York Times*. 18 March.

Cao, M. and Q. Zhang. 2011. Supply Chain Collaboration: Impact on Collaborative Advantage and Firm Performance. *Journal of Operations Management*. 29 (3). pp. 163–180.

Carlsson-Szlezak, P., M. Reeves, and P. Swartz. 2020. What Coronavirus Could Mean for the Global Economy. *Harvard Business Review.* 3 March. https://hbr.org/2020/03/what-coronavirus-could-mean-for-the-global-economy.

Champneys, A. 2015. Robustness and Resilience of Manufacturing Supply Networks. University of Bristol.

Chopra, S. and M. S. Sodhi. 2004. Managing Risk to Avoid Supply-Chain Breakdown. *MIT Sloan Management Review.* 46 (1). pp. 53–61.

Christopher, M. and H. Peck. 2004. Building the Resilient Supply Chain. *The International Journal of Logistics Management.* 15 (2). pp. 1–14. https://doi.org/10.1108/09574090410700275.

Case, A. and A. Deaton. 2020. *Deaths of Despair and the Future of Capitalism.* Princeton, NJ: Princeton University Press.

Chamarbagwala, R. 2006. Economic Liberalization and Wage Inequality in India. *World Development.* 34 (12). pp. 1997–2015.

Cotofan, M., J. de Neve, M. Golin, M. Kaats, and G. Ward. 2021. Work and Well-Being During the COVID-19 Pandemic: Impact, Inequalities, Resilience and the Future of Work. In J. F. Helliwell, R. Layard, J. Sachs, and J-E De Neve, eds. *World Happiness Report 2021.* New York: Sustainable Development Solutions Network.

de Souza, R. and R. Zhou. 2015. Improve Robustness and Resilience of Networked Supply Chains. In proceedings of the 18th Asia Pacific Symposium on Intelligent and Evolutionary Systems. pp. 589–597. DOI:10.1007/978-3-319-13356-0_46.

Donadoni, M., S. Roden, K. Scholten, M. Stevenson, F. Caniato, D. P. van Donk, and A. Wieland. 2019. The Future of Resilient Supply Chains. In G.A. Zsidisin and M. Henke, eds. Revisiting Supply Chain Risk. *Springer Series in Supply Chain Management.* Springer Nature.

Dong, M. 2006. Development of Supply Chain Network Robustness Index. *International Journal of Services Operations and Informatics.* 1 (1–2). pp. 55–66.

Durach, C. F., A. Wieland, and J. A. D. Machuca. 2015. Antecedents and Dimensions of Supply Chain Robustness: A Systematic Literature Review. *International Journal of Physical Distribution and Logistics Management.* 45 (1/2). pp. 118–137. https://doi.org/10.1108/IJPDLM-0 5–201 3–0133.

Dix-Carneiro, R. and B. K. Kovak. 2017. Trade Liberalization and Regional Dynamics. *American Economic Review.* 107 (10). pp. 2908–46.

El Baz, J., and S. Ruel. 2020. Can Supply Chain Risk Management Practices Mitigate the Disruption Impacts on Supply Chains' Resilience and Robustness? Evidence from an Empirical Survey in a COVID-19 Outbreak Era. *International Journal of Production Economics.* No. 233. https://doi.org/10.1016/j.ijpe.2020.107972.

Fawcett, S. E., C. Wallin, C. Allred, A. M. Fawcett, and G. M. Magnan. 2011. Information Technology as an Enabler of Supply Chain Collaboration: A Dynamic-Capabilities Perspective. *Journal of Supply Chain Management.* 47 (1). pp. 38–59.

Fernandes, A., and H. Tang. 2020. How Did the 2003 SARS Epidemic Shape Chinese Trade? *Covid Economics, Vetted and Real-Time Papers.* No. 22. pp. 154–176.

Fernandez-Stark, K., P. Bamber, and G. Gereffi. 2014. Global Value Chains in Latin America: A Development Perspective for Upgrading. In R. Hernandez, J. M. Martinez, and N. Mulder, eds. Economic Commission for Latin America and the Caribbean: Santiago.

Field, A. 2009. Supply Chain Braces for Swine Flu Pandemic But Will It Be Too Late? *Economy Watch*. pp. 1–7.

Furceri, D., P. Loungani, and J. D. Ostry. 2017. The Aggregate and Distributional Effects of Financial Globalization. Unpublished paper. Washington, DC: International Monetary Fund.

Gentilini, U., M. Almenfi, P. Dale, J. Blomquis, R. Palacios, V. Desai, and V. Moreira. 2020. Social Protection and Jobs Responses to COVID-19. Washington, DC: World Bank https://openknowledge.worldbank.org/handle/10986/33635.

Golan, M. S., L. H. Jernegan, and I. Linkov. 2020. Trends and Applications of Resilience Analytics in Supply Chain Modeling: Systematic Literature Review in the Context of the COVID-19 Pandemic. *Environment Systems and Decisions*. No. 40. pp. 222–24. DOI: 10.1007/s1066 9–02 0–09777-w.

Goldin, I., and R. Muggah. 2020. COVID-19 is Increasing Multiple Kinds of Inequality. Here's What We Can Do About It. Geneva: World Economic Forum.

Govindan, K., H. Mina, and B. Alavi. 2020. A Decision Support System for Demand Management in Healthcare Supply Chains Considering the Epidemic Outbreaks: A Case Study of Coronavirus Disease 2019 (COVID-19). *Transportation Research Part E Logistics and Transportation Review*. 138:101967. Amsterdam: Elsevier.

Gray, J. V., A. V. Roth, and M. J. Leiblein. 2011. Quality Risk in Offshore Manufacturing: Evidence from the Pharmaceutical Industry. *Journal of Operations Management*. 29 (7–8). pp. 737–752.

Gregory, M. and C. Greenhalgh . (1997). International Trade, Deindustrialization and Labour Demand: An Input-Output Study for the UK (1979–90). *International Trade and Labour Markets*. pp. 62–89. London: Palgrave Macmillan.

Grotsch, V. M., C. Blome, and M. C. Schleper. 2013. Antecedents of Proactive Supply Chain Risk Management–A Contingency Theory Perspective. *International Journal of Production Research*. 51 (10). pp. 2842–2867. DOI:10.1080/00207543.2012.746796.

Güller, M. and M. Henke. 2019. Resilience Assessment in Complex Supply Networks. In G. A. Zsidisin and M. Henke, eds. *Revisiting Supply Chain Risk*. Switzerland: Springer Nature.

Helble, M. and B.-L. Ngiang. 2016. From Global Factory To Global Mall? East Asia's Changing Trade Composition and Orientation. *Japan and the World Economy*. No. 39. pp. 37–47.

Henriet, F., S. Hallegatte, and L. Tabourier. 2012. Firm-Network Characteristics and Economic Robustness to Natural Disasters. *Journal of Economic Dynamics and Control*. No. 36. pp. 150–167.

Holweg, M., A. Reichhart, and E. Hong. 2011. On Risk and Cost in Global Sourcing. *International Journal of Production Economics*. 131 (1). pp. 333–341.

Hosseini, S., D. Ivanov, and A. Dolgui. 2019. Review of Quantitative Methods for Supply Chain Resilience Analysis. *Transportation Research Part E: Logistics and Transportation Review*. No. 125. pp. 285–307. DOI: 10.1016/j.tre.2019.03.001.

Husdal, J. 2008. Robustness, Flexibility and Resilience. 28 April. http://husdal.com/2008/04/28/robustness-flexibility-and-resilience-in-the-supply-chain/.

Hynes, W., B. Trump, P. Love, and I. Linkov. 2020. Bouncing Forward: A Resilience Approach to Dealing with COVID-19 and Future Systemic Shocks. *Environment Systems and Decisions*. DOI: 10.1007/s1066 9–02 0–09776-x.

Immers, B. n.d. Robustness of Multimodal and Multi-Commodity Supply Chains. Katholieke Universiteit Leuven.

International Labour Organization (ILO). 2019. The Future of Work and Migration: Thematic Background paper for the 12th ASEAN Forum on Migrant Labour. Geneva.

International Monetary Fund (IMF). 2003. *World Economic Outlook: Economic Prospects and Policy Issues.* Washington, DC.

Ireland, R., and R. Bruce. 2000. CPFR: Only the Beginning of Collaboration. *Supply Chain Management Review.* 4 (4). pp. 80–88.

Ivanov, D. 2020a. Predicting the Impacts of Epidemic Outbreaks on Global Supply Chains: A Simulation-Based Analysis on the Coronavirus Outbreak (COVID-19/SARS-CoV-2) Case. *Transportation Research Part E: Logistics and Transportation Review.* DOI: 10.1016/j.tre.2020.101922.

_____. 2020b. Viable Supply Chain Model: Integrating Agility, Resilience and Sustainability Perspectives—Lessons From and Thinking Beyond the COVID-19 Pandemic. *Annals of Operations Research.* DOI: 10.1007/s1047 9–02 0–0364 0–6.

Ivanov, D., and B. Sokolov. 2010. *Adaptive Supply Chain Management.* New York: Springer-Verlag London Limited.

_____. 2013. Control and System-Theoretic Identification of the Supply Chain Dynamics Domain for Planning, Analysis and Adaptation of Performance under Uncertainty. *European Journal of Operational Research.* 224 (2). pp. 313–323. DOI:10.1016/j.ejor.2012.08.021.

Ivanov, D., A. Dolgui, B. Sokolov, and M. Ivanova. 2017. Literature Review on Disruption Recovery in the Supply Chain. *International Journal of Production Research.* 55 (20). pp. 6158–6174. DOI:10.1080/00207543.2017.1330572.

Jaumotte, F., S. Lall, and C. Papageorgiou. 2013. Rising Income Inequality: Technology, or Trade and Financial Globalization? *IMF Economic Review.* 61 (2). pp. 271–309.

Javorcik, B. 2020. Global Supply Chains Will Not Be the Same in the Post COVID-19 World. In R. Baldwin and S. Evenett (eds.). *COVID-19 and Trade Policy: Why Turning Inward Won't Work.* pp. 111–116. London: CEPR Press.

Jurzykm, E.M., M. M. Nair, N. Pouokam, T. S. Sedik, A. Tan, and I. Yakadina. 2020. COVID-19 and Inequality in Asia: Breaking the Vicious Cycle. *IMF Working Papers.* https://www.imf.org/en/Publications/WP/Issues/2020/10/16/COVID-19-and-Inequality-in-Asia-Breaking-the-Vicious-Cycle-49807.

Jüttner, U., and S. Maklan. 2011. Supply Chain Resilience in the Global Financial Crisis: An Empirical Study. *Supply Chain Management: An International Journal.* 16 (4). pp. 246–259.

Kohpaiboon, A. and J. Jongwanich. 2013. Global Production Sharing and Wage Premium: Evidence from Thai Manufacturing. In H. H. Chin and D. Narjoko. Impact of Globalization on Labor Market. *ERIA Research Project Report 2012.* No. 4. Jakarta.

Kostova, D., C. H. Cassell, J. T. Redd, D. E. Williams, T. Singh, L. D. Martel, and R. E. Bunnell. 2019. Long-Distance Effects of Epidemics: Assessing the Link between the 2014 West Africa Ebola Outbreak and U.S. Exports and Employment. *Health Economics.* 28 (11). pp. 1248–1261.

Kumar, U., and P. Mishra. 2008. Trade Liberalization and Wage Inequality: Evidence From India. *Review of Development Economics.* 12 (2). pp. 291–311.

Lengnick-Hall, C. A. and T. E. Beck. 2005. Adaptive Fit Versus Robust Transformation: How Organizations Respond to Environmental Change. *Journal of Management.* 31 (5). pp. 738–757. https://doi.org/10.1177/0149206305279367.

Lim, M. 2014. Globalization, Export-Led Growth and Inequality: The East Asian Story. *South Centre Research Paper.* No. 57.

Liu, H., Z. Tian, A. Huang, and Z. Yang. 2017. Analysis of Vulnerabilities in Maritime Supply Chains. *Reliability Engineering and System Safety.* No. 169. pp. 475–484. http://researchonline.ljmu.ac.uk/.

Liu, Y., J. M. Lee, and C. Lee. 2020. The Challenges and Opportunities of a Global Health Crisis: The Management and Business Implications of COVID-19 from an Asian Perspective. *Asian Business and Management*. 19 (3). pp. 277–297. DOI: 10.1057/s4129 1–02 0–00119-x.

Ma, X., X. Yao, and Y. Xi. 2009. How Do Interorganizational and Interpersonal Networks Affect a Firm's Strategic Adaptive Capability in a Transition Economy? *Journal of Business Research*. 62 (11). pp. 1087–1095. DOI:10.1016/j.jbusres.2008.09.008.

Mackay, J., A. Munoz., and M. Pepper. 2019. Conceptualising Redundancy and Flexibility Towards Supply Chain Robustness and Resilience. *Journal of Risk Research*. pp. 1541–1561. https://doi.org/10.1080/13669877.2019.1694964.

Mah, J. S. 2013. Globalization, Decentralization and Income Inequality: The Case of China. *Economic Modelling*. No. 31. pp. 653–658.

Mandal, S., and R. Sarathy. 2018. The Effect of Supply Chain Relationships on Resilience: Empirical Evidence from India. *Global Business Review*. 19 (3S). pp. 1–22.

Meepetchdee, Y. and N. Shah. 2007. Logistical Network Design with Robustness and Complexity Considerations. *International Journal of Physical Distribution and Logistics Management*. 37 (3). pp. 201–222.

Melitz, M. J. 2003. The Impact of Trade on Intra-industry Reallocation and Aggregate Industry Productivity. *Econometrica*. 71 (6). pp. 1695–725.

Milanovic, B. 2016. Global Inequality: A New Approach for the Age of Globalization. *Harvard University Press*. p. 320. http://www.jstor.org/stable/j.ctvjghwk4.

Miroudot, S. 2020. Resilience versus Robustness In Global Value Chains: Some Policy Implications. In R. Baldwin and S. Evenett. COVID-19 and Trade Policy: Why Turning Inward Won't Work. CEPR Policy Portal. https://voxeu.org/content/covid-19-and-trade-policy-why-turning-inward-won-t-work.

Monostori, J. 2018. Supply Chains Robustness: Challenges and Opportunities. In *Procedia CIRP*. 67. pp. 110–115. Elsevier B.V. https://doi.org/10.1016/j.procir.2017.12.185.

Mugan, T. S.2020. Trade, technology, Foreign Firms, and the Wage Gap: Case of Vietnam Manufacturing Firms. In *The Effects of Globalisation on Firm and Labour Performance*. pp. 113-133. Routledge.

Organisation for Economic Co-operation and Development (OECD). 2007. Globalisation, Jobs and Wages. *OECD Policy Brief*. Paris. https://www.oecd.org/els/emp/Globalisation-Jobs-and-Wages-2007.pdf.

Pal, P. and J. Ghosh. 2007. Inequality in India: A Survey of Recent Trends. United Nations *DESA Working Paper*. No. 45. New York.

Park, C. and A. M. Inocencio. 2020. COVID-19 is No Excuse to Regress on Gender Equality. *ADB Briefs*. No. 157. Manila. https://www.adb.org/sites/default/files/publication/651541/covid-19-no-excuse-regress-gender-equality.pdf.

Pettit, T.J., J. Fiksel, and K. L. Croxton. 2010. Ensuring Supply Chain Resilience: Development of a Conceptual Framework. *Journal of Business Logistics*. 31 (1). pp. 1–21.

Pradhan, J. P. 2006. How Do Trade, Foreign Investment and Technology Affect Employment Patterns in Organized Indian Manufacturing? *Indian Journal of Labour Economics*. 49 (2). pp. 249–72.

Rashid, A. H. M. and S.-P. Loke. 2016. Supply Chain Robustness and Resilience for Firm's Sustainability: Case Studies on Electronics Industry. In 1st AAGBS International Conference on Business Management 2014. Singapore: Springer. https://doi.org/10.1007/97 8-98 1–28 7–42 6–9_16.

Rassy, D. and R. D. Smith. 2012. The Economic Impact of H1N1 on Mexico's Tourist and Pork Sectors. *Health Economics*. 22 (7). pp. 824–834.

Rodrik, D. 1997. *Has Globalization Gone Too Far?* Washington, DC: Institute for International Economics.

_____. 2021. A Primer on Trade and Inequality. *IFS Deaton Review*.

Scheve, K. and M. J. Slaughter. 2004. Economic Insecurity and the Globalization of Production. *American Journal of Political Science*. 48 (4). pp. 662–674.

Seery, E. 2022. Rising to the Challenge: The Case for Permanent Progressive Policies to Tackle Asia's Coronavirus and Inequality Crisis. *Oxfam Briefing Paper*. Nairobi.

Settanni, E. 2020. Those Who Do Not Move, Do Not Notice Their (Supply) Chains - Inconvenient Lessons from Disruptions Related to COVID-19. *AI and Society*. DOI: 10.1007/s0014 6–02 0-00988-y.

Shahin, A. 2020. Supply Chain Risk Management under Covid-19: A Review and Research Agenda. In *Second International Conference on Innovations in Business Administration and Economics*. Tehran. https://www.researchgate.net/publication/343852256_Supply_Chain_Risk_Management_under_Covid-19_A_Review_and_Research_Agenda.

Sharma, A., A. Adhikary, and S. Bikash Borah. 2020. COVID-19's Impact on Supply Chain Decisions: Strategic Insights for NASDAQ 100 Firms using Twitter Data. *Journal of Business Research*. No. 117. pp. 443–449. DOI: https://doi.org/10.1016/j.jbusres.2020.05.035.

Sheffi, Y. 2002. Supply Chain Management Under Threat of International Terrorism. *International Journal of Logistics Management*. 12 (2).

Sheffi, Y., and J. B. Rice. 2005. A Supply Chain View of the Resilient Enterprises. *MIT Sloan Management Review*. 47 (1). pp. 41–48.

Shingal, A. and P. Agarwal. 2020. How Did Trade in GVC-Based Products Respond to Previous Health Shocks? Lessons for COVID-19. *EUI Working Paper*. RSCAS 2020/68.

Siddiqui, R. 2009. Modeling Gender Effects of Pakistan's Trade Liberalization. *Feminist Economics*. 15 (3). pp. 287–321.

Simchi-Levi, D. and E. Simchi-Levi. 2020. Building Resilient Supply Chains Won't Be Easy. *Harvard Business Review*. https://hbr.org/2020/06/building-resilient-supply-chains-wont-be-easy.

Siu, A. and V. C. R. Wong. 2004. Economic Impact of SARS: The Case of Hong Kong. *Asian Economic Papers*. MIT Press. 3 (1): pp. 62–83. DOI: 10.1162/1535351041747996.

Sodhi, M. S., B. G. Son, and C. S. Tang. 2012. Researchers' Perspective on Supply Chain Risk Management. *Production and Operations Management*. 21 (1). pp. 1–13.

Stauffer, D. 2003. Risk: The Weak Link in Your Supply Chain. *Harvard Management Update*. 8 (3). pp. 3–5.

Stevenson, M., and M. Spring. 2007. Flexibility from a Supply Chain Perspective: Definition and Review. *International Journal of Operations and Production Management*. 27 (7). pp. 685–713. DOI:10.1108/01443570710756956.

Stolper, W. F. and P. A. Samuelson. 1941. Protection and Real Wages. *The Review of Economic Studies*. 9 (1). pp. 58–73.

Strange, R. 2020. The 2020 Covid-19 Pandemic and Global Value Chains. *Journal of Industrial and Business Economics*. No. 47. pp. 455–465.

Stringfellow, A., M. B. Teagarden, and W. Nie. 2008. Invisible Costs in Offshoring Services Work. *Journal of Operations Management.* 26 (2). pp. 164–179.

Taleb, N.N. 2007. *The Black Swan: The Impact of the Highly Improbable.* London: Penguin Books.

Tang, C. S. 2006a. Perspectives in Supply Chain Risk Management. *International Journal of Production Economics.* 103 (2). pp. 451–488.

_____. 2006b. Robust Strategies for Mitigating Supply Chain Disruptions. *International Journal of Logistics Research and Applications.* 9 (1). pp. 33–45.

Tejani, S. and W. Milberg. 2016. Global Defeminization? Industrial Upgrading and Manufacturing Employment in Developing Countries. *Feminist Economics.* 22 (2). 24–54.

Thun, J.H., M. Drüke, and D. Hoenig. 2011. Managing Uncertainty—An Empirical Analysis of Supply Chain Risk Management in Small and Medium-Sized Enterprises. *International Journal of Production Research.* 49 (18). pp. 5511–5525. DOI:10.1080/00207543.2011.563901.

Turner, J. and T. Aknremi. 2020. The Business Effects of Pandemics—A Rapid Literature Review. *Enterprise Research Centre Insight Paper.* 1 (April). pp. 1–24.

United Nations Conference on Trade and Development (UNCTAD). 2019a. Trade Policies and their Impact on Inequalities. Geneva.

_____. 2019b. Trade Policies for Combating Inequalities: Equal Opportunities to Firms, Workers and Countries. Geneva.

Urata, S. 2020. Reimagining Global Value Chains after COVID-19. *ERIA.* 2 July. https://www.eria.org/news-and-views/reimagining-global-value-chains-after-covid-19/.

Urata, S. and D. A. Narjoko. 2017. International Trade and Inequality. *ADBI Working Paper.* No. 675. Tokyo: Asian Development Bank Institute. https://www.adb.org/publications/international-trade-and-inequality.

van Hoek, R. 2020. Research Opportunities for a More Resilient Post-COVID-19 Supply Chain—Closing the Gap Between Research Findings and Industry Practice. *International Journal of Operations and Production Management.* 40 (4). DOI: 10.1108/IJOPM-0 3–202 0–0165.

Wieland, A. and C. Wallenburg. 2013. The Influence of Relational Competencies on Supply Chain Resilience: A Relational View. *International Journal of Physical Distribution and Logistics Management.* 43 (4). pp. 300–320.

World Bank. 2020. *East Asia and Pacific in the Time of COVID-19.* Washington, DC: World Bank.

World Economic Forum. 2019. *Outbreak Readiness and Business Impact: Protecting Lives and Livelihoods across the Global Economy.* Geneva.

World Trade Organization (WTO). 2020a. WTO Report Draws Attention to Impact of COVID-19 Trade Disruptions on Women. *WTO News.* 5 August.

WTO. 2020b. Women and Trade: The Role of Trade in Promoting Gender Equality. Geneva. https://www.wto.org/english/res_e/publications_e/women_trade_pub2807_e.htm.

Zitzmann, I. 2014. How to Cope with Uncertainty in Supply Chains? Conceptual Framework for Agility, Robustness, Resilience, Continuity and Anti-Fragility in Supply Chains Standard-Nutzungsbedingungen. In W. Kersten, T. Blecker, and C. M. Ringle, eds. *Next Generation Supply Chains: Trends and Opportunities. Proceedings of the Hamburg International Conference of Logistics (HICL).* Berlin: epubli GmbH.

Appendix 2: Assessment of Geographic Concentration of Global Value Chains

Methodology

The methodology involves classifying global value chain (GVC)-based HS6-digit products traded by Asian Development Bank (ADB) members as highly concentrated goods–exports (HCGx) and highly concentrated goods–imports (HCGm). To enable this analysis, we begin by computing export and import Herfindahl-Hirschman indices (HHIx, HHIm) of geographical concentration and/or diversification for ADB member i and product k at the HS6-digit level. For each country, HS6-digit products with an HHIx or HHIm exceeding 95th percentile of the respective HHI distribution are classified as "highly concentrated goods", which are then further analyzed to identify major regional or international suppliers (for imports) and destinations (for exports).

For all HCG identified above, we compute indices of revealed comparative advantage for all countries to compare the competitiveness of ADB members with existing suppliers. The analysis aims to enable us to make policy recommendations about the most competitive alternative suppliers in the world (or regionally) to ADB members with highly concentrated imports. The five largest alternative world exporters of the specific HCG with revealed comparative advantage values exceeding 1 could be considered viable alternatives for diversifying imports.

The largest world importers of a specific HCG that are not part of the main export destinations of a given Asian country are considered good candidates for potential export diversification.[21]

Data

The analysis is based on bilateral merchandise trade data sourced at the HS6-digit level from UN Comtrade via BACI at two different points in time separated by a decade, i.e., 2010–2011 and 2018–2019. We average the years in each case to minimize fluctuations in reporting practices. The definition of GVC-based products is based on the World Bank World Integrated Trade Solution classification for GVC-based intermediates and final products.

Discussion on the definition of highly concentrated goods

The definition of highly concentrated goods—exports (HCGx) and imports (HCGm)—depends on the respective HHI percentile distribution used as the threshold; in each case, a good is classified as highly concentrated if the corresponding HHI at the HS6-digit level exceeds the threshold.

Obviously, the absolute number of HCGx and HCGm declines as the HHI percentile distribution threshold is increased. Interestingly, the rate of decline varies by income status, with countries classified as lower-middle-income countries according to the World Bank income classification showing the largest rate of decline; for high-income countries, the rate of decline is virtually constant for both HCGx and HCGm. This is shown in Figure A2.1, where the number of HCGx and HCGm for each income group at the HHI fifth percentile distribution threshold (i.e., the sample maximums) are scaled to 100.

---

[21]   Full results are not reported in the present report but are available upon request.

Figure A2.1: Rate of Decline in the Absolute Number of Highly Concentrated Exports and Highly Concentrated Imports at Different Percentile Distribution Thresholds with Countries' Income Status

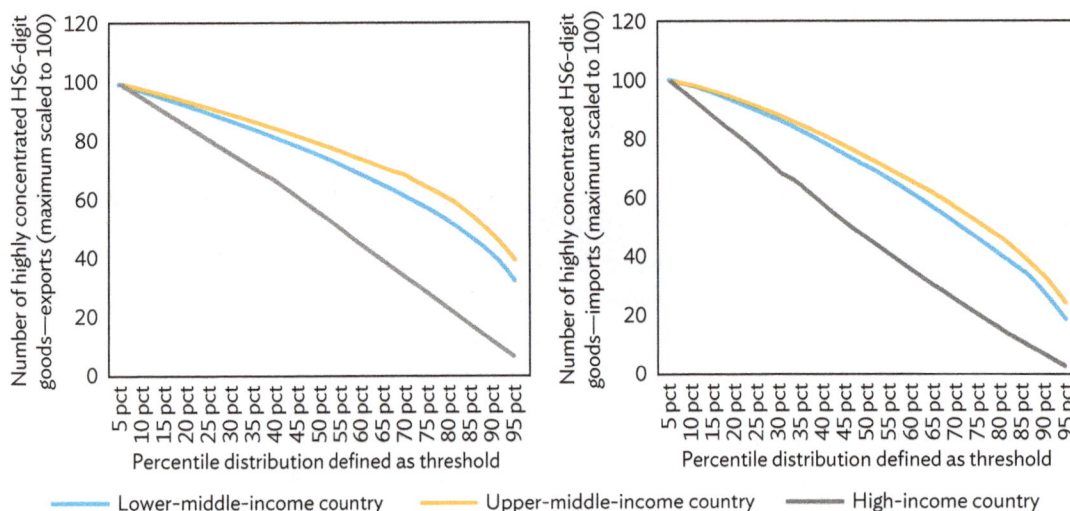

Source: Asian Development Bank calculations based on Base pour l'Analyse du Commerce International database (accessed May 2022).

Table A2.1: Top 20 HS6-Digit Highly Concentrated Exports and Highly Concentrated Imports of ADB Members Over Time

HCGx	2010–2011	Share (%)	HCGx	2018–2019	Share (%)	HCGm	2010–2011	Share (%)	HCGm	2018–2019	Share (%)
392690	106	0.46	392690	146	0.43	392690	124	0.46	392690	167	0.44
851780	104	0.46	870899	123	0.36	847330	107	0.39	610910	132	0.35
851790	99	0.43	610910	115	0.34	870899	101	0.37	870899	130	0.34
847330	97	0.42	610990	114	0.34	300490	96	0.35	840999	125	0.33
610910	90	0.39	847330	113	0.34	851780	96	0.35	870829	118	0.31
300490	87	0.38	630790	108	0.32	840999	92	0.34	300490	117	0.31
870899	87	0.38	851762	107	0.32	903289	85	0.31	610990	112	0.29
847989	82	0.36	903289	102	0.3	847130	83	0.30	847330	110	0.29
840999	80	0.35	847990	99	0.29	870323	83	0.30	847989	109	0.29
844390	78	0.34	300490	98	0.29	610910	82	0.30	847990	109	0.29
852520	77	0.34	847989	98	0.29	847160	82	0.30	903289	107	0.28
854230	77	0.34	840999	96	0.28	851790	82	0.30	847190	104	0.27
847180	75	0.33	847130	96	0.28	852520	82	0.30	851762	104	0.27
870323	73	0.32	851770	90	0.27	382490	81	0.30	852990	104	0.27
630790	71	0.31	847160	89	0.26	847170	81	0.30	847170	103	0.27
847130	71	0.31	620462	88	0.26	847990	81	0.30	630790	102	0.27
903289	70	0.31	870829	88	0.26	610990	80	0.29	640399	99	0.26
854389	68	0.3	620342	87	0.26	844390	80	0.29	840991	99	0.26
610990	67	0.29	650500	86	0.26	847989	79	0.29	851220	96	0.25
847160	67	0.29	852520	85	0.25	870829	79	0.29	620342	95	0.25
Top 20	1,626	7.10	Top 20	2,028	6.00	Top 20	1,756	6.40	Top 20	2242	5.90

HCGm = highly concentrated imports, HCGx = highly concentrated exports.
Source: Asian Development Bank calculations based on BACI database (accessed May 2022).

PART II
LEVERAGING TRADE AND DIGITAL AGREEMENTS TO MEET SUSTAINABLE DEVELOPMENT TARGETS

3. Accelerating Sustainable Trade Through Better Designed and Effective Trade Agreements

3.1 Trends and Opportunities of Regional Trade Agreements in Asia and the Pacific

3.1.1 Trade Liberalization in Asia and the Emergence of the Mega-Regionals

From March 2020—when the World Health Organization characterized the COVID-19 outbreak as a pandemic—to February 2022, trade liberalization negotiations in Asia and the Pacific have continued despite travel restrictions and physical distancing. Twelve regional trade agreements (RTAs) entered into force, four were signed, and one was concluded—that is 17 new trade agreements in 2 years. (Table 3.1).

Table 3.1: New Regional Trade Agreements in Asia and the Pacific Involving Developing Countries, March 2020–February 2022

Name	Status
Intraregional	
PACER Plus	In force, 13 December 2020
RCEP	In force, 1 January 2022
Cambodia–People's Republic of China	In force, 1 January 2022
Cambodia–Republic of Korea	Signed, 26 October 2021
Indonesia–Republic of Korea	Signed, 18 December 2020
Bangladesh–Bhutan[a]	Signed, 6 December 2020
Philippines–Republic of Korea	Concluded, 26 October 2021
Interregional	
Indonesia–EFTA	In force, 1 November 2021
EAEU–Serbia[a]	In force, 10 July 2021
India–Mauritius	In force, 1 April 2021
Azerbaijan–Türkiye[a]	In force, 1 March 2021
PRC–Mauritius	In force, 1 January 2021
Georgia–United Kingdom	In force, 1 January 2021
Republic of Korea–United Kingdom	In force, 1 January 2021
Singapore–United Kingdom	In force, 1 January 2021
Viet Nam–United Kingdom	In force, 1 January 2021
Republic of Korea–Israel	Signed, 13 March 2021

EAEU = Eurasian Economic Union, EFTA = European Free Trade Association, PACER Plus = Pacific Agreement on Closer Economic Relations Plus, PRC = People's Republic of China, RCEP = Regional Comprehensive Economic Partnership.
[a] Goods only.
Source: ADB compilation based on information available as 28 February 2022.

The pace and scope of economic integration in Asia and the Pacific are unprecedented. Regional trade agreements are proliferating and expanding. The region is now home to two so-called mega-regionals, the Regional Comprehensive Economic Partnership (RCEP) and the Comprehensive and Progressive Agreement for Trans-Pacific Partnership (CPTPP). Several established intraregional agreements exist and, increasingly, interregional agreements. Bilateral agreements between regional members are also increasing.

Asia and the Pacific's mega-regionals are the RTAs of the 21st century, with integration partnerships between countries or regions that account for a substantial share of world trade and gross domestic product (GDP). Two or more members are usually in a leading position or are hubs in global value chains. The RCEP is the most recent, a large and significant mega-regional agreement signed in November 2020 after 8 years of negotiations, entering into force in January 2022.[25] Among the 15 signatory states, and unlike the CPTPP, six are lower-middle-income or least developed countries.

In addition to the mega-regionals, the UK has negotiated four RTAs with Asia and Pacific developing nations. The EU and the US also have preferential agreements and RTAs in the region. The RCEP, CPTPP, and others have continuously widened the scope, depth, and complexity of RTAs covering goods, services (in most cases), and increasingly foreign investment, competition policy, and other behind-the-border measures.

The region is also developing the digital economy by forging new deals ahead of the conclusion of any formal agreement at the World Trade Organization. This topic is discussed in section 4.2.

Mechanics of trade liberalization and key factors for effective use of trade preferences

Trade liberalization is about market access and regulatory convergence. Agreements seek to increase exports and imports and improve the business environment. However, the region's ability to assess the effectiveness of these many new agreements is very limited, and specific challenges exist in the inclusion of and benefits to low- and middle-income and least developed countries. The intensity of development of new trade agreements in Asia and the Pacific raises questions that confront all developing countries: What is the incremental value and the cascading effect of successive and often overlapping FTAs? Do they improve market access? Do they increase regulatory convergence?

These questions are important. Free trade agreements with no or minute incremental value are not only a cost to the international trading system, but also to the countries that negotiate and implement them. The most controversial question arising from the region's multiple FTAs is how to measure the value of trade liberalization from each FTA. There are few rigorous analyses of this issue and very little is known of how firms are making use of each of the FTAs.

The CPTPP and RCEP both cover the "classical" elements of trade, i.e., tariffs and behind-the-border measures. ADB has also emphasized that gains will depend on effective implementation of the agreement and the extensive built-in agenda (Crivelli and Inama 2022). Further intergovernmental work and strong political will is needed to unlock the potential of the RCEP and expand its coverage.

---

[25] On 1 January 2022, the RCEP entered into force for 10 out of 15 signatory states: Australia, Brunei Darussalam, Cambodia, the People's Republic of China, Japan, the Lao People's Democratic Republic, New Zealand, Singapore, Thailand, and Viet Nam. The agreement became effective for the Republic of Korea on 1 February 2022 and Malaysia on 18 March 2022.

Developing countries, including the least developed, are particularly challenged in entering new trade agreements, particularly identifying the benefits of new RTAs. These challenges came at a juncture when Asian LDCs—Bangladesh, Cambodia, Myanmar, and Nepal—that traditionally relied on nonreciprocal or unilateral trade preferences, e.g., the EU's Everything but Arms scheme and several other regional and international duty-free and quota-free schemes, were graduating from these preferential arrangements. Least developed country preferences are also eroding because of entry into force of other regional countries' bilateral RTAs with large trading partners such as the EU and other preference-granting countries. Least developed countries, on graduating from unilateral preferential arrangements, are now challenged to identify or negotiate RTAs that will be to their benefit. Negotiating beneficial agreements will require capacities and expertise that LDC governments will need to develop.

Developing countries have recently signed a number of RTAs, but it is unclear what the value-added may be. Viet Nam has signed four RTAs with Japan: the ASEAN–Japan FTA, the Viet Nam–Japan bilateral FTA, the RCEP, and the CPTPP. The value and utilization rates of these overlapping agreements are unclear and require review with greater aid for trade support.

The size and scope of these issues is significant, and in these negotiations, the devil is always in the details. Aid for trade support for research and support for low- and middle-income countries and LDCs, as well as emerging upper-middle-income countries, like Armenia, which attempt to assess the incremental benefits of overlapping negotiations is urgently needed. For example, evaluating the market access of overlapping FTAs for goods requires comparison of overlapping tariffs schedules, complex rules of origin, and thousands of tariff lines. Comparisons also require text-based or side-by-side reviews of legal provisions to (i) identify the meaning of such provisions for market access and national treatment, and (ii) employ a quantification methodology to rank the degree of liberalization. When trade in services, technical barriers to trade, sanitary and phytosanitary measures, and other regulatory issues also require evaluation, the comparison exercise enters complex and uncharted territory.

Aid for trade programs can help address issues by developing neutral methodologies for assessing and quantifying the impacts and benefits of existing RTAs and potential new agreements; and also by providing clear direction to countries on the agreements that are most beneficial. Such analyses will need to address tariffs and rules of origin; sanitary and phytosanitary measures and technical barriers to trade; and trade in services, investment, intellectual property rights, including the most recent issues of e-commerce and digital services. For example, Australia and New Zealand provide ODA support to the Pacific island members of PACER Plus to negotiate and ratify the agreement, and subsequently a A\$25 million AfT package to support its implementation.

Trade policymaking in developing countries, including the least developed, should be based on informed analysis and public–private dialogue. The decision whether to negotiate new RTAs should be informed by technical calculations of perceived advantage and calculations that quantify the specific proposed language in agreements. Aid for trade can help countries with limited capacity and can provide crucial capacity in assessing and negotiating trade agreements in least developed, low-income, and lower-middle-income, and some emerging upper-middle-income countries. This can help ensure they benefit from them. The following sections describe areas that require deeper research and policy options.

Review of preference utilization rates

Preference utilization rates can be used to assess the incremental value of new RTAs (Inama and Crivelli 2021), particularly for market access and regulatory convergence. Utilization rates assess (i) the effectiveness of subsequent and overlapping RTAs; (ii) the extent to which new initiatives provide new trade opportunities for developing countries, especially least developed and lower-middle-income; and (iii) how this progress is measurable and quantifiable.

Cambodia's recent RTAs raise issues of incremental value. Cambodia recently signed an FTA with the PRC—although Cambodia has been a member of the ASEAN–PRC FTA since 2004 and is a member of the RCEP. Again, the RCEP came into force in January 2022, at the same time as the Cambodia–PRC FTA. The PRC and Cambodia both produce textiles and apparel, so Cambodia benefits most under the RCEP from the elimination of many customs duties on its several agricultural exports. Countries with relatively large apparel industries based on intra-RCEP imports, such as Cambodia, should also benefit from the RCEP's Rules of Origin and modern cumulation rules. Observers may ask what additional benefits the PRC–Cambodia agreement offers in better market access for agricultural exports.

These questions point to the need for assessments of preference utilization rates. Studies can reveal a disturbing picture of trade preference utilization, whether unilateral or reciprocal. Low utilization rates suggest that a preference scheme is not working properly. High utilization rates may or may not be a positive sign, since they may hide low trade volumes and/or low coverage of the RTA or the preferential arrangement. This is the case for the US Generalized System of Preferences and the African Growth and Opportunity Act, in which trade flows are relatively low. In contrast, the spectacular rise in utilization rates of the EU's Everything but Arms Initiative and Canada's Least Developed Country Tariff following a reform of rules of origin was accompanied by increasing trade volumes (WTO 2014). Like a medical check-up, the analysis of utilization rates should be carried out by trade experts able to draw conclusions from a variety of datasets and evidence from firms.

Governments have become wary of preference utilization studies. Objections could be raised, as some trade preferences may not be used, simply because these preferences or other competing duty rebates schemes overlap, such as duty drawbacks.[26] Yet, utilization rates are key to increasing transparency by measuring the effectiveness of various overlapping trade preferences. For instance, Cambodia's utilization rates in the ASEAN–Japan FTA were as low as 10% in 2018; but utilization rates were more than 80% for the Japanese Generalized System of Preferences scheme in the same year. The latter provides more lenient product-specific rules of origin, especially in the garment sector.

Given the overlapping nature of RTAs or preference schemes like the Generalized System of Preferences, studies of utilization rates mean that governments will be able to determine the preference scheme that best suits their firms. They will also be better informed on formulating rules of origin, tariff dismantling, and trade facilitating administrative measures for future RTAs.

Aid for trade should be focused on these issues. New research methodologies to measure the effectiveness of overlapping RTAs should support governments in determining the value of sanitary and phytosanitary measures, technical barriers to trade requirements; trade in services; investment; state-owned enterprises;

---

[26] For instance, the Generalized System of Preferences/African Growth and Opportunity Act for unilateral trade preferences might be overlapping. For FTAs, a valuable example is the Viet Nam–Japan preferential trade relations, in which there is (i) a Japan–ASEAN FTA, (ii) a Viet Nam–Japan bilateral FTA, and (iii) CPTPP and RCEP. In addition, Viet Nam is still a beneficiary of the Japan Generalized System of Preferences.

and intellectual property rights. So far, no one has attempted systemically to devise an appropriate and tailored methodology to each of these new disciplines, nor to assist developing countries with tailored capacity building in these new areas. Such rigorous analysis and its results should be put in place to support governments and trade officials, as ignoring findings of low utilization rates may lead to flawed policy decisions and ineffective RTAs.

3.1.2 Preference Erosion: Graduation and New Regional Trade Agreements

Least developed country graduation is an overarching objective of the international community. Most of the 12 LDCs in Asia and the Pacific are on the verge of graduation from the special treatment provided by the international community in trade and in development cooperation. The WTO contains special and differential treatment provisions for LDCs, over and above flexibilities accorded to developing countries. Market access in the form of unilateral and nonreciprocal preferential tariff treatment for products originating in LDCs is one of the most utilized special and differential treatment provisions in the WTO. Least developed countries enjoy unilateral preferences of duty-free and quota -free market access under schemes like the EU's Everything but Arms Initiative and schemes offered by several Asia and Pacific countries. These preferences offer unilateral and nonreciprocal duty- and quota-free market access to least developed countries. Once these countries graduate from that category they will eventually lose this special treatment. The impact of graduation in scope and magnitude will range from high to low depending on countries' export concentrations of products and destinations and the extent of the LDCs' reliance on unilateral trade preferences.

Asian economies are the success stories of trade preferences. During the 1980s and early 1990s, the Asian tigers (Hong Kong, China; the Republic of Korea; Singapore; and Taipei,China) were able to make efficient use of opportunities created by trade preferences. After their graduation from the Generalized System of Preferences schemes, low- and middle-income countries such as Sri Lanka and Viet Nam have increasingly benefitted. The present performance of Asian LDCs has been impressive.

Graduating LDCs have diverse economic profiles, with marked divergences in export structure, as well as diverse utilization rates of—and reliance on—unilateral preferential market access (WTO 2020). Countries such as Bangladesh and Cambodia have been very successful in taking advantage of the preferences to become leading garment exporters. In contrast, the export structure of small islands and developing states of the Pacific, such as Tuvalu, may not allow them to leverage trade preferences in boosting economic performance.

Graduation from preferences is a main concern of the LDCs that have benefited the most. Preference erosion is also being driven by the proliferation of RTAs in Asia and the Pacific. And while LDCs are particularly vulnerable to preference erosion, the phenomenon is not restricted to LDCs but potentially concerns any developing economy, such as Armenia's loss of preferential access to the EU (Box 3.1).

When devising policy options to remedy to the loss of preferences, factors to be examined should go beyond graduation policy to take into account the overall, constantly changing trade scenario in Asia and the Pacific. A most likely option is that LDCs join RTAs. However, given their proliferation, the need is urgent for accurate analysis of tariff and product-specific rules of origin levels across RTAs. Such analyses may show countries and firms the best options for replacing unilateral preferences by RTAs with the most favorable market access and rules of origin. Aid for trade has a role to play in this exercise, as discussed later.

Box 3.1: Preference Erosion—Armenia's Loss of Preferential Access to the European Union

Armenia was a beneficiary country of the European Union (EU) Generalized Scheme of Preferences Plus (GSP+) from 2014 to 2021. GSP+ grants duty-free access to the EU market for 66% of products. However, EU legislation provides that a country classified by the World Bank as high income or upper middle income for 3 consecutive years should no longer benefit from GSP or GSP+ schemes. As it has been classified as an upper-middle income country since 2018, eligibility ceased for Armenia on 1 January 2022 (EU 2020).[a]

According to ADB 2021,[b] the loss of preferential access to the EU market will reduce Armenia's manufacturing exports to the EU by 11.5%, corresponding to $34.5 million (see table). Exports to Germany are projected to be the most affected (–$23 million), followed by exports to Italy (–$6 million) and France (–$2 million). Part of the foregone exports to the EU, however, are expected to be reallocated to other markets. Exports to the Russian Federation are notably expected to increase by 1.6%. Overall, Armenia's total exports of manufactured goods are expected to decline by 0.9%, corresponding to $16.6 million. This reduction in exports is expected to translate into a minimal reduction of Armenia's welfare (or real consumption) of about 0.1%.

Impact of Loss of Preferential Access to the EU Market on Armenia's Welfare and Exports of Manufactured Goods

Scenario	Impact on Welfare %	Impact on Exports		
		$ million	Share of total exports (%)	Share of bilateral exports (%)
Aggregate impact	**(0.13)**	**(16.6)**	**(0.9)**	**—**
of which European Union	—	(34.5)	(1.8)	(11.5)
of which Russian Federation		8.8	0.5	1.6

() = negative, EU = European Union.
Note: For simplicity, the United Kingdom is included within the EU as its withdrawal from the EU also means that it is no longer part of the EU's Generalized Scheme of Preferences Plus program.
Source: Asian Development Bank. 2021. The Impact of Tariff Changes on Armenia's Foreign Trade. Manila.

This moderate effect is mostly due to the low coverage of GSP+ for Armenia's exports to the EU. As of 2018, copper ores accounted for 38% of Armenia's exports to the EU; and the EU does not impose tariffs on copper (see table). GSP+ thus does not provide any advantage for Armenia's top export product to the EU. For ferro-molybdenum alloys—which accounts for 23% of Armenia's exports to the EU—GSP+ does provide an advantage, but only minimal as the default most-favored nation tariff is only 2.7%. The moderate effect of GSP+ on Armenia's exports to the EU thus mostly arise from aluminum foil and textile, which are also significant bilateral exports.

The structure of Armenia's exports makes its case specific. Preferential access to the EU market might be more critical for other beneficiaries of the GSP+ scheme or more generous schemes such as "Everything but Arms". These economies may incur significant losses and suffer long-term adverse effects if the preferential tariff scheme they benefit from are removed. Alternative options therefore need to be explored in a forward-looking trade policy agenda.[c]

continued on next page

Box 3.1 continued

Armenia's Exports to the European Union: 2018

	$ million	Share of exports to the EU (%)	EU's MFN Tariff (%)
Exports to the EU	**831**	**100**	**—**
Copper ores	313	38	0.0
Ferro-molybdenum alloys	193	23	2.7
Aluminum foil	97	12	7.5

– means data not available, ADB = Asian Development Bank, EU = European Union, MFN = most-favored nation.
[a] European Union. 2020. Commissions Delegated Regulation (EU) 2021/114 of 25 September 2020.
[b] ADB. 2021. The Impact of Tariff Changes on Armenia's Foreign Trade. Manila.
[c] See recommendations contained in Chapter 1 of the Cambodia Trade Integration Strategy 2019–2023.
  https://cambodiancorner.files.wordpress.com/2019/12/cambodia-trade-integratio-strategy-2019-2023-1.pdf.
Sources: International Trade Centre. 2021. Market Access Map; and Centre d'Études Prospectives et d'Informations Internationales (CEPII).
2021. Base pour l'Analyse du Commerce International (BACI). This box was written by Pramila Crivelli and Jules Hugot of the Economic
Research and Regional Cooperation Department, ADB.

3.1.3 Global Value Chain Participation

Most developing economies and some LDCs participate heavily in GVCs. Regional trade agreements such as the CPTPP, RCEP, and ASEAN FTAs that address behind-the-border issues, strengthen existing GVCs, and promote new ones. However, we know less about how to attract GVCs and enhance their positive impact through RTA-related institutional and policy reform. Much more analysis is needed of what policies support GVCs and promote GVC investment. Technical and economic assistance are also required to help governments address these issues, as is adjustment assistance that enables labor mobility in line with changes in production and export patterns.

Within the group of lower-middle-income countries—the main beneficiaries of Aid for Trade—GVC participation rates for Indonesia[27] and the Lao PDR are below the regional average (ADB 2021a). Indonesia's ranking is partly explained by the high share of petroleum and agricultural products in its exports. Meanwhile, over the past 20 years, Cambodia, the Lao PDR, and Viet Nam experienced extremely high growth in their gross exports, as well as indirect exports, i.e., the portion of their value added exports embodied as intermediate inputs in other countries' exports. The most striking case is Viet Nam. The big volume of indirect exports ($165 billion in 2019) is mostly related to labor-intensive industries, which account for a continuously declining share in the PRC's exports. The PRC has also been an important source of foreign direct investment flows to Viet Nam.

The relative share of forward and backward linkages[28] in overall GVC participation significantly varies across countries. Forward linkages are more important in countries that are rich in natural resources, such as Indonesia. The Lao PDR's high degree of forward integration can be explained by its landlocked position, which causes the country to use Vietnamese and Thai port facilities for shipping its exports to the rest of the world (ADB 2021b). Conversely, in Cambodia and Viet Nam, backward linkages prevail by far over forward linkages, due to the high share of final, rather than intermediate, products in the composition of their exports.

---

[27] In 2020, Indonesia stepped down from the upper-middle-income category to the lower-middle-income category as a result of the negative impact of COVID-19 on its economy.

[28] Backward linkages: share of foreign value-added in total exports of a country; forward linkages: domestic value-added embodied in intermediate exports that are further re-exported to third countries.

Gains from GVC participation are not inevitable. The benefits of GVCs can vary considerably depending on whether a country operates at the high or low end of the value chain. A study on the textile and clothing sector in graduating, Asian LDCs concluded that a "successful" country like Cambodia has been caught for decades in the low-value segment of the GVC, resulting in extremely low profit margins (Box 3.3).

Governments and trade agreements have a key role to play in promoting GVC participation. Tariff reduction is important to attracting GVCs. Multiple border crossings of intermediate goods magnify costs to GVCs, particularly compared to trade in final goods produced in a single country. Tariffs applied on the gross value of imports, rather than on value added, do the same. Any marginal decrease in gross tariff rates can significantly lower costs for trade in intermediate goods and enhance options for GVC participation.

Nontariff barriers or behind-the-border measures are often more restrictive role than tariffs and quotas. The most important factors affecting developing country participation in GVCs are intellectual property rights protection, standards and logistics, such as trade facilitation. In fact, in the context of RCEP, full implementation of the trade facilitation commitments could have a greater impact on trade liberalization and strengthening GVCs than tariff reductions alone (ADB 2022).

3.1.4 Mega-Regional Trade Agreements: A Role in Supporting Recovery from COVID-19 and Building Resilience?

The long-standing stalemate in multilateral trade negotiations within WTO's Doha Round means that RTAs and, more recently, the mega-regionals, are attempting to fill the gap in global governance of the international trading system. In Asia and the Pacific, two mega-regionals stand out: the CPTPP, which entered into force in December 2018, and the more recent RCEP.[29] These agreements are similar, but stark differences outweigh the similarities. Seven countries are parties to both agreements—Australia, Japan, New Zealand, and the four ASEAN countries of Brunei Darussalam, Malaysia, Singapore, and Viet Nam. They share the ultimate goals of greater market access and enhanced trade and investment flows. They also use the same approaches to achieve these goals: cutting tariffs and lowering behind-the-border barriers to trade and investment. However, they have five key areas of difference: genesis, geographical coverage and size, scope, depth, and accessions (Box 3.2).

---

[29] ADB (2022) provides a detailed analysis of the RCEP and how it differs from the CPTPP.

Box 3.2: Comparing the Comprehensive and Progressive Agreement for Trans-Pacific Partnership and the Regional Comprehensive Economic Partnership

Genesis. The Regional Comprehensive Economic Partnership (RCEP) is the result of a long-standing integration effort centered on the Association of Southeast Asian Nations (ASEAN), starting with the ASEAN Free Trade Agreement (FTA), followed by FTAs between ASEAN and five Asia and the Pacific countries: Australia, the People's Republic of China (PRC), Japan, New Zealand, and the Republic of Korea. The RCEP's content has been shaped by the "ASEAN way" of conducting step-by-step negotiations by consensus and postponing unresolved issues to future negotiations under a robust built-in agenda. In fact, the RCEP has been termed a "work in progress" (Park, Petri, and Plummer 2021).

The Comprehensive and Progressive Agreement for Trans-Pacific Partnership (CPTPP) originated in the Trans-Pacific Partnership. In 2017, the United States (US) withdrew from the agreement, and remaining parties concluded the agreement as CPTPP by suspending a number of provisions, especially in the investment area. The CPTPP is a high-quality and ambitious regional trade agreement, with no built-in agenda.

Geographical coverage and size. The CPTPP has a smaller membership of 11 countries; the RCEP has 15. The CPTPP has no least developed countries and only one lower-middle-income country. Unlike the RCEP, four of its members are extraregional—Canada, Chile, Mexico, and Peru. The CPTPP features smaller income disparities between parties than the RCEP. With the exception of Viet Nam, the CPTPP is composed of high-income and upper-middle-income countries exclusively. The RCEP covers six lower-middle-income countries, including three least developed countries. Furthermore, the RCEP is the first agreement in which the PRC, Japan, and the Republic of Korea—all non-ASEAN nations—share membership.

The RCEP covers 30% of the world population, versus the CPTPP's 7%. It also covers 31% versus 13% of global gross domestic product and 29% versus 14% of global merchandise exports. In 2020, intra-RCEP trade accounted for 44% of members' global trade, against 36% for the CPTPP. However, the CPTPP's gross domestic product per capita ($19,000 in 2020) was about twice the RCEP's ($11,000).

Scope. Both agreements deal with areas covered by the World Trade Organization (WTO)—trade in goods, in services, movement of natural persons, intellectual property, and government procurement—as well as WTO-plus commitments in investment, competition, electronic commerce, and small and medium-sized enterprises. The CPTPP covers three behind-the-border areas that do not appear in the RCEP, namely, state-owned enterprises, labor, and environment.

Depth. The CPTPP is considered more comprehensive than the RCEP because of its wider coverage and more ambitious commitments. Such differences include:

Trade in goods. Unlike the CPTPP, the RCEP is composed of 38 different tariff schedules with very long timelines of 20 years (or even slightly more). Some countries—Australia, Brunei Darussalam, Cambodia, the Lao People's Democratic Republic, Malaysia, New Zealand, Singapore, and Thailand—created a single tariff schedule to apply equally to all other trading partners. Japan used a "hybrid" schedule. Other RCEP members, such as Indonesia and Viet Nam, have made differentiated offers depending on RCEP partners. This complexity has in turn generated other layers of provisions in reading and understanding tariff schedules, including the potential for tariff differentials to impact cumulation.

Trade in services. In comparison to the CPTPP, the RCEP annex on financial services is more weighted toward prudential regulations and states' right to regulate over financial liberalization. Furthermore, the RCEP lacks an investor-state dispute settlement mechanism, which is available in the CPTPP for the enforcement of financial service suppliers' rights, including minimum standards of treatment. The CPTPP's annex on professional services is far more detailed than the RCEP's. In fact, it contains not only general provisions but also specific commitments in a number of areas.

continued on next page

Box 3.2 continued

Intellectual property. The RCEP aims to reconcile "the rights of intellectual property right holders and the legitimate interests of users and the public interest." The CPTPP instead is tilted toward the rights of intellectual property rights holders. However, the RCEP's chapter on intellectual property can be defined as a quantum leap compared to the shallow treatment in ASEAN+1 FTAs.

Government procurement. While the RCEP focuses only on transparency and technical cooperation, the CPTPP deals with market access.

Competition. The CPTPP's and the RCEP's chapters on competition are quite similar. However, the RCEP has no specific provisions on state-owned enterprises, while the CPTPP devotes a separate chapter to them.

Investment. The RCEP's market access commitments on investment appear to be below those offered under the CPTPP. The latter also contains specific provisions for investor-state dispute settlement, which are absent from the RCEP. Admittedly, this agreement offers a state-state dispute settlement mechanism. This means that if a host state does not meet its obligations under the investment chapter, investors can request their home state to support their claims, which it can eventually bring against the host state.

Electronic commerce. The RCEP provisions are neither as comprehensive nor as strict as those in the CPTTP. The RCEP does not address issues related to source code, such as the one underpinning Microsoft Office, a fundamental component of software. Unlike the CPTTP, the RCEP's electronic commerce chapter is not now subject to dispute settlement. The RCEP's rules on data flows and data localization, allowing slightly wider policy space.

Accessions. So far, Hong Kong, China alone has announced its desire to apply for RCEP membership once the Agreement opens for accession from 1 July 2023. India opted out of negotiations in November 2019. The RCEP remains open for India to commence accession discussions at any time (RCEP Article 20.9). The United Kingdom (February 2021); the PRC (September 2021); Taipei,China (September 2021); and Ecuador (December 2021) have applied to join the CPTPP. Indonesia, the Republic of Korea, the Philippines, and Thailand have expressed interest in acceding to the agreement.

Source: Asian Development Bank.

Economic effects and the future of mega-regional trade agreements

The RCEP and the CPTPP have the potential to shape future regional trade and investment patterns and international economic cooperation in the post-COVID-19 era. However, their impact will be uneven. Except for Viet Nam, the benefits accruing to LDCs and lower-middle-income countries—Cambodia, the Lao PDR, Indonesia, and the Philippines—in terms of increase in income and exports are expected to be much smaller than those of Japan and the Republic of Korea, *unless the RCEP's built-in agenda is fully implemented* (see Crivelli and Inama 2022). Several Asia and Pacific lower-middle-income and LDCs are not parties to the CPTPP and are expected to be hurt by trade diversion (Park, Petri, and Plummer 2021).

A recent study by the World Bank, also based on computable general equilibrium modeling, indicates that RCEP tariff liberalization alone brings little benefit, but when it is accompanied with flexible rules of origin, the gains in real income could be substantial (Estrades et al. 2022). The study estimates that trade among RCEP members could increase 12.3% in 2035 relative to the baseline. However, the study also argues that these aggregate effects mask a large variety of outcomes across countries, with Viet Nam expected to register the highest trade and income gains.

As with several other studies,[30] this research relies on the econometric assumptions of full implementation of the commitments contained in the RCEP and its built-in agenda.

Aid for trade has a role in assisting least developed and other developing countries in identifying how to enhance gains from the mega-regionals and offset losses stemming from the deals and/or to address trade diversion, preference erosion, and graduation.

Can mega-regionals promote trade resilience? Widening market access and input sourcing possibilities through cumulation benefits?

Mega-regionals and RTAs have mitigated the COVID-19 downturn. In developing Asia, intra-RTA trade declined significantly less than trade under no agreement. Trade within deep RTAs was more resilient than trade within shallow RTAs. Inevitably, during an economic crisis, demand turns to more reliable suppliers and lower trade costs, such as lower tariffs and smaller regulatory differences, both associated with RTAs. On the supply side, suppliers can be selective in complying with contracts. As forfeiting of contracts covered by RTA enforcement rules can be costly, intra-RTA trade becomes less volatile (Nicita and Saygili 2021).

Cumulation is the plumbing of global value chains as it allows countries to consider inputs originating in other countries as domestic inputs for duty-free purposes. More specifically, cumulation provisions allow identification of intermediate materials, work, and processing in a region to be considered as originating in the country of export. This allows ease of market access for firms by facilitating compliance with the origin criteria and the application of reduced duties or duty-free treatment.

Mega-regional RTAs are expected to streamline the "spaghetti bowl" of overlapping regulations, boosting creation of regional value chains. However, firms will use these mega-regional deals only if they provide value added over existing RTAs including a competitive margin of preferences, flexible product-specific rules of origin, and related administrative procedures (Crivelli, Inama, and Pearson 2022). It remains to be seen if the RCEP's trade preferences are fully utilized: assessing that will require close monitoring of utilization rates.

The absence of a most-favored nation clause in the Trade in Goods chapter of RCEP and the differentiated tariff offers among member countries are likely to make cumulation provisions difficult to use. Specific provisions to determine the country of final origin when different preferential tariffs apply are contained in the tariff schedules of each RCEP member, formulated with different wording and, at times, different criteria. In contrast, the CPTPP adopts one single pragmatic criterion for determining the country of origin for the application of tariff differentials for all CPTPP members: the country where the last production process took place unless such process is a minimal operation.

The RCEP parties should therefore rapidly activate article 2.5 to accelerate and simplify tariff commitments as well as article 2.21 on sectoral initiatives to facilitate trade. In addition, they should extend the application of cumulation to working and processing undertaken in the RCEP, as provided for in article 3.4, and where possible, introduce self-certification as a preferred proof of origin. They should also implement promptly the approved exporters mechanism and self-certification.[31]

---

[30]   See Economic Research Institute for ASEAN and East Asia (2022).

[31]   These recommendations are drawn from Crivelli and Inama (2022).

3.2 Support Developing Asia to Increase the Efficiency and Design of Trade Agreements

3.2.1 Supporting Least Developed Countries in Addressing Preference Erosion and Graduation Challenges

The evolving contest for market access further marginalized Asian LDCs such as Bangladesh, Cambodia, Myanmar, and Nepal that have been relying on unilateral trade preferences such as the EU Everything but Arms initiative or other duty-free quota-free schemes. Several LDCs so far have not engaged in new RTAs, because of the lack of capacity to engage in negotiations or implement such agreements.

Exports of the 12 Asia and Pacific LDCs represent close to half of the total exports of the 47 LDCs. Bangladesh, Cambodia, and Myanmar are the three largest Asia and Pacific LDC exporters. These graduating LDCs show differences in destination and product concentration of exports and trade context. For some of these countries (e.g., Bhutan, Nepal, and Pacific LDCs) exports are predominantly intraregional, while for other LDCs (e.g., Bangladesh and Cambodia) exports are mainly concentrated in the EU and North America. The direction of exports will to a large extent determine decisions on market access and on membership of RTAs following graduation.

According to the United Nations Conference on Trade and Development (UNCTAD), Cambodia has attracted dedicated analysis within the country's Diagnostic Trade Integration (UNCTAD 2020), illustrating these various challenges and outlining a series of detailed trade policy initiatives needed in the region's LDCs to surmount a difficult juncture. These trade policy initiatives require capacities and expertise that LDC governments may lack.

Least developed country governments may be motivated to seek additional market access to compensate preference erosion due to graduation by entering quickly into new RTAs. However, this policy option requires building considerable technical competence and negotiating capacity within these LDCs, particularly given uneven distribution of benefits in some RTAs.

Assessing the incremental value of RTAs or mega-regionals that LDCs may consider is a challenging task. An in-depth analysis of utilization rates of trade preferences under current and future RTAs would need to be carried out, including identification of the best cumulation options. Governments of LDCs will also need to identify the complex and challenging issues surrounding regulatory concessions or proposals for concessions that may be elaborated in the context of RTA negotiations.

Cost-benefit analysis also needs to be undertaken on the coverage and ambition of LDC accession to RTAs. Even more challenging would be to build a framework and design mechanism in RTAs for regulatory convergence on areas of special interest to least developed countries. These are areas in which aid for trade can play a role.

Country-specific analysis of least developed country graduation challenges

The stakes are not the same across graduating LDCs in Asia and the Pacific. Exports of Bhutan, the Lao PDR, Myanmar, and Timor-Leste are concentrated in primary commodities (including fuels and minerals) and selected markets. Bangladesh and Cambodia are dependent on clothing, and Nepal's reliance on certain textile items such as carpets is very high. Kiribati, Solomon Islands, Tuvalu, and Vanuatu mainly export agricultural and fishing products. Differences in destination, product concentration, and general trade contexts determines, to a large extent, the market access scenario following graduation.

The following illustrates challenges faced by Bangladesh, Cambodia, the Lao PDR, Nepal, and Solomon Islands on graduation from duty-free and quota-free preferences.

Bangladesh and Cambodia face particular challenges, as they are both heavily dependent on market access to few export destinations, and export a limited range of products under trade preferences.

Bangladesh relied on the EU market for 57% of its exports in 2020 (Figure 3.1, panel A). Bangladesh garments (HS 61 and 62) accounted for 85% of total exports in 2020 (Figure 3.1, panel B).

Panels D and E show a slightly less pronounced picture for Cambodia, with the US (30.8% share), the EU (23.4%), and ASEAN (21.5%) as the main export destinations in 2020. It is remarkable that the US is the first export destination, even if in that market Cambodia does not benefit from trade preferences. The US Generalized System of Preferences in fact does not provide trade preferences for textile and clothing apparel. By export composition, the basket of Cambodia exports also appears to be less dependent on garments, since it also includes shoes (HS 64), bags (HS 42), and bicycles (HS 87).

Panels C and F show the main market destinations of Bangladesh and Cambodia, including alternative market access opportunities provided by mega-regionals such as the RCEP and CPTPP. It is evident that destinations are heavily skewed toward preference-granting countries, with Bangladesh ranking first, with a 57.2% share in the EU alone. Panel F shows that in 2020 Cambodia's exports to member countries of mega-regionals (RCEP and CPTPP) reached a share of 40.5%.

Figure 3.2, panel A shows the reliance of Bangladesh exports of garments on the EU Everything but Arms preferences. Utilization rates have been well over 90% since 2011, also showing an additional dependence of the favorable rules of origin associated with Everything but Arms after the reform of the EU rules of origin[32] in 2011. Utilization rates of HS 62 show a vertical increase from around 43% in 2010 to over 90% in 2011 after the EU reform of rules of origin, allowing a single transformation: fabrics to garments replacing the former requirement of double transformation, i.e., yarn to fabrics and fabrics to garments. This change allowed Bangladesh garments producers to use nonoriginating fabric from the PRC, making compliance much easier.

---

[32]   On the impact and significance of the EU reform of rules of origin for LDCs, see Crivelli and Inama (2021).

Figure 3.1: Export Destinations and Export Shares by HS Chapter, Bangladesh, and Cambodia
(%)

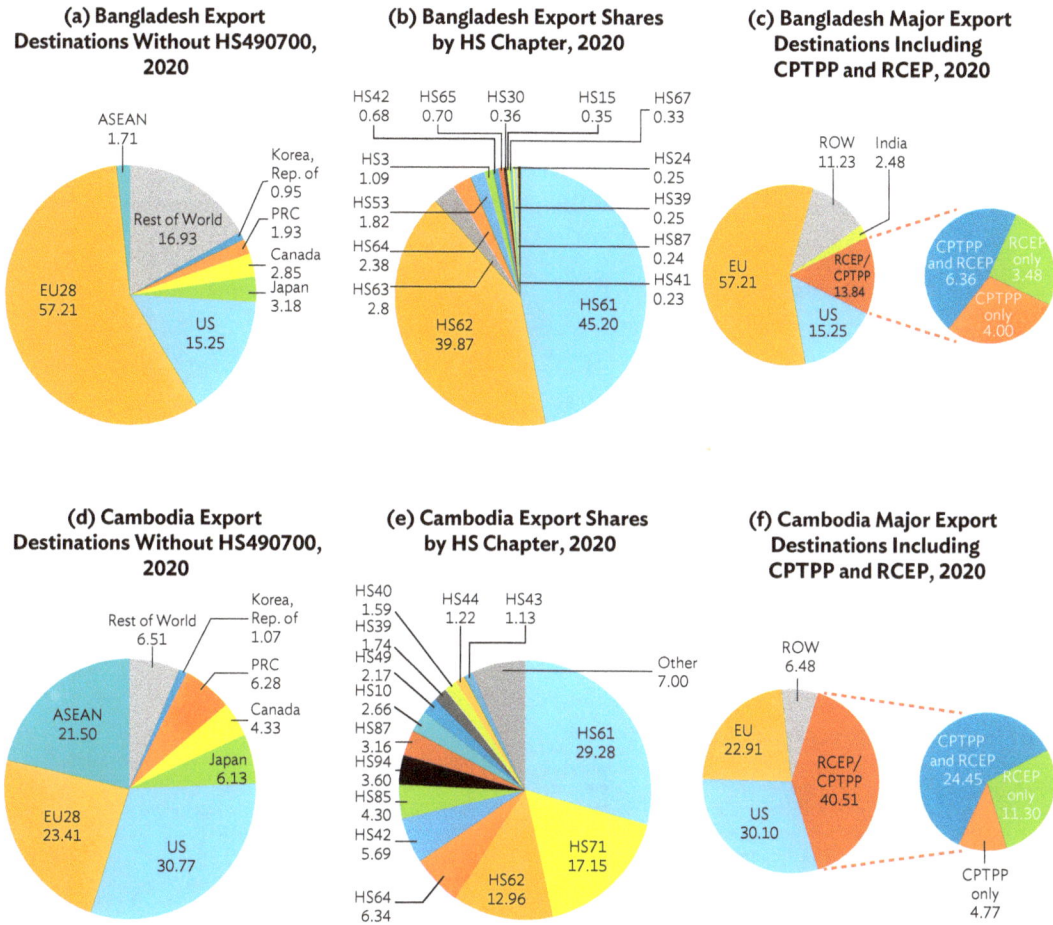

(a) Bangladesh Export Destinations Without HS490700, 2020

ASEAN 1.71
Korea, Rep. of 0.95
PRC 1.93
Canada 2.85
Japan 3.18
Rest of World 16.93
EU28 57.21
US 15.25

(b) Bangladesh Export Shares by HS Chapter, 2020

HS42 0.68
HS65 0.70
HS30 0.36
HS15 0.35
HS67 0.33
HS3 1.09
HS53 1.82
HS64 2.38
HS63 2.8
HS24 0.25
HS39 0.25
HS87 0.24
HS41 0.23
HS62 39.87
HS61 45.20

(c) Bangladesh Major Export Destinations Including CPTPP and RCEP, 2020

ROW 11.23
India 2.48
EU 57.21
US 15.25
RCEP/CPTPP 13.84
CPTPP and RCEP 6.36
RCEP only 3.48
CPTPP only 4.00

(d) Cambodia Export Destinations Without HS490700, 2020

Rest of World 6.51
Korea, Rep. of 1.07
PRC 6.28
Canada 4.33
Japan 6.13
ASEAN 21.50
EU28 23.41
US 30.77

(e) Cambodia Export Shares by HS Chapter, 2020

HS40 1.59
HS44 1.22
HS43 1.13
HS39 1.74
HS49 2.17
HS10 2.66
HS87 3.16
HS94 3.60
HS85 4.30
HS42 5.69
HS64 6.34
HS62 12.96
HS71 17.15
HS61 29.28
Other 7.00

(f) Cambodia Major Export Destinations Including CPTPP and RCEP, 2020

ROW 6.48
EU 22.91
US 30.10
RCEP/CPTPP 40.51
CPTPP and RCEP 24.45
RCEP only 11.30
CPTPP only 4.77

ASEAN = Association of Southeast Asian Nations; CPTPP = Comprehensive and Progressive Agreement for Trans-Pacific Partnership; EU = European Union; HS = Harmonized System; HS3 = Fish and crustaceans, molluscs and other aquatic invertebrates; HS10 = Cereals; HS15 = Animal or vegetable fats and oils and their cleavage products prepared edible fats; animal or vegetable waxes; HS24 = Tobacco and manufactured tobacco substitutes; HS30 = Pharmaceutical products; HS39 = Plastics and articles thereof; HS40 = Rubber and articles thereof; HS41 = Raw hides and skins (other than furskins) and leather; HS42 = Articles of leather; saddlery and harness; travel goods, handbags and similar containers; articles of animal gut (other than silkworm gut); HS43 = Furskins and artificial fur; manufactures thereof; HS44 = Wood and articles of wood; wood charcoal; HS49 = Printed books, newspapers, pictures and other products of the printing industry; manuscripts, typescripts and plans; HS53 = Other vegetable textile fibers; paper yarn and woven fabric of paper yarn; HS61 = Articles of apparel and clothing accessories, knitted or crocheted; HS62 = Articles of apparel and clothing accessories, knitted or crocheted; HS63 = Other made up textile articles; sets; worn clothing and worn textile articles; rags; HS64 = Footwear, gaiters and the like; parts of such articles; HS65 = Headgear and parts thereof; HS67 = Prepared feathers and down and articles made of feathers or of down; artificial flowers; articles of human hair; HS71 = Natural or cultured pearls, precious or semi-precious stones, precious metals, metals clad with precious metal and articles thereof; imitation jewelry; coin; HS85 = Electrical machinery and equipment and parts thereof; sound recorders and reproducers, television image and sound recorders and reproducers, and parts and accessories of such articles; HS87 = Vehicles other than railway or tramway rolling stock, and parts and accessories thereof; HS94 = Furniture; bedding, mattresses, mattress supports, cushions and similar stuffed furnishings; lamps and lighting fittings, not elsewhere specified or included; illuminated sign illuminated nameplates and the like; prefabricated buildings; PRC = People's Republic of China; RCEP = Regional Comprehensive Economic Partnership; US = United States.
Source: ADB calculations based on United Nations Comtrade Database. https://comtrade.un.org/data (accessed May 2022).

Figure 3.2, panel B depicts Cambodian rates in using the Everything but Arms preferences for HS 61 and 62, showing that the garment sector remains the driver of the country's performance in the EU, one of its major export markets. Notably, Cambodia was temporarily suspended from Everything but Arms preferences in August 2020.[33] As with Bangladesh, Cambodia's dependence on the more favorable rules of origin contained in the EU reform is remarkable, as utilization rates have increased impressively since its introduction, from slightly above 50% in 2010 to over 90% in 2011 and beyond, for HS 62 and for HS 61, from around 70% to 90% and over in the following years.

Figure 3.2: European Union Imports from Bangladesh and Cambodia and Generalized System of Preferences Utilization Rates

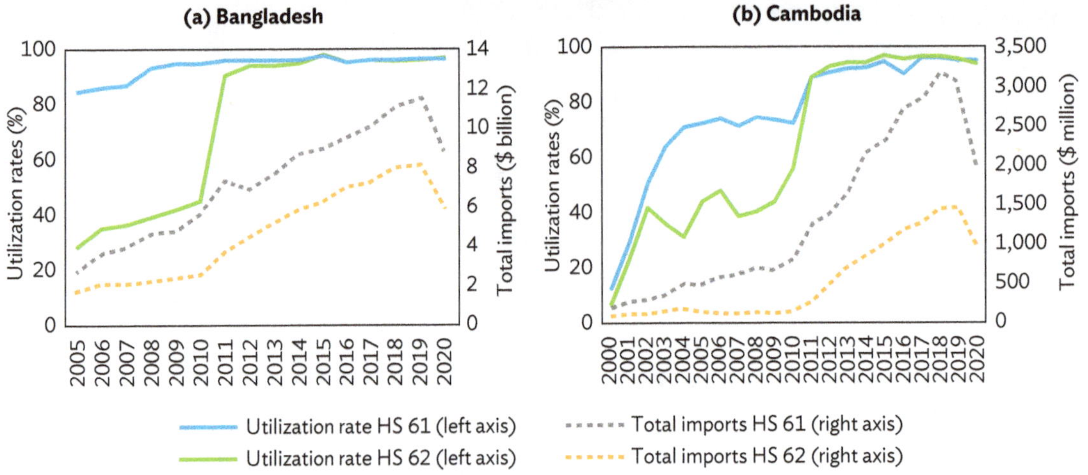

HS = Harmonized System, GSP = Generalized System of Preferences.
Note: Articles of apparel and clothing accessories, HS 61 (knitted/ crocheted) and HS 62 (not knitted/ crocheted clothing and accessories).
Source: Asian Development Bank calculations based on United Nations Conference on Trade and Development. UNCTAD Database on GSP Utilization. https://gsp.unctad.org (accessed May 2022).

Notably, Figure A3.2 panels A and B show a dramatic decrease in total imports of garments in 2020 compared to earlier years, mainly due to COVID-19. Yet, Bangladesh and Cambodia utilization rates exhibit no significant variation, showing that high rates remained a constant feature, even during the pandemic. The figure also shows that the importance of trade preferences, especially when coupled with lenient rules of origin, cannot be overstated for these Asian countries.

The potential loss of the EU trade preferences for the Lao PDR may be mitigated by the country's reliance on regional markets

The Lao PDR records a trade volume of $190 million to the EU market for garments and enjoys a preference utilization rate of around 90%. However, extreme reliance on the regional market with ASEAN (57%) and the PRC (29%) as the main destinations can help the country mitigate the potential loss of trade preferences (Figure 3.3, panels A and B).

---

[33] See Commission Delegated Regulation (EU) 2020/550 of 12 February 2020 amending Annexes II and IV to Regulation (EU) No 978/2012 of the European Parliament and of the Council as regards the temporary withdrawal of the arrangements referred to in Article 1(2) of Regulation (EU) No 978/2012 in respect of certain products originating in the Kingdom of Cambodia.

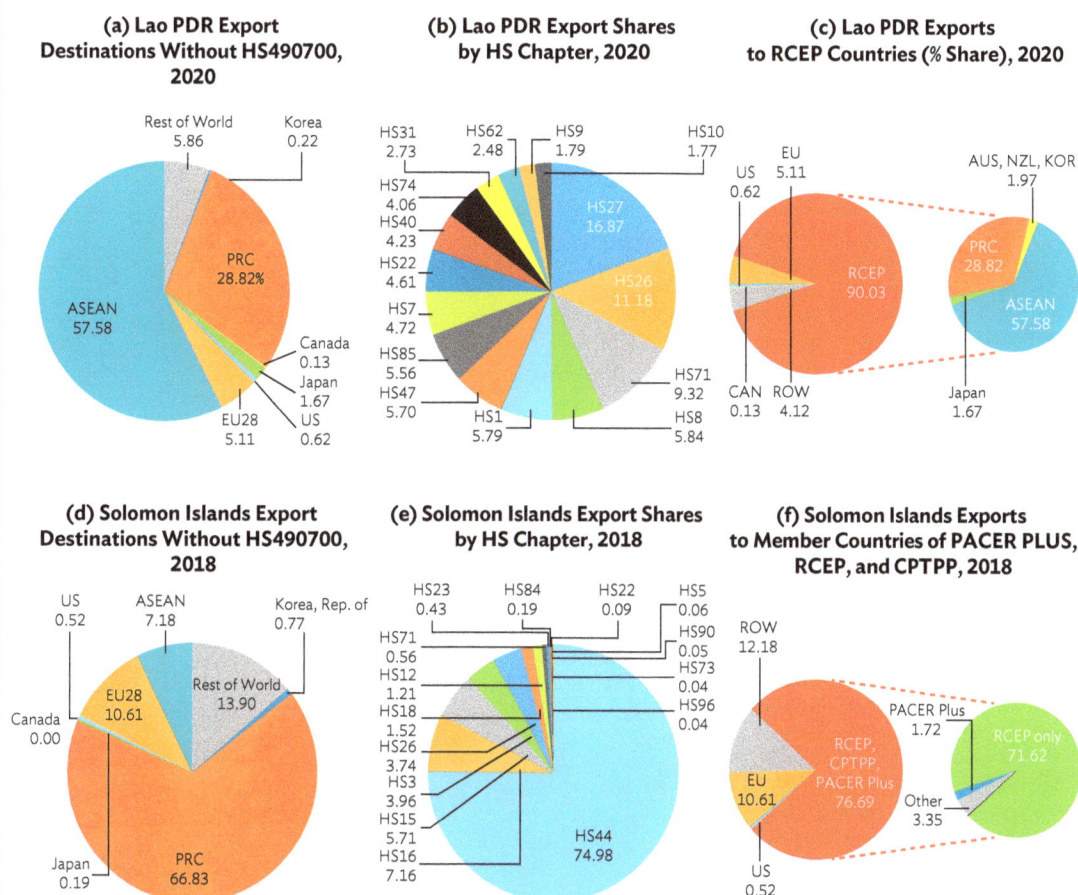

Figure 3.3: Export Destinations and Export Shares by HS Chapter, Lao PDR, and Solomon Islands (%)

ASEAN = Association of Southeast Asian Nations; AUS = Australia; CPTPP = Comprehensive and Progressive Agreement for Trans-Pacific Partnership; EU = European Union; HS = Harmonized System; HS1 = Live animals; HS3 = Fish and crustaceans, molluscs and other aquatic invertebrates; HS7 = Edible vegetables and certain roots and tubers; HS8 = Edible fruit and nuts; peel of citrus fruit or melons; HS9 = Coffee, tea, maté and spices; HS10 = Cereals; HS12 = Oil seeds and oleaginous fruits; miscellaneous grains, seeds and fruits; industrial or medicinal plants; straw and fodder; HS15 = Animal or vegetable fats and oils and their cleavage products prepared edible fats; animal or vegetable waxes; HS16 = Preparations of meat, of fish or of crustaceans, molluscs or other aquatic invertebrates; HS18 = Cocoa and cocoa preparations; HS22 = Beverages, spirits and vinegar; HS26 = Ores, slag and ash; HS27 = Mineral fuels, mineral oils and products of their distillation; bituminous substances; mineral waxes; HS31 = Fertilizers; HS40 = Rubber and articles thereof; HS44 = Wood and articles of wood; wood charcoal; HS47 = Pulp of wood or of other fibrous cellulosic material; waste and scrap of paper or paperboard; HS62 = Articles of apparel and clothing accessories, not knitted or crocheted; HS71 = Natural or cultured pearls, precious or semi-precious stoned, precious metals, metals clad with precious metal and articles thereof; imitation jewelry; coin; HS74 = Copper and articles thereof; HS85 = Electrical machinery and equipment and parts thereof; sound recorders and reproducers, television image and sound recorders and reproducers, and parts and accessories of such articles; KOR = Republic of Korea; NZL = New Zealand; PACER Plus = Pacific Agreement on Closer Economic Relations Plus; PRC = People's Republic of China; RCEP = Regional Comprehensive Economic Partnership; USA = United States.
Source: Asian Development Bank calculations based on UN Comtrade Database. https://comtrade.un.org/data (accessed May 2022).

The Lao PDR's export basket is also diversified, even with significantly lower trade volumes than Bangladesh and Cambodia. Energy products and minerals represent a combined 37% of the total export basket. Panel C shows the importance of the RCEP for the Lao PDR as the main destination of its exports, with a share as high as 90%. In contrast to Bangladesh and Cambodia, the potential loss of trade preferences may not be as high. The Lao PDR enjoys trade preferences in the EU market for garments, recording a trade volume of around $190 million and a utilization rate well above 90%. Given the Lao PDR's export destinations, mainly focused on ASEAN and the PRC, the main issue is determining what the RCEP brings in incremental value in addition to existing FTAs with ASEAN countries (ASEAN Trade in Goods Agreement and the ASEAN-PRC FTA). In addition, it would be necessary to identify the preferential margin under these FTAs. While exports to the EU may appear of relatively small value compared to overall export markets, it should also be noted that they represent a significant share of manufactured products.

19% of exports to the EU and the US may suffer from the loss of preferential market access

Nepal's main bilateral partner is India, with a 68% share of export destinations. The US and the EU still represent 10% and 9%, respectively, as destinations for manufactured products exported from Nepal (Figure 3.4), suggesting that trade preferences still play a role.[34]

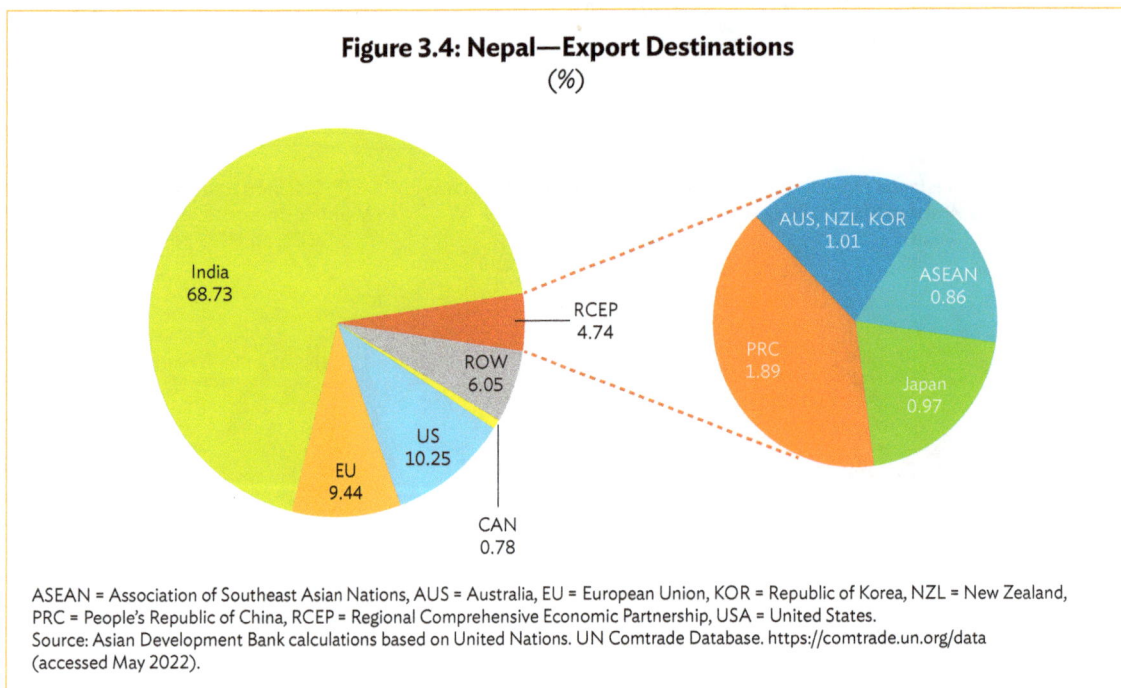

Figure 3.4: Nepal—Export Destinations
(%)

ASEAN = Association of Southeast Asian Nations, AUS = Australia, EU = European Union, KOR = Republic of Korea, NZL = New Zealand, PRC = People's Republic of China, RCEP = Regional Comprehensive Economic Partnership, USA = United States.
Source: Asian Development Bank calculations based on United Nations. UN Comtrade Database. https://comtrade.un.org/data (accessed May 2022).

The share of the RCEP economies as export destinations, somewhat below 5%, does not yet represent a significant alternative. However, given that as much of the combined 19% of exports to the EU and the US may suffer from the loss of preferential market access, possible accession to RCEP should be assessed, taking into account the RCEP's future development and possible enlargement to Nepal's neighboring countries.

---

[34] The US is granting a special preference program to Nepal since 2015 following the earthquake that devastated the country. The program covers a number of products such as carpets and bags that are not covered under the US GSP and lasts until 2025 (US Federal Code 19 US Code § 4454 - Trade Preferences for Nepal).

With high export concentration, Solomon Islands will face challenges in diversifying exported products and market destinations

As in the Lao PDR and Nepal, the export composition and destinations of Solomon Islands show a unique pattern (Figure 3.3, panels D and E): a heavy dependence for exports of wood products (HS 44) on the PRC (66.7% share in 2018) and an even more pronounced one in export composition, since such exports represented 75% of total exports in 2018. Solomon Islands benefits from Everything but Arms access to the EU for its exports of canned tuna ($56 million in 2018) and palm oil ($15 million, in the same year) with high utilization rates over 90%.

The RCEP appears to be the main export destination, given the inclusion of the PRC. Solomon Islands is also a member of the Pacific Agreement on Closer Economic Relations Plus (PACER Plus). However, as Figure 3.3 panel F shows, PACER Plus countries represent a minute share of Solomon Islands' export destinations (1.72%).

Trade policy responses

Each least developed country will need to elaborate its own trade policy responses to graduation and the resulting preference erosion. The loss of LDC status may also have negative implications for GVC market access due to exclusion or changes in the cumulation criteria in the rules of origin.

In addition, many Asian countries have negotiated bilateral FTAs with main preference, giving countries. These agreements are further eroding the market access of Asian LDCs independently from graduation. It follows that after graduation some Asian LDCs may find themselves facing negative market access relative to non-LDCs in Asia that have entered into FTAs to build up their networks.

For example, Cambodia's bicycle sector represents a success for the country's export diversification strategy. But according to non-LDC EU rules of origin, Cambodia's bicycle producers will no longer be able to use for cumulation purposes parts of bicycles originating in Viet Nam. This restriction will severely disrupt the existence of the regional value chain. The Cambodian bicycle industry has initiated a procedure for requesting the continuation of LDC cumulation requirements to the European Union.

Bangladesh and Cambodia, the most severely affected countries, have the option to apply for the EU's GSP+ (Special Incentive Arrangement for Sustainable Development and Good Governance) upon graduation. Attaining GSP+ would provide Cambodia and Bangladesh with duty-free market access for textile and clothing products, but not the lenient rules of origin that have made their recent success story possible. Falling back to normal GSP status would see clothing exports levied with tariffs of 8% to 9.3%, or even with higher MFN rates (Box 3.3). Further, for nontrade reasons, such an option may not be viable for Cambodia and it may also be difficult to achieve for Bangladesh.

The current GSP regime of the EU expires in 2023 and will be replaced by a new one from the beginning of 2024. However, the new GSP of the EU, including the GSP+ possibilities, does not provide market access similar to what is currently provided under the Everything but Arms. Least developed countries may attempt to embark on FTAs with previous preference-giving countries. This seems to be an option for ASEAN LDCs since other ASEAN countries (Singapore and Viet Nam) have already entered an FTA with the EU, while some other ASEAN countries are at different negotiating stages.

Box 3.3: Textile and Clothing Exports in Graduating Asian Least Developed Countries

A recent study, produced by World Trade Organization (WTO) and some United Nations entities,[a] argues that Asian graduating least developed countries are placed in the low-value stages of the textile and clothing global value chains (GVCs) and the loss of trade preferences would hurt their competitiveness and export performance. The findings of a survey carried out in the context of the study are the following:

Most textile and clothing factories, which are currently subject to lenient rules of origin for "cut, make and trim" processing under trade preference programs, will have difficulties in complying with more stringent rules of origin.

In Bangladesh, knitwear producers are more likely to meet rules of origin requirements than those making woven apparel. Almost two-thirds of knitwear firms said they are currently using domestic-made inputs (such as yarns, dyes, chemicals, and accessories), in comparison with just 36% of woven apparel factories.

In Cambodia, textiles and clothing manufacturers corroborated the general opinion that low value-added sewing work, associated with a high proportion of imported textiles as raw materials, results in extremely low profit margins. Their production and exports are focused on relatively simple and basic clothing items targeting primarily low-end markets, mostly in the European Union, the United States, Japan, and the People's Republic of China. For about two-thirds of manufacturers, at least 40% of their export receipts derive from one or two key export markets. Some 60% of firms do not source any domestic textile raw materials because of their limited availability. For nearly 40% of respondents, domestic inputs (mostly packaging materials and label printing services) constitute below 10% of their total inputs.

The findings of the study basically replicate those of an earlier research[b] carried out in 2003 especially for Bangladesh and Cambodia, where the heavy dependence on fabrics imported from the People's Republic of China and other suppliers was highlighted, together with the scarcity of alternative local sourcing and backward linkages. However, some progress may have been achieved in Bangladesh for knitted garments. Nevertheless, the consistency of the findings at an interval of twenty years suggests that alternative solutions have to be pursued.

[a] World Trade Organization, United Nations Conference on Trade and Development, International Trade Centre, and United Nations Department of Economic and Social Affairs. 2022. *Textiles and Clothing In Asian Graduating Least Developed Countries: Challenges and Options*.
[b] United Nations Conference on Trade and Development. 2003. *Trade Preferences for Least Developed Countries: An Early Assessment of Benefits and Possible Improvements*. New York and Geneva: UNCTAD.
Source: Asian Development Bank.

Another possible option is an ASEAN-EU FTA. Yet, the timing, feasibility, and content of such negotiating option may not offer the expected outcome for ASEAN LDCs since the design and objectives of the negotiations may be tailored to fit the interests of the larger economies.

Alternatives provided by RCEP and CPTPP may be of some importance as possible substitution of the market access granted by preference-granting countries. Recent studies have shown that tariff preferences under RCEP are complex to detect and with long phasing out periods and tariff differentials (ADB 2022, Crivelli and Inama 2022). CPTPP's rules of origin for textile and clothing are stringent requiring a triple transformation while RCEP's are more lenient allowing cumulation with the PRC, the main fabric supplier. However, the main limitation on LDC options is that RCEP countries, the PRC in particular, are major producers of textiles and apparel, and are therefore unlikely to serve as alternative destination markets for Bangladeshi and Cambodian exports.

3.2.2 Lessons in Drafting and Negotiating Regional Trade Agreements for Developing and Least Developed Countries

Developing Asia will need to raise its capacity to increase the efficiency and effectiveness of trade agreements. This includes developing a roster of lessons and best practices as well as developing human and institutional capacity to negotiate trade agreements that work in its favor. Asian LDCs face a particularly urgent situation in the multiple challenges of graduation. They will need to assess their export structure, reliance on market access, and most of all a new factor: the capacity of the public and private sectors to develop and implement credible trade policy strategy. This will require urgent attention from the aid for trade community, as outlined in section 3.2.3.

Creation of effective and trade liberalizing RTAs is one of the most important challenges for developing and LDCs in Asia and the Pacific. The design and drafting of chapters of RTAs dealing with behind-the-border measures require uncommon skills and a capacity from trade negotiators to enter into dialogue with regulators of such policies. A public–private dialogue on domestic reforms and regulations is also needed.

The UNCTAD Global Nontariff Measures Database reveals that such measures in Asia are rising and that major potential markets, such as the PRC, have imposed the largest number of nontariff measures (Suvannaphakdy 2022). More than 50% of total nontariff measures in the PRC and ASEAN are accounted for by sanitary and phytosanitary measures. At the same time, the mechanisms inserted in the various FTAs are not showing any WTO-plus disciplines that could diminish the increasing incidence of nontariff measures.

As such, how to build research and capacity on trade and regulatory issues to diminish the impact of nontariff measures should be a key topic in debate on aid for trade in the Asia and the Pacific. Trade liberalization and economic growth require capacities to evaluate proposals, draft legislation related to domestic regulatory frameworks, and constructively negotiate positions that many Asian developing countries may not possess, especially the least developed. Limited human capacity is a major obstacle to these countries' participation in the global economy.

Without enhanced capacity to research, quantify, negotiate, and implement, governments risk having their trade reform agenda frustrated by lack of technical capabilities. The drafting of trade language during trade negotiations should be based on the coordinated involvement of the national authorities and the private sector and should rely on substantive research carried out at national level to enhance clarity and precision and achieve the best possible deal.

Lack of capacity can ultimately result in nonimplementation of commitments and may contribute to lack of confidence of investors and trade policymakers in genuine effort to implement domestic reforms. The following suggestions on how to increase aid for trade support for trade policy making and drafting of trade agreements could address the pitfalls existing in certain FTAs. These considerations address the systemic issues that need consideration when confronted with nontariff measures in the complex and sophisticated Asia and Pacific region and how further work may be carried out under a focused and research-based aid for trade agenda.

Research, design, and drafting

An example of thorough research on a trade agreement was the preparatory work for the EU–US Transatlantic Trade and Investment Partnership negotiations, the kind of exercise that AFT could support in Asia and the Pacific. The research focused on expected and unusual ways to identify gains and losses and establish cooperation among regulatory bodies in the US and the EU while maintaining their independence. This architecture of regulatory convergence may be usefully adapted to Asia and the Pacific, including the possibility of third parties joining the progressive building up of a regulatory hub.

The research found that overall dismantling of nontariff measures in all sectors was by far the most economically beneficial measure for both the EU and the US. The EU, in its initial negotiating position papers, set out an ambitious agenda for the elimination of nontariff measures. The agenda went beyond reducing existing barriers by establishing a horizontal chapter containing principles and procedures on consultation, transparency, impact assessment, and a framework for future cooperation. The intention of the EU was to establish a "gateway" for handling sectoral regulatory issues via a consultation procedure that discussed and addressed issues arising in EU or US regulations or regulatory initiatives. Either party could request the consultation.

Great attention was paid to the use of multilateral instruments as the baseline for the negotiations. For instance, the WTO technical barriers to trade and sanitary and phytosanitary agreements were taken as the baselines to create WTO–plus disciplines in the Transatlantic Trade and Investment Partnership. The EU intention was to foster cooperation on regulatory issues without creating an EU-US regulatory authority. Where the new regulatory standards arising from the partnership did not require significant adjustments for third countries, they were to be offered less time to adjust and comply than the original parties, the EU and the US. This was expected to be an incentive for third countries willing to join or align to the regulatory standards in the partnership.

3.2.3 Scaling Up Aid for Trade to Address Implementation Challenges

Trade integration can contribute to important development goals, particularly if trade regimes are resilient, stable, and less volatile. Nicita and Saygili (2021) note that (i) the proliferation of RTAs, (ii) the deepening of RTAs and behind-the-border measures, and (iii) LDCs facing preference erosion and graduation challenges point to the need for regulatory convergence and stronger trade policy.

The case is strong for a research and capacity building program with extensive coverage of disciplines that leads to establishment of a mature class of trade policy officials capable of using research findings to negotiate, draft, and implement trade agreements. Aid for trade assistance is required to develop an innovative research and capacity building program tailored to identification of appropriate methodologies to assess incremental values in all these areas and lessons learned.

Initiatives should fall within the aid for trade category "trade policy and regulations" and include "institutional and technical support to facilitate implementation of trade agreements". Trade adjustment assistance should also be given priority to ensure that trade is inclusive, and its gains are shared equally among workers and businesses (Chapter 2).

The beneficiaries of the proposed program would be all Asia and Pacific developing countries and institutions with a strong focus on lower-middle-income countries and LDCs. The initiative could involve a coordinated effort by donors and recipients, the ASEAN and RCEP secretariats, ADB, Asian Infrastructure Investment Bank, World Bank, and the EU institutions. This new aid for trade instrument should be designed and carried out at the multilateral level as a unifying factor for a renewed spirit of multilateralism and implemented by trade-related international organizations and bilateral donor initiatives. This will be important to ensure contemporary challenges and needs of developing countries in Asia and the Pacific are addressed. Action should be targeted and demand-driven. Lessons from and experience of previous programs such as the Joint Integrated Trade Assistance Programme and the current Enhanced Integrated Framework (Box 3.4) can be considered. The program components of this proposed initiative are developed in Chapter 5.

Box 3.4: Two Multilateral Trade-Related Capacity-Building Programs: Joint Integrated Trade Assistance Programme and Enhanced Integrated Framework

The Joint Integrated Trade Assistance Programme, implemented by the International Trade Centre, United Nations Conference on Trade and Development, and the World Trade Organization (WTO) began in 1996 to address the capacity building needs of selected countries in implementing new disciplines arising from the Uruguay Round agreement and the establishment of the WTO as a negotiating forum for future WTO agreements. It continued in a second phase from February 2003 until December 2007. By design, the Joint Integrated Trade Assistance Programme built or strengthened human, institutional, and entrepreneurial capacities in five main areas:[a]

- **Trade negotiations, implementation of WTO agreements, and related trade policy formulation:** Through the Inter-Institutional Committees, the official frameworks for organizing national stakeholder discussions and decision-making on the multilateral trading system.

- **Provision of reliable technical information on multilateral trading system, with attention to standards and quality requirements:** Through MTS Reference Centres and national enquiry points.

- **Development of the national knowledge base on multilateral trading system:** Through training of trainers and creation of trainers' networks.

- **Development of goods, commodities and services policy frameworks, and sectoral strategies:** Including market knowledge of exporting and export-ready enterprises to develop and increase production and exports.

- **Networking of the institutional and human capacities built in each country:** To encourage synergy and the exchange of expertise and experiences (including at the subregional level) to ensure sustainability of such capacities beyond the program's life.

The Enhanced Integrated Framework replaced, to some extent, the Joint Integrated Trade Assistance Programme with a focus on least developed countries and the ambition to assist them in mainstreaming trade into their development policies. The second phase of the EIF will operationally end in 2024.

[a] Based on UNCTAD. 2004. The Joint Integrated Technical Assistance Programme: Capacity Building in Assuring Developmental Gains from the Multilateral Trading System. Joint background note by the ITC, UNCTAD and WTO secretariats.
Source: Asian Development Bank.

Bibliography

Asian Development Bank (ADB). 2021a. *Global Value Chain Development Report 2021. Beyond Production.* Manila: ADB.

_____. 2021b. *Key Indicators for Asia and the Pacific 2021.* Manila.

_____. 2022. *The Regional Comprehensive Economic Partnership (RCEP) Agreement: A New Paradigm in Asian Regional Cooperation?* Manila.

Crivelli, P. and S. Inama. 2021. *Improving Market for Least Developed Countries: The Impact of the EU Reform of Rules of Origin on Utilization Rates and Trade Flows under the Everything But Arms Initiative (EBA).* https://www.un.org/ldc5/sites/www.un.org.ldc5/files/t6_inama_eu_reform_2021_16_helsinki_final_20210816_clean.pdf.

_____. 2022. Preliminary Assessment of the Regional Comprehensive Economic Partnership. *ADB Briefs.* No. 206. Manila: Asian Development Bank. http://dx.doi.org/10.22617/BRF220009-2.

Crivelli, P., S. Inama, and M. Pearson. 2022. *An Analysis of the Product-Specific Rules of Origin of the Regional Comprehensive Economic Partnership.* Manila: Asian Development Bank.

Economic Research Institute for ASEAN and East Asia (ERIA). 2022. *Regional Comprehensive Economic Partnership (RCEP): Implications, Challenges, and Future Growth of East Asia and ASEAN.* Jakarta.

Estrades, C., M. Maliszewska, I. Osorio-Rodarte, and M. Seara e Pereira. 2022. *Estimating the Economic and Distributional Impacts of the Regional Comprehensive Economic Partnership.* Washington, DC: World Bank.

Inama, S. and P. Crivelli. 2021. Getting to Better Rules of Origin for LDCs Using Utilization Rates. Geneva: UN Conference on Trade and Development. https://unctad.org/webflyer/getting-better-rules-origin-ldcs-using-utilization-rates.

Nicita, A. and M. Saygili. 2021. Trade Agreements and Trade Resilience During COVID-19 Pandemic. *Research Paper.* No. 70. UN Conference on Trade and Development, Geneva. https://unctad.org/webflyer/trade-agreements-and-trade-resilience-during-covid-19-pandemic#:~:text=Using%20an%20econometric%20approach%20where,global%20trade%20collapse%20of%202020.

Park, C. Y., P. A. Petri, and M. G. Plummer. 2021. Economic Partnership for Asia and the Pacific. *ADB Economics Working Paper No. 206.* Manila: Asian Development Bank. http://dx.doi.org/10.22617/WPS210371-2.

Suvannaphakdy, S. 2022. ASEAN and China in RCEP: Time to Liberalise Trade. *ASEANFocus.* No. 38. March. Singapore: ASEAN Studies Centre at ISEAS-Yusof Ishak Institute.

United Nations Conference on Trade and Development (UNCTAD). 2020. *Cambodia Diagnostic Trade Integration Study 2019-2023. UNCTAD's Contribution to Chapter 1. Trade Policy and Regional Integration (RCEP, BRI, CP-TPP, FTAs).* Geneva.

World Trade Organization (WTO). 2014. Challenges Faced by LDCs in Complying with Preferential Rules of Origin under Unilateral Trade Preferences. G/RO/W/148. Paper presented by Uganda on Behalf of the LDCs Group. 28 October. https://docs.wto.org/dol2fe/Pages/FE_Search/FE_S_S009-DP.aspx?language=E&CatalogueIdList=128174&CurrentCatalogueIdIndex=0&FullTextHash=371857150&HasEnglishRecord=True&HasFrenchRecord=True&HasSpanishRecord=True.

_____. 2020. Trade Impacts of LDC Graduation. Geneva.

World Trade Organization, United Nations Conference on Trade and Development, International Trade Centre, and United Nations Department of Economic and Social Affairs. 2022. *Textiles and Clothing in Asian Graduating LDCs: Challenges and Options.*

4. Preparing for the Digital Economy

4.1 Increased Digital Connectivity and Its Implications for Digital Trade

The COVID-19 pandemic has accelerated the digital transformation of businesses of all sizes and across all industries. The pandemic caused a deep contraction of international trade in 2020 and services trade is still lagging, particularly transport and tourism. However, merchandise trade has largely rebounded and reached record highs in 2021. Digitally delivered services have also grown, meeting the benchmarks of "robustness" and "resilience" defined in Chapter 2.

This accelerated digital transformation could boost global output, trade and commerce, and employment (ADB 2021a). For example, a 20% increase in the size of the digital sector over the baseline by 2025 will increase global output an average of $4.3 trillion yearly from 2021 to 2025 (equivalent to 5.4% of the 2020 baseline) or a cumulative impact of $21.4 trillion in 5 years. Asia would reap an economic dividend of more than $1.7 trillion yearly (equivalent to 6.1% of the 2020 regional gross domestic product [GDP] baseline) or more than $8.6 trillion from 2020 to 2025.

Yet, access to the digital economy and even the internet generally remains the biggest challenge. One billion adults in Asia have no access to financial services and over 2 billion do not have access to the internet. This lack of access to the digital economy, and of education on how to use it, risks worsening inequality between and within countries, particularly if this "digital divide" widens. If countries, businesses, and individuals are not equipped with the infrastructure, skills, technologies and an enabling regulatory environment, then only a limited number of individuals and businesses will be able to take advantage of digital opportunities. Countries may find themselves as rule-takers rather than rule-makers, and their businesses and communities may be marginalized. Some low- and middle-income countries and many LDCs face challenges in this area.

Digital services trade holds substantial promise for developing Asia and the Pacific. Countries with better digital connectivity have a greater degree of trade openness and enable more products to be sold in more markets: more digitalization means more trade (López-González and Ferencz 2018). Digitally deliverable services trade is also more robust and resilient (see Chapter 2), and is thus valuable both as a strategy for long-term economic development and short-term support for pandemic recovery.

This chapter examines the development of digital services trade, digital domestic regulations, and ways to foster the participation of developing countries and LDCs in this trade. It proposes refocusing aid for trade on capacity building for digital economy governance and digital trade policymaking. Refocusing aid for trade (of which only 0.4% currently goes to digital service trade) will help equip developing countries in Asia and the Pacific to participate more actively in domestic, regional, and global digital trade initiatives and more fully realize the potential of digital trade for inclusive and sustainable growth.

4.1.1 Recent Trends in Services Trade During the COVID-19 Pandemic

The establishment of digital platforms, and the proliferation of new digital business models offers enormous economic opportunities. In 2019, digital platform business-to-consumer revenues reached $3.8 trillion, equivalent to 4.4% of global GDP. Asia accounted for about 48% ($1.8 trillion; equivalent to 6% of regional GDP), the US for 22% ($836.7 billion, 3.9%), and the euro area 12% ($445.3 billion, 3.3%). Asia will continue its rise as a major player in the global digital platform market as wider access reaches more users and generates higher revenue growth (ADB 2021a).

Asia and the Pacific is the world's second-largest exporter and importer of services and of digitally deliverable services.[35] From 2005 to 2019, trade in services in the region almost tripled, while trade in digitally deliverable services expanded from $403.4 billion in 2005 to $1.4 trillion in 2019, significantly faster than in other emerging regions.

Both intraregional and extraregional trade in digitally deliverable services expanded. Intraregional exports grew from 36% to 48%. Exports to the rest of the world grew faster from 48% in 2005 to 54%. In 2019, East Asia (excluding Japan) was the top exporter and importer of digitally deliverable services in developing Asia. The PRC accounted for half of all exports and 55% of imports. Exports grew faster than imports over 2005–2020 in most subregions. Some economies—India, the PRC, Singapore, Japan, and the Republic of Korea— became hubs for imports and exports of digitally delivered services. The Philippines and India were the main drivers of this rapid expansion. Bangladesh (growth rate in 2005–2020 of 13.3%), Cambodia (11%), the Lao PDR (20.2%), and Nepal (14%) have also recently experienced rapid growth albeit from a low base.

However, in the last 2 years, the COVID-19 pandemic dramatically reversed the growth trajectory of global and regional trade in services. Nondigitally deliverable services fell 39% globally, 38% in Asia and the Pacific. In contrast, nondigitally deliverable services experienced a mere 3% year-on-year contraction globally, and a 1% increase in Asia and the Pacific.

Three main sectors dominate services trade in the region: travel services, transport, and "other business services". Of these three, the services that could not be digitally delivered—travel and transport—fell precipitously during the pandemic, with severe implications for tourism-dependent and heavily transport-dependent economies, such as small islands and landlocked states. By contrast, demand for services that could be digitally delivered, many falling under "other business services," grew significantly.[36]

Trade by mode

Figure 4.1 breaks down services exports by mode of supply across 35 countries in Asia and the Pacific in 2017 (the latest year of available data for these countries). East Asian economies are significant exporters of mode 3 (commercial presence) services, but for many other economies in the region, mode 1 "cross border" services are prominent. In Southeast Asia and the Pacific, mode 2 "consumption abroad" is also

---

[35]   The discussion draws on key findings from the Asian Economic Integration Report 2022 on trends in services trade in the region (ADB 2022a). "Digitally deliverable" services are those than can be supplied over the internet, including insurance and pension services; financial services; charges for the use of intellectual property not identified elsewhere; telecommunications, computer and information services; other business services; and personal, cultural, and recreational services. Nondigitally deliverable services include manufacturing services on physical inputs owned by others, maintenance and repair services not identified elsewhere, transport, travel, construction, and government goods and services not identified elsewhere.

[36]   This subsector includes professional services such as legal, accounting, and management consulting services; engineering and scientific services; technical, trade-related, and other business services; and research and development services.

common. Less trade is taking place via mode 4 "movement of natural persons" across the region, with only a few countries (such as Afghanistan, Armenia, India, and the Philippines) registering close to 10% of mode 4 services.

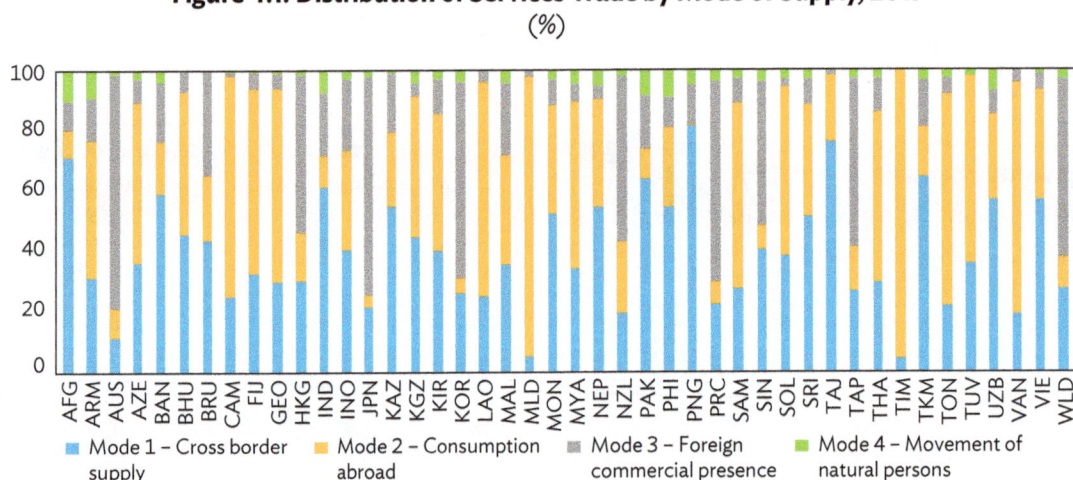

Figure 4.1: Distribution of Services Trade by Mode of Supply, 2017
(%)

AFG = Afghanistan; ARM = Armenia; AUS = Australia; AZE = Azerbaijan; BAN = Bangladesh; BRU = Brunei Darussalam; BHU = Bhutan; CAM = Cambodia; FIJ = Fiji; GEO = Georgia; HKG = Hong Kong, China; IND = India; INO = Indonesia; JPN = Japan; KAZ = Kazakhstan; KGZ = Kyrgyz Republic; KIR = Kiribati; KOR = Republic of Korea; LAO = Lao People's Democratic Republic; MAL = Malaysia; MLD = Maldives; MON = Mongolia; MYA = Myanmar; NEP = Nepal; NZL = New Zealand; PAK = Pakistan; PHI = Philippines; PNG = Papua New Guinea; PRC = People's Republic of China; SAM = Samoa; SIN = Singapore; SOL = Solomon Islands; SRI = Sri Lanka; TAJ = Tajikistan; THA = Thailand; TIM = Timor-Leste; TKM = Turkmenistan; TON = Tonga; TUV = Tuvalu; TAP=Taipei,China; UZB = Uzbekistan; VAN = Vanuatu; VIE = Viet Nam; WLD=World.
Source: World Trade Organization Trade in Services by Mode of Supply database (Shingal and Agarwal 2021).

By value, mode 3 predominates for both exports and imports, with Australia; the PRC; Japan; the Republic of Korea; and Taipei,China leading the way. The World Trade Organization (WTO) *Trade in Services by Mode of Supply* database shows that major mode 3 exports in East Asia prior to the pandemic included construction, recreation services, and other personal services.

There were significant disparities in the impact of the pandemic on trade in digitally delivered services across the region. In Timor-Leste, the Lao PDR, Brunei Darussalam, and Papua New Guinea declines exceeded 40%; by contrast, Afghanistan increased exports of such services by 37.2% and Georgia 24.1%, (Shingal and Agarwal 2021). These differences may reflect pandemic-related impacts on demand across particular destination markets.

Modes 2 and 4, both requiring person-to-person contact, declined significantly during the pandemic. Mode 2, tourism-related services, declined 68.3% in 2020 relative to 2019. Tourism accounts for 50%–80% of total services exports in Armenia, Cambodia, Fiji, Georgia, Indonesia, the Lao PDR, and Thailand. Exports declined significantly in these countries.

Figure 4.2 shows the decline in total services exports in 2020 relative to 2019, mapped against the share of services exports in total exports delivered via modes 1 and 2, respectively. It shows that the fall in the value of services exports in 2020 was less pronounced for countries whose services were transacted via mode 1; it was more pronounced for countries where the share of mode 2 in total services exports was large. Mode 2 (tourism-related services) declined 68.3% in 2020 relative to 2019, with significant negative implications for Pacific island countries and several regional countries.

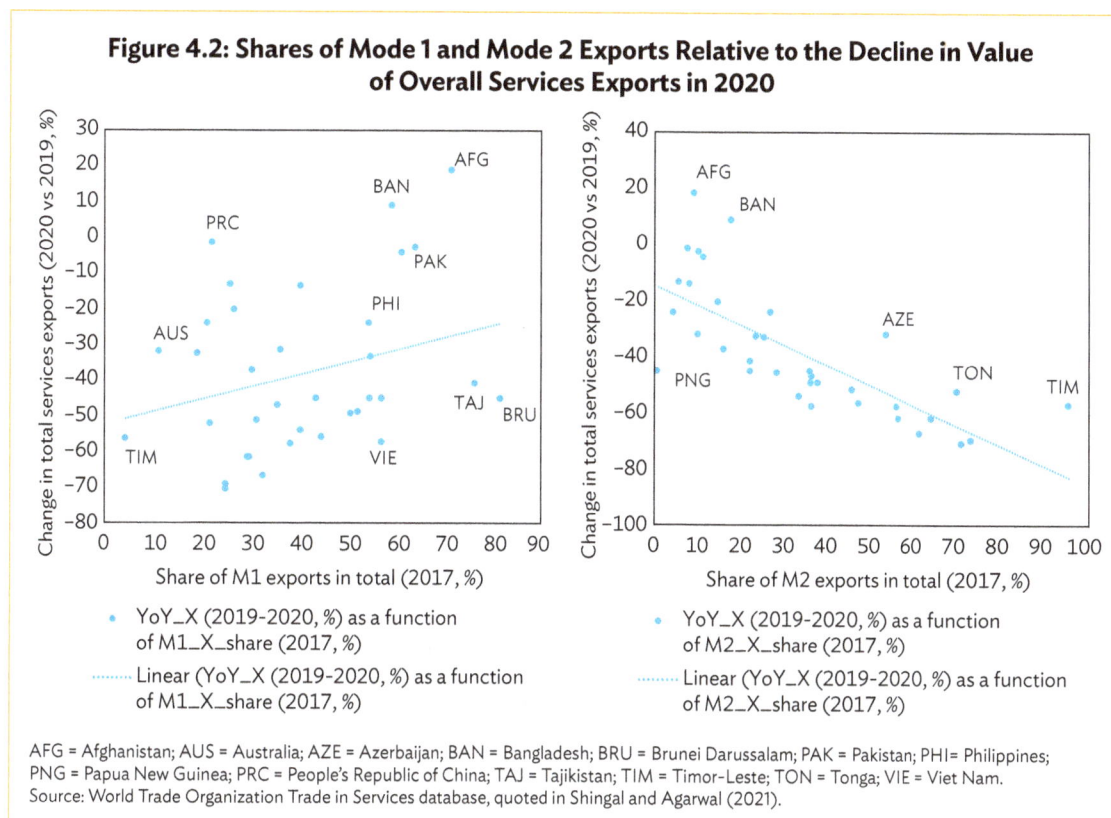

Figure 4.2: Shares of Mode 1 and Mode 2 Exports Relative to the Decline in Value of Overall Services Exports in 2020

AFG = Afghanistan; AUS = Australia; AZE = Azerbaijan; BAN = Bangladesh; BRU = Brunei Darussalam; PAK = Pakistan; PHI= Philippines; PNG = Papua New Guinea; PRC = People's Republic of China; TAJ = Tajikistan; TIM = Timor-Leste; TON = Tonga; VIE = Viet Nam.
Source: World Trade Organization Trade in Services database, quoted in Shingal and Agarwal (2021).

The pivot to digital

Firms pivoted to digital products, tools, and channels in response to lockdowns, social distancing, and supply-chain disruption. The share of partially or fully digitalized offerings by businesses in Asia and the Pacific may have grown by more than a decade's equivalent in the first few months of 2020 (McKinsey 2020). Businesses that were more digitalized prior to the pandemic, or that rapidly undertook digitalization post-pandemic, tended to be more resilient. Digital platforms and digitally delivered services have many positive impacts, such as bolstering economic growth, growing businesses, generating value chains, and creating jobs (ADB 2021a and 2022a).

The pandemic saw business, consumers, and governments making more use of "tradetech"—technologies to enable trade, such as blockchain—and governments shifting toward digital trade facilitation measures such as digital "single windows" and electronic signatures. Tools such as paperless trading increased about 6% from 2019 to 2021, with rates now above 80% in East and Northeast Asia, over 70% in North and Central Asia and Southeast Asia, and close to 100% in Australia and New Zealand.

4.1.2 Economic Risks and Opportunities for Developing Countries from Digital Trade

Digitalization has fundamentally altered the scale, scope, and speed of trade and business models. The ADB Asian Economic Integration Report 2022 highlights the important role that digital technology plays in linking firms participating in global value chains—not only to coordinate sophisticated networked production processes and for enabling communications, legal, and payments elements of global value chain transactions, but also as inputs into services and manufacturing-based global value chains (ADB 2022a). Digitalization has also substantially transformed the nature of work, consumer behavior, and perspectives on social and environmental protection. The pandemic has hastened this transformation.

Digital technologies are transforming trade in myriad ways, from what is bought and sold, the channels through which trade takes place, to the way production and value chains are coordinated. Asia already enjoys high internet penetration (around 61%) and high mobile subscriptions (OECD 2021b). The broader Asia and the Pacific is already the most vibrant hub in the world for e-commerce, accounting for over two-thirds of global e-commerce sales in 2020, and a key player in digital services, as noted. About 800 million people came online for the first time during the COVID-19 pandemic lockdowns. The region should accordingly be well positioned to benefit from a shift toward digital trade.

Research by OECD (López-González and Ferencz 2018) suggests that a 10% increase in digital connectivity between countries raises goods trade by nearly 2% and trade in services by over 3%. There are also synergies between digital services trade and other sectors of the economy. An increase in physical goods e-commerce, for example, creates opportunities for digitally delivered financial, logistics, and other services. Digitally deliverable services also unlock opportunities for participation in global value chains; the largest share of services trade, precrisis, was in demand for services inputs by firms operating within a global value chain.

Access by micro, small, and medium-sized enterprises (MSMEs) to digitally deliverable business services such as internet banking or cloud accounting helps drive export competitiveness. MSMEs with a digital presence such as a webpage are more likely to become exporters. Digital tools can help women entrepreneurs overcome impediments to establishing businesses, growing and exporting by improving access to credit and information

Digitalization also supports overall productivity and inclusion. With the "servicification" of manufacturing, blurring the lines between goods and services, access to more digitally delivered services can help even domestically focused businesses to be more resilient to external shocks. Digital technologies improve financial inclusion by providing access to financial services to the unbanked: 1 billion adults in Asia do not have access to financial services, but 4.1 billion have a mobile phone which means they could potentially access such services online.

These benefits may also accelerate the currently slow progress toward realization of the UN Sustainable Development Goals. A large share of the UN SDG targets—one study puts it at two-thirds—are directly influenced by digital technologies. In particular, digital technologies can help achieve "decent work and economic growth" (SDG8); build resilient infrastructure and promote sustainable and inclusive industrialization (SDG9); provide the means to progress goals relating to poverty through financial inclusion (SDG1), gender equality (SDG5); and reduced inequalities (SDG10).

Economic risks

Digitalization also risks worsening inequality if the "digital divide" widens. Only 1.7 billion people in Asia have access to the internet. If countries, businesses, and individuals are not able to access the internet, nor equipped with infrastructure, skills, and technologies—as well as an enabling regulatory environment— they may not be able to take advantage of digital opportunities. Without strong policy capabilities, they may also find themselves as rule-takers rather than rule-makers on digital trade governance. This is a particular risk for LDCs in the region (UNCTAD 2022a).

Equally there are risks to broader societal interests, if cybersecurity threats are not addressed at both the domestic and international level. There are also risks in relation to privacy violations, the reduction of competition and innovation in markets, financial instability and other challenges.

Regulatory heterogeneity can also add to the costs of exporting, with small businesses least able to absorb the high fixed trade costs. As discussed further below, divergent regulatory approaches are increasingly common in the digital economy. Opaque or overly burdensome regulatory barriers are emerging in many countries.. Since MSMEs make up the majority of the business community around the region—over 97% of businesses and employing 69% of the workforce in Asia—these barriers are serious risks to growth and employment.

Accordingly, a stronger and more coherent regulatory environment for digital trade is needed, something on which participation in digital trade agreements can make a meaningful contribution (particularly those designed as building blocks to broader outcomes, such as the Digital Economy Partnership Agreement). Even simply achieving greater certainty in the trade environment and barriers that exporters face has a value (Handley and Limão 2022), especially for the rapid transformation that characterizes the digital economy.

4.1.3 Regulatory Approaches to the Digital Economy

Domestic regulations

If all trade costs declined, the share of developing countries in services trade would rise substantially, from 35% to almost 40%. Developing Asia and Pacific countries would benefit disproportionately from lower trade costs because of the strong projected growth in the number of skilled workers in these countries (WTO 2019). There is accordingly a strong case for seeking to ensure that good regulatory practices are used in all economies.

The WTO *Reference Paper for Services Domestic Regulation* (WTO 2021a) seeks to facilitate services trade in three main areas: transparency, legal certainty, and predictability of authorization requirements and procedures, and regulatory quality and facilitation. The new disciplines seek to make information about requirements and procedures for authorization of services suppliers more accessible, ensure that fair treatment is given during licensing and authorization of services providers, and to require independence and impartiality of regulatory authorities when dealing with authorization applications. The acceptance of electronic applications is also encouraged (WTO 2021b). It therefore provides important guidance on how economies ensure that the domestic and trade-related regulatory and policy settings are transparent, enabling, trusted, and sufficiently responsive to tackle new challenges raised by ongoing digital transformation.

Recent trade agreements in Asia and the Pacific include relatively strong commitments on services domestic regulations. While the ASEAN–Australia–New Zealand Free Trade Agreement was comparatively unambitious, for example, the Regional Comprehensive Economic Partnership establishes binding commitments in a number of areas, in some cases even going beyond the WTO reference paper. According to WTO analysis, South Asia scores lowest on approaches that are coherent with the reference paper, with East Asia, the Pacific, and Central Asia all scoring higher. For example, the Pacific Agreement on Closer Economic Relations Plus trade agreement (PACER Plus) between Australia; New Zealand; and nine Pacific islands (the Cook Islands, Kiribati, Nauru, Niue, Samoa, Solomon Islands, Tonga, Tuvalu, and

Vanuatu) strengthens regulation and establishes obligations on the publication of measures relevant for service suppliers, procedural guarantees for the treatment of applications, and measures on consultation of interested stakeholders (PACER Plus, Chapter 7, Articles 10 and 17, and Chapter 13 Article 2). South Asia scored lowest in coherence with the reference paper, while East Asia, the Pacific and Central Asia scored higher.

Regulatory approaches to digital trade

Digital transformation creates a wide range of policy and regulatory issues for governments, which will need to balance commercial interests and market liberalization against sociocultural and security interests, among others. Issues include foundational regulatory issues such as the development of overall frameworks for electronic transactions and data protection; the protection of privacy, cybersecurity, and consumer protection; and a more level playing field in the digital economy. They also include cross-border regulatory divergences, opaque regulatory approaches, and a lack of interoperability at the technical and legal or regulatory level. Domestic reforms for sound regulatory practices in services will also be key.

Regulation in digital services trade (along with investment in digital infrastructure) will be crucial to establish countries' comparative advantages in digitally enabled services sectors. Regulatory coherence is particularly important. Domestic regulatory reform is needed alongside trade liberalization in order to achieve changes to real incomes. This is because economies may tend to source the bulk of their inputs in "digitally enabled" sectors domestically and sell their outputs there as well, meaning that price implications of policy reforms are maximized when reforms are implemented in the domestic market and internationally (ADB 2022).

Regulation can promote the development of the digital economy in several ways. It can create a level playing field for business, advance consumer protection, and enable domestic objectives and international commitments. Good regulation will promote digitalization within an economy by ensuring that the economy stays open to digital competition while ensuring consumers are protected from privacy violations and fraud.

Free trade agreements in Asia and the Pacific demonstrate aspects of regulatory promotion, coherence, and convergence, along the spectrum of services, investment, and digitalization. Regulatory *convergence* happens as regulatory requirements across countries become more similar or aligned over time, facilitating trade and business. Regulatory *cooperation* can encourage interoperability of divergent digital regulatory approaches through common standards, thus reducing redundancy, duplication of efforts, and trade costs. Regulatory *coherence* refers to efforts by countries to create a more seamless and coherent digital market for exporters. As the previous chapter noted, there are many such efforts, and approaches differ, making it confusing for low- and middle-income countries and LDCs to determine optimal policy choices, not least because of the sheer number of issues to be addressed. Further, regulatory barriers are appearing in many countries, impeding liberalization efforts.

Table 4.1, which draws from the United Nations Conference on Trade and Development Summary of Adoption of E-Commerce Legislation, illustrates the uneven legislative coverage of digital economy issues across countries in Asia and the Pacific. Of the 49 countries in the table, 35 have electronic transactions legislation (another 3 have draft legislation under preparation); 19 have consumer protection legislation (3 with draft legislation); 25 have privacy and data protection legislation (3 with draft legislation in train);

and 34 have cybercrime legislation (5 with draft legislation to come).[37] Nor does the table reflect the quality of the regulations it includes.

Table 4.1: Inventory of Domestic Digital Legislation

Economy	UNCITRAL Model Law on E-Commerce	Electronic Transactions Legislation	Consumer Protection Legislation	Privacy and Data Protection Legislation	Cybercrime Legislation
Afghanistan		Draft			Y
Armenia		Y	No data	Y	Y
Australia	Y	Y	Y	Y	Y
Azerbaijan		Y	Draft	Y	Y
Bangladesh	Y	Y	Y		Y
Bhutan		Y	Y	Y	Y
Brunei Darussalam	Y	Y			Y
Cambodia	Y	Y	Y	Y	Draft
Cook Islands	not included	not included			
Fiji	Y	Y			Y
FSM		No data	No data	No data	
Georgia		Y	No data	Y	Draft
Hong Kong, China	Y	not included			
India	Y	Y	No data	Y	Y
Indonesia		Y	Y	Y	Y
Japan		Y	Y	Y	Y
Kazakhstan		Y	Y	Y	Y
Kiribati			No data		Y
Republic of Korea	Y	Y	Y	Y	Y
Kyrgyz Republic		Y	Draft	Y	Y
Lao PDR		Y	Draft	Y	Y
Malaysia	Y	Y	Y	Y	Y
Maldives		Draft		Draft	Draft
Marshall Islands		No data	No data		
Mongolia		Y	No data	Y	Y
Myanmar		Y	Y	Draft	Draft
Nauru		No data	No data		
Nepal		Y	Y	Y	Y
New Zealand		Y	Y	Y	Y
Niue		No data	No data	No data	No data
Pakistan	Y	Y	No data	Draft	Y
Palau		No data	No data	No data	
Papua New Guinea		Draft	No data		Y
Philippines	Y	Y	Y	Y	Y
PRC	Y	Y	Y	Y	Y
Samoa	Y	Y			Y
Solomon Islands		Y	No data		
Singapore	Y	Y	Y	Y	Y
Sri Lanka	Y	Y	Y		Y
Taipei,China					

continued on next page

---

[37]   Based on UNCTAD (2022) and on author's own calculations.

Table 4.1 continued

Economy	UNCITRAL Model Law on E-Commerce	Electronic Transactions Legislation	Consumer Protection Legislation	Privacy and Data Protection Legislation	Cybercrime Legislation
Tajikistan		Y	No data	Y	Y
Thailand	Y	Y	Y	Y	Y
Timor-Leste		No data	No data		Y
Tonga		Y	No data	No data	Y
Turkmenistan		Y	No data	Y	Y
Tuvalu			No data		Draft
Uzbekistan		Y	No data	Y	Y
Vanuatu	Y	Y	Y		
Viet Nam	Y	Y	Y	Y	Y

FSM = Federated States of Micronesia, Lao PDR = Lao People's Democratic Republic, PRC = People's Republic of China, UNCITRAL = United Nations Commission on International Trade Law
Sources: United Nations Conference on Trade and Development (accessed April 2022). Summary of Adoption of E-Commerce Legislation Worldwide; and Nemoto and López-González (2021).

Electronic transactions laws, the prerequisite for conducting commercial transactions online, recognize the legal equivalence between paper-based and electronic forms of exchange. Nearly three-quarters of ADB members have or are developing such legislation. Cybersecurity is a common feature of digital trade agreements; around four-fifths of the countries surveyed have such legislation in place or in draft (UNCTAD 2022b).

Consumer protection legislation supports consumer confidence, particularly business-to-consumer e-commerce. However, only one-third of countries have such legislation in place. Privacy and data protection laws govern the collection, use and/or sharing of personal and other types of data. These laws are increasingly a core element in digital trade provisions, but only around half of the ADB countries have them in place.

Eighteen ADB countries are signatories to the United Nations Commission on International Trade Law Model Law on Electronic Commerce (Table 4.1). This law (and the earlier UN Electronic Communications Convention) encourages harmonization of domestic laws and regulations on e-commerce transactions, including provisions for functional equivalence between electronic communications and paper documents. However, the need for digital economy regulation goes far beyond these five basic areas.

Rise in digital trade barriers

While Asia and the Pacific encompass some of the most open markets for digital trade in the world, the region also includes some of the most restrictive. The OECD's Digital Trade Restrictiveness Index notes that Hong Kong, China; New Zealand; and Singapore are among the most open globally and regionally.

The index similarly ranks digital service trade restrictions across 44 economies, including 17 countries in Asia and the Pacific. It finds that Cambodia, Kazakhstan, the Lao PDR, and the PRC, and are among the most restrictive, while Australia, Japan, Malaysia, New Zealand, and Vanuatu are some of the least restrictive. For 17 Asian economies with available data from the index, the total number of restrictions increased from 138 in 2015 to 153 in 2020, with barriers related to cross-border data flows accounting for around 20%, on average, over the period. On the other hand, Cambodia, Indonesia, the Lao PDR, Nepal, and Vanuatu improved in restrictiveness.

Regulations that restrict the flow of data are both increasingly widespread and can be costly for businesses and economies. Restrictions apply to the location of the processing or storage of data, i.e., "forced data localization". They include local storage requirements as well as conditional flow regimes (where, for example, a copy must be kept in-market, or ready access must be provided to the data on request). Such restrictions often aim to address legitimate goals around protecting privacy, cybersecurity, law enforcement, consumer protection, or public security. These goals are legitimate and important, but data restrictions, particularly forced data localization, are not necessarily fit for purpose or not even the most effective way to achieve those aims (Cory and Dascoli 2021).

Data localization is economically inefficient, with impacts on economic growth, competitiveness, and investment. It constrains businesses' ability to access networks, customers, and digital infrastructure, as well as to make use of the synthesis of large data sets to enhance value-adding, productivity, and innovation. Data flow restrictions create significant trade barriers to MSMEs in particular—reducing the potential inherent in digital trade for low-cost scale and reach. Around the world, 13 countries within Asia and the Pacific have imposed data localization requirements.

A further potential barrier may be the imposition of customs duties on electronic transmissions— something currently prohibited by a WTO Moratorium on Customs Duties on Electronic Transmissions but about which there is ongoing debate.[38] Analysis shows that the revenues to governments would be small, but the broader negative economic impacts would be significant.

A further impediment to participation in digital trade is lack of interoperability in regulatory or policy approaches. Potential for cross-border trade cannot be fully realized without interoperability. Regulatory heterogeneity is particularly challenging for MSMEs, as they may lack resources to handle the higher costs of regulation compliance or defend their interests compared to larger firms with strong market power.

4.2 Digital Agreements in Developing Asia

4.2.1 Trends in Regulating the Digital Economy Worldwide

Digital trade rules are highly fragmented across the region and around the world. The Digital Trade Restrictiveness Index shows that the global regulatory environment continues to be both complex and fragmented (OECD 2022a). In the multilateral trading system, the core General Agreement on Tariffs and Trade and WTO rulebook largely predates the internet and digital trade. Elements of existing rules apply to digital trade in services through the General Agreement on Trade in Services and other agreements.

However, a more comprehensive and targeted set of rules is needed, particularly as the digital economy continues to expand drawing in new wide-ranging issues. The General Agreement on Trade in Services needs to be updated in areas such as classification of services, scheduling digital trade, a set of minimum regulatory standards, and exceptions that apply to digital trade.

Eighty-six WTO members are considering these issues in the *Joint Initiative on E-Commerce Plurilateral* negotiation in the WTO. These countries, including 15 from developing Asia, account for over 90% of global trade. There is significant overlap in the approaches between the WTO exercise and regional Asia

---

[38] More information on the WTO Work Programme on E-Commerce and Moratorium on Customs Duties on Electronic Transmissions can be found here: WTO. Work Programme on E-Commerce. https://www.wto.org/english/tratop_e/ecom_e/ecom_work_programme_e.htm.

and Pacific agreements, for example, on e-invoicing, paperless trading, or consumer protection. The WTO joint initiative negotiations are considering a range of topics, including digital trade facilitation, data flows, nondiscrimination in the treatment of digital goods, trust in electronic commerce, transparency, cybersecurity, telecommunications services, market access for digital services, and access to online platforms and competition.

Good progress has been made on eight articles: online consumer protection, electronic signatures, spam, open government data, electronic contracts, transparency, paperless trade, and open internet access. Work is ongoing on electronic transactions frameworks and electronic invoicing. Some of the most contentious issues, especially around data flows, will not be easy to resolve (WTO 2021b, 2022). The co-convenors have emphasized the importance of supporting the engagement of developing members and to this end launched the E-Commerce Capacity Building Framework in June 2022.[39] India and South Africa maintain that the plurilateral format is at odds with fundamental WTO principles and are not participating.

Other avenues to regulate digital trade

Other relevant aspects of digital trade, including regulatory design, standards, and measurement, are being discussed in multiple institutions, including the OECD, International Organization for Standardization, International Telecommunication Union, World Wide Web Consortium, various United Nations bodies, World Customs Organization, World Intellectual Property Organization, and business organizations such as the International Chamber of Commerce (Nemoto and Lopez-Gonzalez 2021).

These approaches tend to be piecemeal, and may be overlapping or inconsistent. The OECD's Digital Trade Inventory identifies 52 instruments that are directly relevant to digital trade discussions, currently being addressed in 24 different forums. The number of jurisdictions that have ratified, signed, committed to, or adhere to different regulations, treaties, or approaches varies by body, region, and topic (Nemoto and Lopez-Gonzalez 2021).

Role of regional (and digital) trade agreements

Until the WTO reaches consensus, RTAs remain the primary source of development for cross-border digital trade rules, bilateral, and plurilateral. Between 2000 and 2020, 188 out of 353 trade agreements included at least *some* provisions relating to digital trade, 113 including specific e-commerce provisions, and 83 with dedicated e-commerce chapters. Sixty-one percent of the trade agreements of the last decade have included digital provisions and two-thirds of WTO members are now party to an agreement with e-commerce provisions.

Diversity in these agreements and regulations is a challenge (Table 4.2). Just under half of the countries in the region have negotiated trade agreements with digital trade provisions, with Australia, Japan, the Republic of Korea, New Zealand, and Singapore active since the early 2000s, as well as ASEAN. Japan led the development of an initiative in the G7 and G20 on "Data Free Flow with Trust" (WEF 2020).

---

[39]   Projects under the Framework, including the World Bank-managed DATA Fund, will provide capacity building and technical assistance to help developing and least developed countries benefit from ambitious digital trade rules.

Table 4.2: Participation in Bilateral, Regional, and Plurilateral Initiatives on Digital Trade

Economy	WTO JI on Services Domestic Regulation	WTO JI on E-Commerce	RCEP	CPTPP	AANZ-FTA	Other Free Trade Agreement (digital provisions)	DEPA	DEA
Afghanistan								
Armenia						VN-EAEU		
Australia	Y	Y	Y	Y	Y	Singapore; US; Thailand; PRC; Chile; Malaysia; Indonesia; Republic of Korea; Japan; Hong Kong, China; PACER Plus		SADEA
Azerbaijan								
Bangladesh								
Bhutan								
Brunei Darussalam		Y	Y	Y	Y			
Cambodia			Y		Y	Republic of Korea, Chile, Singapore		
Cook Islands						PACER Plus		
Fiji								
FSM								
Georgia		Y						
Hong Kong, China	Y	Y				NZ, Australia		
India						Singapore		
Indonesia		Y	Y		Y	Australia		
Japan	Y	Y	Y	Y		Singapore, EU, Australia, Mongolia, Switzerland, US		
Kazakhstan	Y	Y				VN-EAEU		
Kiribati						PACER Plus		
Kyrgyz Republic						VN-EAEU		
Korea, Republic of	Y	Y	Y			Singapore, EU, Australia, Canada, US VN, Colombia	Applied	SKDPA
Lao PDR		Y			Y			
Malaysia		Y	Y	Y	Y	Australia, Türkiye		
Maldives								
Marshall Islands								
Mongolia		Y				Japan		
Myanmar		Y	Y		Y			
Nauru								
Nepal								

continued on next page

Table 4.2 continued

Economy	WTO JI on Services Domestic Regulation	WTO JI on E-Commerce	RCEP	CPTPP	AANZ-FTA	Other Free Trade Agreement (digital provisions)	DEPA	DEA
New Zealand	Y	Y	Y	Y	Y	Singapore; PRC; Thailand; Hong Kong, China; Taipei,China; PACER Plus	Y	
Niue						PACER Plus		
Pakistan								
Palau								
Papua New Guinea								
Philippines	Y	Y	Y		Y			
PRC	Y	Y	Y	Applied		Australia	Applied	
Samoa						PACER Plus		
Singapore	Y	Y	Y	Y	Y	NZ, Australia, US, Republic of Korea, India, EU Jordan, Panama, Peru, GCC, CR, PRC, Sri Lanka, Türkiye, Taipei,China	Y	SADEA, UKSDEA, SKDPA
Solomon Islands						PACER Plus		
Sri Lanka						Singapore		
Taipei,China	Y	Y				NZ, Singapore		
Tajikistan								
Thailand	Y	Y	Y		Y	Australia, NZ		
Timor-Leste								
Tonga						PACER Plus		
Turkmenistan								
Tuvalu								
Uzbekistan								
Vanuatu								
Viet Nam			Y	Y	Y	Republic of Korea, EAEU, EU		

AANZFTA = ASEAN-Australia-New Zealand FTA, CPTPP = Comprehensive and Progressive Agreement for Trans-Pacific Partnership, CR = Costa Rica, DEA = Digital Economy Agreement, DEPA = Digital Economy Partnership Agreement, EAEU = Eurasian Economic Union (Armenia, Belarus, Kazakh, Kyrgyz Republic, Russian Federation), EU = European Union, FSM = Federated States of Micronesia, GCC = Gulf Cooperation Council, Lao PDR = Lao People's Democratic Republic, NZ = New Zealand, PACER Plus = Pacific Agreement on Closer Economic Relations, PRC = People's Republic of China, RCEP = Regional Comprehensive Economic Partnership Agreement, SADEA = Singapore-Australia DEA, SKDPA = Singapore-Korea Digital Partnership Agreement, UKSDEA = United Kingdom-Singapore DEA VN-EAEU = Viet Nam-EAEU; US = United States.
Source: Adapted from Nemoto and López-González (2021) and Gao (2022).

Data and digital trade models

Observers of the global digital economy identify three major "data realms": the US, the PRC, and the EU (Aaronson and Leblond 2018). The US and the PRC together account for about 90% of the market capitalization of the world's largest digital platforms, half of the world's hyperscale data centers, and some of the highest rates of technological innovation in the world, including in robotics and artificial intelligence. The US and the PRC approaches have, respectively, influenced the design of the e-commerce chapters in the CPTPP and the RCEP, the two "mega-regional" FTAs in the region. The RCEP e-commerce chapter is similar to the CPTPP in many respects (Box 3.2 in the previous chapter discusses the differences), but provides considerably greater regulatory flexibility in the application of exception provisions to protect essential security interests. The RCEP e-commerce chapter is not covered by the agreement's dispute settlement mechanism, unlike CPTPP.

Understanding the distinctions between CPTPP and RCEP

The differences among these three "models" are best understood in relation to the way that the US, the PRC, and the EU seek to reconcile the respective roles and interests of individuals, businesses, and the state. Broadly:

    (i)   the EU prioritizes the privacy of individuals as a fundamental right,

    (ii) the US prioritizes the commercial interests of firms, and

    (iii) the PRC prioritizes security (or national security) above all.

These various approaches drive management of cross-border data flow regulation in key regional trade agreements, including the CPTPP and RCEP.

The CPTPP model

The pioneering CPTPP agreement includes many digital trade forerunners, including Australia, Canada, Chile, Japan, New Zealand, and Singapore. The US, a nonmember, is widely seen as having driven the design of the approach to data flows before it withdrew from negotiations.

The CPTPP provides for free flow of information or data across borders for business, but gives the parties the ability to enact measures to regulate flows for a "legitimate public policy objective". These measures must not constitute a "means of arbitrary or unjustifiable discrimination or a disguised restriction on trade" and must not impose restrictions on transfers of information "greater than are required to achieve the objective". There is no definition of "legitimate public policy objective". There is also a prohibition on forced data localization, with an exceptions clause along the same lines as the "legitimate public policy" exception for data flows (see CPTPP Articles 14.11 and 14.13). Neither of these articles applies to financial services (see definition of 'covered person' in article 14.1), but there is a related provision on the transfer of information for financial services in Section B of Annex 11.B.

These two data provisions provide strong protection of the interests of the firm, given—as has been discussed above—data flows play a critical role in digital trade models, and restrictions on data flows can inhibit the ability of businesses to engage across borders.

The CPTPP includes provisions for privacy protection and cybersecurity cooperation. Privacy provisions require Parties to have in place legal frameworks for data protection, taking into account already established international principles, and encouraging the development of mechanisms to promote compatibility in protection of personal information. Cybersecurity provisions simply recognize the importance of building national capabilities in computer security and using existing collaboration mechanisms to identify and mitigate malicious intrusions "that could affect the electronic networks of the Parties" (CPTPP Article 14.6).

Other core rules include the following:

(i)   prohibition of customs duties on electronic transmissions,

(ii) nondiscriminatory treatment for digital goods,

(iii) implementation of an electronic transactions framework, and

(iv) prohibition of forced transfer of source code as a condition for market access.

The CPTPP also includes a number of other measures to facilitate digital trade and increase trust. These span paperless trade rules, online consumer protection, and frameworks to minimize spam (CPTPP Article 14.1).

The United Kingdom is currently engaged in the formal accession process, and the PRC; Taipei,China; and Ecuador have asked to join. Other Southeast Asian countries and the Republic of Korea have also signaled interest. Commentators are divided on the technical feasibility of the PRC's application as the PRC recently implemented a number of digital regulations that suggest a roll back from the CPTPP's data model. However, PRC's membership of the CPTPP would be highly significant for the overall heft and reach of the FTA. It may have positive dimensions for some, especially those already in the CPTPP, but also raises complex and potentially adverse implications for ASEAN's least developed countries.

The RCEP model

The RCEP agreement includes seven signatories to the CPTPP (Australia, Brunei Darussalam, Japan, Malaysia, New Zealand, Singapore, and Viet Nam) along with the Republic of Korea, all other ASEAN economies, and the PRC. In contrast to the CPTPP, on the core issue of data flow regulation, the RCEP takes a considerably more flexible approach, preserving significant policy space for governments. This likely reflects the central focus of the PRC on data security, national security, and sovereignty.

The RCEP's e-commerce chapter is similar to the CPTPP, but the provisions on data flows and forced data localization are more flexible. Members are allowed to "adopt any measure that they consider necessary for the protection of its essential security interests." Nothing prevents parties from adopting or maintaining any measure that the party "considers necessary to achieve a legitimate public policy objective", provided that this is not applied in an arbitrary or protectionist manner." (RCEP Article 12.14 and Article 12.15). Unlike CPTPP, the chapter is not covered by the dispute settlement mechanism.

The RCEP provisions on privacy are weaker than the CPTPP, while the cybersecurity provisions in the RCEP essentially mirror the CPTPP approach. On privacy, parties are required to adopt or maintain a legal framework "which ensures the protection of personal information" of e-commerce users and takes into account international standards, principles and guidelines. There is a grace period of 5 years for the LDCs Cambodia, the Lao PDR, and Myanmar. The RCEP provisions merely instruct the parties to "cooperate, to the extent possible, for the protection of personal information transferred from a Party" (RCEP Article 12.8.5).

The RCEP includes two provisions that could help to deepen policy coherence on digital trade. A cooperation provision directs members "where appropriate" to work together to help SMEs, and identify areas for targeted cooperation. This "will help Parties to implement or enhance their electronic commerce legal framework, such as research and training activities, capacity building, and the provision of technical assistance" and sharing best practices, encouraging businesses to enhance accountability and consumer confidence, and participating in regional and multilateral forums (RCEP Article 12.4).

Second, the RCEP also includes "Dialogue on Electronic Commerce", with the involvement of stakeholders where appropriate, on the cooperation topics noted above, along with current and emerging issues (the treatment of digital products, source code, data flow and data localization), competition policy, online dispute resolution and skills development (RCEP Article 12.6). This provides a forum in which business interests could be reconciled with wider sociopolitical objectives emerging from a multistakeholder approach (ADB 2022b).

These CPTPP and RCEP models, particularly on data, reflect the different trade and economic interests of the US and the PRC: the US perspective of a large digital services exporter versus the PRC's perspective of a large producer, consumer, and exporter of platform-based physical goods trade. The agreements also reflect their different underlying political and governance philosophies. The PRC's application to join the CPTPP merits watching closely. If it were to go ahead, the inclusion of the PRC in the CPTPP would necessitate a shift for the PRC's approach to digital trade rules on data flows and forced data localization and, in particular, a tighter set of exceptions including around "security" and dispute settlement.

The EU model

In contrast, the EU model centers on the privacy of the individual. The EU sees privacy as a core human right and until recently did not negotiate on data flows. Instead, it relied on its 2018 General Data Protection Agreement to prohibit the transfer of personal data outside the EU unless the privacy protection standards in the foreign market are deemed adequate. Later, the EU has sought to develop a new approach with a raft of new legislation including the Digital Services Act, Digital Single Market, and a new Data Act under development. Its December 2020 Trade and Cooperation Agreement with the UK includes a digital chapter with data flow and data localization provisions, as well as a number of other topics (e-contracts, e-signatures, paperless trade, consumer protection, spam, and cooperation on emerging technologies such as artificial intelligence and quantum computing).

4.2.2 Recent Advances in Digital Trade Rules: Digital Economy Agreements

A new approach to (DEAs) is being developed by some of the smaller economies in the region. These countries have a strong interest in seeing a more seamless and coherent digital market for their exporters, but also seek to address a range of broader policy issues. The DEA model accordingly includes core disciplines on data flows and data localization drawn from the CPTPP, but also brings in a far wider range of topics. Fundamentally, it is a governance model based in collaborative approaches, the development of soft norms as pointers toward eventual legally binding commitments, and a bias toward interoperability as a first step toward eventual harmonization.

The Digital Economy Partnership Agreement (DEPA), signed by Chile, New Zealand, and Singapore in mid-2020 is an "open plurilateral", which includes a formal accession process (DEPA Article 16.4). The DEPA parties have publicly encouraged other countries to join provided they can meet the high standards of the agreement.

The Republic of Korea is in the process of accession, and the PRC and Canada have both signaled that they would like to accede.[40] PRC accession would mark a notable evolution in its digital trade approach, building on its RCEP commitments. The accession of the Republic of Korea would likewise be significant given the relatively limited scope of its previous digital trade commitments and the potential size and dynamism of its digital economy.

Other DEAs negotiated or under negotiation in the region are bilateral agreements or new digital chapters of existing FTAs, rather than standalone agreements. Singapore has led this approach with the Singapore-Australia DEA, which entered into force December 2020. It constitutes a new chapter in the 2003 bilateral FTA. The United Kingdom-Singapore DEA, signed in February 2022, builds on the bilateral FTA of February 2021. A digital partnership agreement between the Republic of Korea and Singapore was substantially concluded (but not yet finalized) in December 2021.

The digital trade chapters of the Australia-UK FTA and New Zealand-UK FTA, signed in December 2021 and March 2022, respectively, follow a similar model, as does the December 2021 ASEAN E-Commerce Agreement , although to a less ambitious extent. Nascent initiatives include: Singapore's negotiations for a DEA with Viet Nam, informal talks with the EU launched in December 2021, and a new "partnership" on digital and green economy cooperation signed with France in March 2022.[41]

Coverage of Digital Economy Agreements

These agreements include a far wider range of issues than the preceding RTA e-commerce chapters. The basic building block is the CPTPP template, in particular, affirmation of CPTPP-style commitments on data flows, data localization, electronic transactions frameworks, and nondiscrimination in the treatment of digital products. Other elements of the CPTPP e-commerce chapter are also included. Three of the original country-authors of the DEPA were also founder-members of CPTPP.

However, the scope of the DEPA and DEAs is much wider than previous models. They seek a more holistic "digital economy" approach rather than the narrower notion of "digital trade" in the CPTPP and RCEP. Article 1 of the DEPA discusses "trade in the digital economy" (DEPA Article 1.1.1). Conversely, these new DEAs do not necessarily encompass the full range of digitally relevant provisions in a typical regional trade agreement, such as market access commitments for cross-border services, financial services, or intellectual property.

This "holistic" conceptualization is consistent with OECD analysis which points out that the approach to digital trade is not just about cross-border transactions, but needs to take account the entire value chain, such as logistics or e-payments. The OECD notes that what is needed is to approach market openness "thinking about measures affecting goods, services and digital connectivity more jointly, and about measures affecting the full value chain, including the enablers of digital trade, and tackling all these through greater international cooperation" (López-González and Ferencz 2018).

---

[40] For more information, see Damien O'Connor. 2021. New Zealand Welcomes the Republic of Korea's Formal Request to Joint the Digital Economy Partnership Agreement. 6 October; Ministry of Commerce. 2021. China Has Submitted an Official Application to Join the Digital Economy Partnership Agreement. 3 November 2021; Global Affairs Canada. Undated. Background: Canada's Possible Accession to the Digital Economy Partnership Agreement. https://www.international.gc.ca/trade-commerce/consultations/depa-apen/background-information.aspx?lang=eng.

[41] The Straits Times. 2021. Singapore, Vietnam to Work On Digital Economy Agreements. 22 June 2021; The Straits Times. 2021. Singapore, EU in Talks on Strengthening Bilateral Digital Trade, Forming Partnership. 8 December 2021; Ministry of Trade and Industry Singapore. 2022. Singapore and France Sign Partnership on Digital and Green Economy Cooperation. 14 March.

These new agreements cover four groups of issues, grouped within subject-specific "modules" in the case of DEPA (see Box 4.1).

Box 4.1: Digital Economy Partnership Agreement Broad Categories of Groups of Issues

Category 1 comprises core disciplines around data, including data flows, data localization, and a prohibition on the imposition of customs duties on electronic transmissions. Digital Economy Partnership Agreement (DEPA) reaffirms the existing Comprehensive and Progressive Agreement for Trans-Pacific Partnership (CPTPP) commitments, but does not create new obligations through the DEPA itself. Both the Singapore-Australia Digital Economy Agreement (DEA) and United Kingdom-Singapore DEA, but not DEPA, include financial services in the coverage of the prohibition on forced data localization. These provisions are potentially valuable for business, given the central role of electronic payment services in trade.

Category 2 includes provisions to support the facilitation of end-to-end digital trade transactions and to build up business and consumer trust. These include gold-standard rules on paperless trade and personal information protection which go further than the CPTPP and Regional Comprehensive Economic Partnership (RCEP) approaches. The DEPA approach mandates nondiscriminatory practices in protecting users' privacy, greater transparency in privacy protections, and directs parties "to pursue the development of mechanisms to promote compatibility and interoperability between their different regimes". These include autonomous or mutual recognition, reference to international frameworks, use of trust marks, and other avenues of transfer of personal information (DEPA Article 4.2).

This second group of issues also encompasses a host of novel issues, such as electronic invoicing, electronic payments, online consumer protection, and transparency. Other CPTPP-style provisions, on spam and cybersecurity cooperation (which do not go significantly further than the CPTPP template), are also included (DEPA Modules 2, 4, 5 and 6).

Category 3 sets up cooperative processes and frameworks for emerging technologies and policy issues including artificial intelligence, digital identities, fintech, data innovation, open government data, including the importance of a rich and accessible public domain. There are also undertakings for future cooperation on competition policy, logistics and government procurement, as well as other issues. In most of these rapidly developing areas, progress is on a best-endeavors basis, rather than through binding commitments, reflecting that the collective understanding of the economic, legal, regulatory, and societal implications of these technologies for trade is still evolving and they may not yet be ready for binding hard law (DEPA Modules 7–9).

The category 4 group of issues reflects the broader societal context of the agreement: there are modules that seek to foster greater participation in digital trade by small and medium-sized enterprises (including through greater access to information, knowledge-sharing on best practices, and the establishment of an "SME Dialogue"), as well as an inclusion module that seeks to support the participation of women, Indigenous communities, and other groups with untapped potential. There is also a brief best-endeavors nod to the growing importance of a safe online environment (DEPA Modules 10 and 11).

Source: Authors.

As Table 4.3 shows, this inventory of issues goes well beyond the core elements of CPTPP (although it should be noted that the table gives only a broad indication of the level of ambition of the various provisions). Nor is the coverage fully consistent across the agreements. DEPA goes further in some respects, for example, with a Module on "Inclusion" and provisions on logistics and cooperation on government procurement. The Singapore-Australia DEA goes further in other areas, for example with its provisions on standards and conformity assessment, fintech and regulatory technology (digital technologies to manage regulatory compliance in the financial sector), submarine cables, internet interconnection charges, stakeholder engagement, and regional capacity building. The United Kingdom-Singapore DEA similarly includes submarine cables and capacity building, but additionally introduces the novel topics of "lawtech" cooperation and electronic contracts.

Table 4.3: Topic Coverage in Regional Trade Agreements, Digital Economy Partnership Agreement, and Digital Economy Agreement

PROVISION	CPTPP 2018	USJDTA 2019	ASEAN 2019	RCEP 2020	DEPA 2020	SADEA 2020	UKSDEA 2022
No customs duties on e-transmissions	▲	▲		▲	▲	▲	▲
Nondiscrimination on digital goods	▲	▲			▲	▲	▲
Free data flows	▲	▲	▲	▽	▲	▲	▲
No forced data localization	▲	▲	▲	▽	▲	▲	▲
No forced data localization in financial services		▲				▲	▲
Electronic transactions framework	▲	▲	▲	▲	▲	▲	▲
Personal information protection	▲	▲	▲	▲	▲	▲	▲
Online consumer protection	▲	▲	▲	▲	▲	▲	▲
E-signatures, e-authentication	▲	▲	▲	▲		▲	▲
No forced transfer of source code	▲	▲				▲	▲
Cybersecurity cooperation	▲	▲	▲	▲	▲	▲	▲
Cooperation			▲	▲	▲	▲	▲
Paperless trading	▲		▲	▲	▲	▲	▲
Spam	▲	▲		▲	▲	▲	▲
Open government data		▲	▲		▲	▲	▲
Cooperation on competition policy			▽		▲	▲	▲
E-invoicing					▲	▲	▲
E-payments			▲		▲	▲	▲
Transparency			▲	▲	▲	▲	▲
Data innovation					▲	▲	▲
Digital identities					▲	▲	▲
Emerging technologies or artificial intelligence					▲	▲	▲
FinTech and regtech					▲	▲	▲
Products containing cryptography	▲	▲			▲		▲
SMEs					▲	▲	▲
Digital inclusion					▲		▲
Safe online environment					▲	▲	▲
Access to the internet	▲				▲	▲	
Interactive services intermediary liability		▲					

continued on next page

Table 4.3 continued

PROVISION	CPTPP 2018	USJDTA 2019	ASEAN 2019	RCEP 2020	DEPA 2020	SADEA 2020	UKSDEA 2022
Logistics			△		▲		▲
Government procurement cooperation					△		▲
Standards and conformity assessment						▲	▲
Submarine cable						▲	▲
Interconnection charge sharing	▲					▲	
Stakeholder engagement			△	△		△	△
Capacity building						▲	▲
Lawtech cooperation							▲
Public domain					▲		

DEA = digital economy agreement, DEPA = Digital Economy Partnership Agreement, fintech = financial technology, regtech = regulatory technology, SMEs = small and medium-sized enterprises.
Note: Darker triangles denote a higher level of ambition than paler triangles. Inverted triangles denote a partial or low-ambition commitment.
Source: Asian Development Bank.

The level of ambition across these topics varies among DEAs, as Table 4.3 shows. In some areas of the bilateral agreements, a higher level of binding commitments has been achieved than in DEPA. By contrast, as a potential "building block" to broader outcomes, DEPA is designed to appeal to range of viewpoints, not just like-minded partners, so focuses on building coherence over time. DEPA is intended as a "living" agreement to which new issues can be added (DEPA Article 12.2). This reflects something fundamental about the nature of the digital economy: its rapid transformation means that regulators are challenged to design good trade rules in an unpredictable context, but also to design those rules in a way that adequately addresses this continual evolution (Burri 2021). The DEPA approach is a more agile approach than many previous RTA models, which have often required multiyear negotiating processes and lengthy periods before upgrading. Potentially, innovations from subsequent DEAs could be added into the DEPA if the parties wish it.

An important thread running through DEPA and the other DEAs is a strong focus on interoperability. This is a critical concept when seeking to design rules that can apply across a range of jurisdictions that potentially have quite different approaches to digital regulation. DEPA explicitly recognizes that the regulatory and legal frameworks across the parties may be different, for example in relation to personal information protection or digital identities, and seeks to encourage the parties to development mechanisms for cross-border interoperability where possible (DEPA Modules 4 and 7).

These mechanisms are identified as including autonomous or mutual recognition of regulatory approaches, the use of international standards, and technical mechanisms such as application programming interfaces. For example, for electronic payments, the parties "agree to support the development of efficient, safe and secure cross border electronic payments by fostering the adoption and use of internationally accepted standards, promoting interoperability and the interlinking of payment infrastructures..." (DEPA Module 2, Article 2.7).

Other DEAs establish institutional mechanisms to deepen coherence. The Singapore-Australia DEA includes a detailed article on Digital Standards and Conformity Assessment, which seeks to build common ground for potential harmonization. The Singapore-Australia DEA and the United Kingdom-

Singapore DEA are both accompanied by memorandums of understanding detailing work programs on specific topics—for the Singapore-Australia DEA, covering personal data protection, digital identities, artificial intelligence, data innovation, electronic certification of agricultural commodities, digital trade facilitation, and e-invoicing; and for the United Kingdom-Singapore DEA, covering cybersecurity cooperation (collaboration in areas such as IOT security, cyber resilience, and capacity building); digital trade facilitation; and digital identities. The United Kingdom-Singapore DEA also includes side letters on fintech (launching negotiations on a revitalized UK-Singapore FinTech Bridge), and on customs cooperation (to work on single window interoperability and supply chain digitalization).

A further key characteristic of this new model of digital trade agreement is a strong focus on collaboration and cooperation. These agreements serve as a vehicle to allow the parties to deepen their shared understanding of rapidly evolving technologies and policy. In DEPA's case, the agreement also establishes the Joint Committee to drive implementation and the continuing evolution of its coverage (DEPA Article 10.4 and Module 12). The agreements also emphasize the need for engagement with the business community and technical experts—for example, establishing various forms of stakeholder outreach including to small and medium-sized enterprises and the fintech sector.

ASEAN e-Commerce Agreement

A collaborative, holistic approach also underpins the e-Commerce agreement of the Association of Southeast Asian Nations, another important agreement in the region, which entered into force in December 2021. As with the DEPA, it is largely based on cooperation and best endeavors, and designed as a pathfinder toward a "regionally integrated digital economy" (ASEAN 2021).

The ASEAN agreement contains core commitments on maintaining or adopting domestic laws and regulations governing electronic transactions and transparency. It also includes provisions on accessing and moving data across borders, subject to certain safeguards, including relatively soft language about "working toward eliminating or minimizing barriers to the flow of information across borders", and on personal information protection and online consumer protection. It commits ASEAN members to expand use of paperless trading, electronic signatures and authentication, and electronic payments, to be more transparent about consumer protection measures, and to endeavor to lower the cost of logistics.

There is also a list of areas for cooperation, including on information and communication technology infrastructure, digital skills development, online consumer protection, trade facilitation, e-payments, logistics for e-commerce, intellectual property rights, competition policy, and cybersecurity. The agreement provides for stakeholder engagement, creates an institutional structure to make progress on these issues, and mandates a review in 3 years. Overall, however, the balance of the provisions is toward best-endeavors rather than binding commitments (Tham 2021).

PACER Plus

The PACER Plus agreement, involving Australia and New Zealand as well as most Pacific Forum Island Countries, includes a range of development cooperation activities during the negotiation of the agreement, including aid for trade in relation to the development of a digital customs border management and trade facilitation system, ASYCUDA World. In services, PACER Plus includes a range of measures, including access to specialized skills and transfer of technology from other PACER Plus Parties (Zhuawu 2021).

Future directions

The DEPA was explicitly intended to foster broader coherence across the region and globally. The New Zealand Ministry of Foreign Affairs and Trade website expresses the "hope that this new agreement will generate new ideas and approaches that can be used by members in the WTO negotiations, and by other countries negotiating free trade agreements or engaging in international digital economy or digital trade work" (MFAT 2022a). Individual modules from the DEPA can also be used by others in their own regional trade agreements, contributing to greater coherence across agreements.

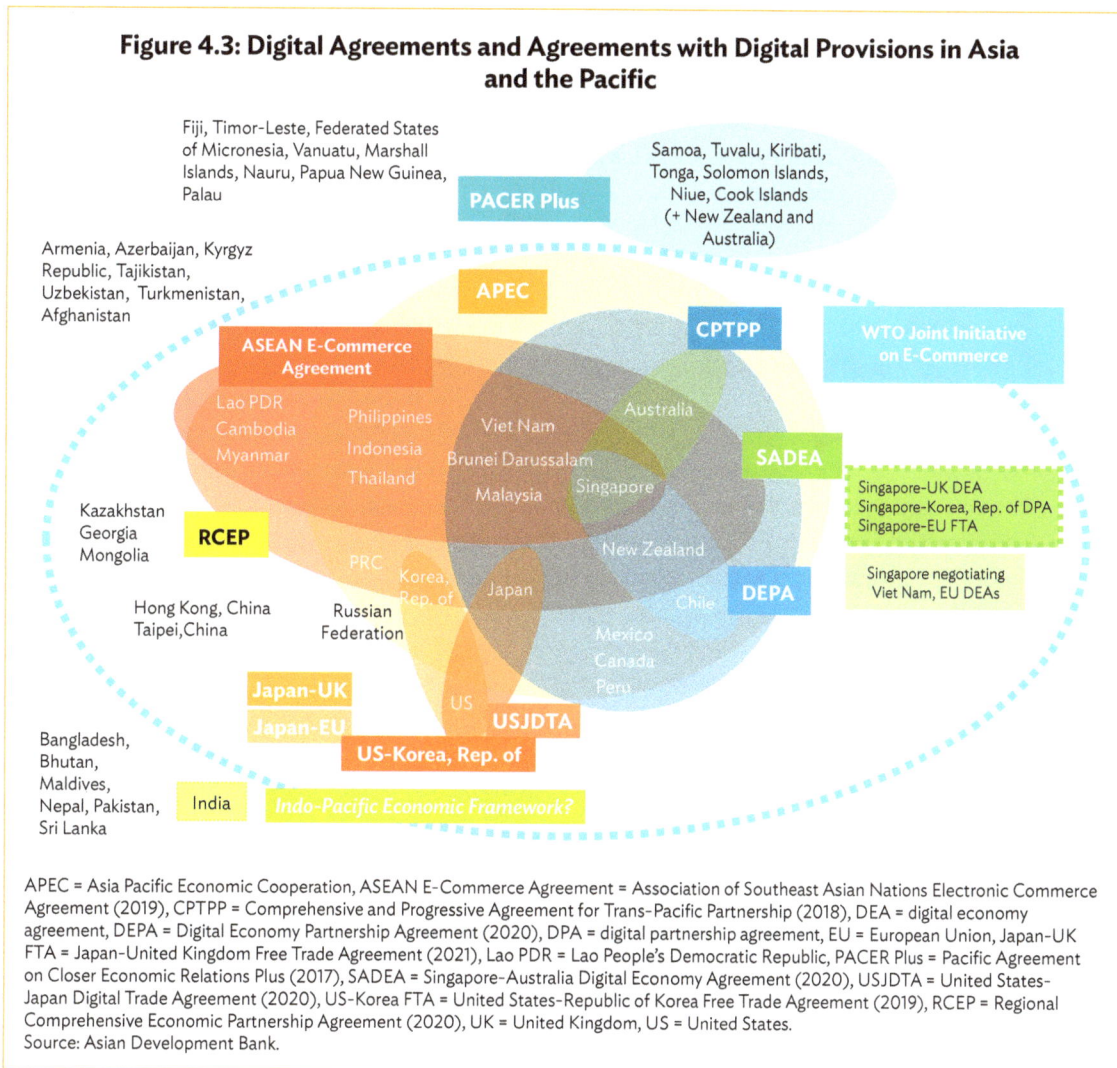

Figure 4.3: Digital Agreements and Agreements with Digital Provisions in Asia and the Pacific

APEC = Asia Pacific Economic Cooperation, ASEAN E-Commerce Agreement = Association of Southeast Asian Nations Electronic Commerce Agreement (2019), CPTPP = Comprehensive and Progressive Agreement for Trans-Pacific Partnership (2018), DEA = digital economy agreement, DEPA = Digital Economy Partnership Agreement (2020), DPA = digital partnership agreement, EU = European Union, Japan-UK FTA = Japan-United Kingdom Free Trade Agreement (2021), Lao PDR = Lao People's Democratic Republic, PACER Plus = Pacific Agreement on Closer Economic Relations Plus (2017), SADEA = Singapore-Australia Digital Economy Agreement (2020), USJDTA = United States-Japan Digital Trade Agreement (2020), US-Korea FTA = United States-Republic of Korea Free Trade Agreement (2019), RCEP = Regional Comprehensive Economic Partnership Agreement (2020), UK = United Kingdom, US = United States.
Source: Asian Development Bank.

Bringing on board a broader range of economies would help to counter one of the challenges of the increase in digital trade agreements, namely a growing regulatory heterogeneity. Figure 4.3 illustrates the complexity of the current digital trade regulation landscape in Asia and the Pacific, with many overlapping agreements potentially creating a "digital noodle bowl" of divergent provisions on core regulatory issues. It is interesting to note that some of the strongest performers in growth of digitally deliverable services in the region, such as Nepal, are not part of this web of agreements—nor is digital services giant, India.

Potentially, the DEPA or DEA-style model may help streamline trade rules across the region—but equally may struggle to build sufficient critical mass to achieve greater coherence overall.

Some elements of the DEPA could be included in the revision of existing agreements or negotiation of new trade agreements in the region, such as a possible upgrading of the CPTPP (CPTPP Commission 2021). Another good candidate is the ASEAN-Australia-New Zealand Free Trade Agreement, which is undergoing an upgrade negotiation that will focus, among other things, on e-commerce (MFAT 2022b). The US also recently announced its intention to negotiate an "Indo-Pacific Economic Framework" involving some countries in the region, which will have a digital component (White House 2022).

On the other hand, there is room for confusion about how these individual DEA models or upgraded free trade agreements will interact with other agreements. For example, for the seven countries party to both the CPTPP and RCEP, the exceptions clause in the e-commerce chapter for data flows and data localization is more flexible in the latter than the former. Article 20 of RCEP provides that if a party considers a provision of the agreement to be inconsistent with another agreement, the relevant parties will consult with a view to reaching a mutually satisfactory solution. How this might work in practice remains to be seen.

4.2.3 Fostering the Participation of Developing Countries in Digital Agreements

Several conclusions can be drawn from the discussion above. First, digital services trade holds substantial promise for developing Asia and the Pacific. Countries with better digital connectivity have a greater degree of trade openness and sell more products to more markets: more digitalization means more trade (López-González and Ferencz 2018). Digitally deliverable services trade is also more robust and resilient. This is valuable as a strategy for long-term economic development and short-term support for recovery from the pandemic.

Second, digital transformation can contribute importantly to the achievement of many of the UN SDGs, as noted, particularly SDG1 (poverty), SDG5 (gender equality), SDG8 (decent work and economic growth), SDG9 (industry, innovation and infrastructure), and SDG10 (reduced inequalities). Developing countries will need to take full advantage of digital trade to achieve broader policy goals.

Digitally delivered services face a range of barriers in international markets, and services exporters can struggle if regulatory settings at home or in foreign markets are opaque, costly, or highly heterogenous. Even simply achieving greater certainty in the trade environment and barriers that exporters face has value—especially for the rapid transformations of the digital economy (Handley and Limão 2022). Accordingly, need exists to develop a stronger and more coherent regulatory environment for digital trade—something on which participation in digital trade agreements (particularly those designed as building blocks to broader outcomes, such as the DEPA) can make a meaningful contribution.

Governments face challenges related to the "digital divide" and inclusion. This is an issue both within and across countries. Governments must grapple with challenges including the development of adequate infrastructure, skills and technologies, as well as creating an enabling regulatory environment, in order to support broader uptake of digital opportunities. At the same time, there are potent benefits for inclusion: small and medium-sized enterprises, women entrepreneurs, and those from other underserved groups may be able to leapfrog structural and other impediments that would otherwise curtail their ability to participate in trade.

Despite its importance, little aid for trade has gone toward supporting the digital economy. A mere $0.4 billion went to aid for trade for digital economy issues in 2017–2019, representing only 0.4% of total aid for trade disbursements. Developing economies and the international community will need to invest in (or be supported to invest in) a range of important challenges around infrastructure and digital connectivity, investment in and access to technologies, and digital literacy and skills; indeed, this has been a focus of aid for trade to date (Mbise 2022, ADB 2022a). Even within the "infrastructure" category of aid for trade, ICT is a small proportion relative to transport and storage (see section 1.1). Aid for trade has an important role to play in meeting several related challenges, but doing so will mean ramping up the portion devoted to the digital economy.

Bibliography

Aaronson, S. A. and P. Leblond. 2018. Another Digital Divide: The Rise of Data Realms and Its Implications for the WTO. *Journal of International Economic Law*. 21 (2). pp. 245–272.

Andrenelli, A. and J. López-González. 2019. Electronic Transmissions and International Trade: Shedding New Light on the Moratorium Debate. *OECD Trade Policy Papers*. No. 233. Paris: OECD Publishing.

Asia-Pacific Economic Cooperation (APEC). 2021. Leaders' Declaration. 12 November.

Asian Development Bank (ADB). 2018. *Embracing the e-Commerce Revolution in Asia and the Pacific*. Manila.

_____. 2020. *Asia Small and Medium-Sized Enterprise Monitor 2020*. Manila.

_____. 2021a. *Asian Economic Integration Report 2021: Making Digital Platforms Work for Asia and the Pacific*. Manila.

_____. 2021b. *Asia-Pacific Financial Inclusion Forum 2021: Emerging Priorities in the COVID-19 Era*. December. Manila.

_____. 2022a. *Asian Economic Integration Report: Advancing Digital Services Trade in Asia and the Pacific*. Manila.

_____. 2022b. *The Regional Comprehensive Economic Partnership Agreement. A New Paradigm in Asian Regional Cooperation*. Manila.

Association of Southeast Asian Nations (ASEAN). 2021. ASEAN Agreement on Electronic Commerce Official Enters into Force. 3 December. https://asean.org/asean-agreement-on-electronic-commerce-officially-enters-into-force/.

Baiker, L., E. Bertola, and M. Jelitto. 2021. Services Domestic Regulation—Locking in Good Regulatory Practices. *WTO Staff Working Paper* ERSD-2021-1 4. Geneva: World Trade Organization.

Baldwin, R. 2019. *The Globotics Upheaval: Globalisation, Robotics and the Future of Work*. New York, NY: Oxford University Press

Burri, M., and R. Polanco. 2020. Digital Trade Provisions in Preferential Trade Agreements: Introducing a New Dataset. *Journal of International Economic Law*. 23 (1): pp. 187–220.

Burri, M. 2021. Digital Transformation. Heralding in a New Era for International Trade Law. *Trade, Law and Development*. 13 (1): pp. 38–62.

CPA Australia . 2021. *Asia-Pacific Small Business Survey 2020–21*.

Chang, L. 2021. Ensuring Cyber Security for Digital Services Trade. Manuscript.

Cirera, X., D. Comin, M. Cruz, K. Lee, and J. Torres. 2022. Technology and Resilience. *CEPR Discussion Paper*. No. 16885.

Coghi, J. 2021. 5 Ways a New WTO Agreement Will Remove Barriers to Trade in Services. Geneva: World Economic Forum.

Cory, N. and L. Dascoli. 2021. How Barriers to Cross-Border Data Flows are Spreading Globally, What they Cost, and How to Address Them. Information Technology & Innovation Foundation. Washington, DC.

CPTPP Commission. 2021. Decision by the Commission of the CPTPP Regarding Establishment of a Committee on Electronic Commerce. Fifth CPTPP Commission Meeting, 1 September.

Crivelli, P. and S. Inama. 2022. China's CPTPP Accession and Implications for ASEAN. *ASEAN Focus* No. 38. ASEAN Studies Centre, ISEAS-Yusof Ishak Institute.

Dingel, J. and B. Neiman. 2020. How Many Jobs Can Be Done at Home? *NBER Working Paper.* No. 6948. Cambridge, MA: National Bureau of Economic Research.

Drake-Brockman, J. 2020. Australia-Singapore Digital Trade Agreement: Setting New Benchmarks in Trade Governance. *Institute for International Trade.* 24 August.

eMarketer. 2020. *Global E-Commerce 2020.* https://www.emarketer.com/content/global-ecommerce-2020.

European Union (EU). Digital Strategy. https://digital-strategy.ec.europa.eu/en/policies/strategy-data.

Ferracane, M. H. Lee-Makiyama, and E. van der Marel. 2018. *Digital Trade Restrictiveness Index.* European Centre for International Political Economy, https://ecipe.org/dte/dte-report/.

Ferracane, M. and M. Li. 2021. What Kinds of Rules Are Needed to Support Digital Trade? In B. Hoekman, X. Tu, and D. Wang, eds. *Rebooting Multilateral Trade Cooperation: Perspectives from China and Europe.* London: CEPR Press.

Global Enabling Sustainability Initiative (GeSI) and Deloitte. 2019. Digital with a Purpose—Delivering a Smarter 2030. http://gesi.org/platforms/digital-with-a-purpose-delivering-a-smarter2030.

Gao, H. and W. Zhou. 2021. China's entry to CPTPP trade pact is closer than you think. Nikkei Asia, 20 September 2021.

Gao, H. 2022a. *Data Sovereignty and Trade Agreements: Three Digital Kingdoms.* Hinrich Foundation: Singapore.

_____. 2022b. *Digital Services Trade and Trade Agreements.* Manuscript.

Global Affairs Canada. Undated. Background: Canada's Possible Accession to the Digital Economy Partnership Agreement. https://www.international.gc.ca/trade-commerce/consultations/depa-apen/background-information.aspx?lang=eng.

Handley, K. and N. Limão. 2022. Trade Policy Uncertainty. *NBER Working Paper Series.* No. 29672. Cambridge, MA.

Hass, R., P.M. Kim, and E. Kimball. 2021. US–China Technology Competition. Brookings Global China Interview, Brookings Institution, 23 December.

Honey, S. 2021. Asia-Pacific Digital Trade Policy Innovation. In I. Borchert and A. Winters. *Addressing Impediments to Digital Trade.* VoxEU/CEPR.

International Telecommunication Union (ITU). 2021. Digital Technologies to Achieve the UN SDGs. December 2021. Geneva.

Kim, M. 2021. Background Paper on Digital Trade Agreements and Services Trade: The Case of Korea. Manuscript.

Korinek, J., E. Moïsé, and J. Tange. 2021. Trade and Gender: A Framework of Analysis. *OECD Trade Policy Papers.* No. 246. Paris: OECD Publishing.

López-González, J. and J. Ferencz. 2018. Digital Trade And Market Openness. *OECD Trade Policy Papers.* No. 217. Paris: OECD Publishing.

López-González, J., and S. Sorescu. 2021. Trade in the Time of Parcels. *OECD Trade Policy Papers,* No. 249. Paris: OECD Publishing.

Mbise, T. 2022. *Aid for Trade Monitoring and Evaluation—Preliminary Insights.* Aid for Trade Unit, WTO Secretariat.

McKinsey. 2020. How COVID-19 Has Pushed Companies over the Technology Tipping Point. 5 October.

Meltzer, J. and P. Lovelock. 2018. Regulating for a Digital Economy: Understanding the Importance of Cross-Border Data Flows in Asia. *Brookings Working Paper.* No. 113. Washington, DC.

Meltzer, J. 2020. China's Digital Trade and Data Governance. How Should the United States Respond? *The Brookings Institution.* Washington, DC.

Ministry of Commerce. 2021. China Has Submitted an Official Application to Join the Digital Economy Partnership Agreement. 3 November.

Ministry of Foreign Affairs and Trade (MFAT). 2022a. New Zealand Ministry of Foreign Affairs and Trade. https://www.mfat.govt.nz/en/trade/free-trade-agreements/free-trade-agreements-in-force/digital-economy-partnership-agreement-depa/overview/.

_____. 2022b. Upgrading AANZFTA. https://www.mfat.govt.nz/en/trade/free-trade-agreements/free-trade-agreements-in-force/asean-australia-new-zealand-free-trade-agreement-aanzfta/upgrading-aanzfta/.

Ministry of Trade and Industry Singapore. 2022. Singapore and France Sign Partnership on Digital and Green Economy Cooperation. 14 March.

Mishra, N. 2022. *Can Trade Agreements Narrow the Global Data Divide? A Novel Agenda for Digital Trade.* Hinrich Foundation: Singapore.

Nemoto, T. and J. López-González. 2021. Digital Trade Inventory: Rules, Standards and Principles. *OECD Trade Policy Paper.* No. 251. Paris: OECD.

O'Connor, D. 2021. New Zealand Welcomes the Republic of Korea's Formal Request to Joint the Digital Economy Partnership Agreement. 6 October.

Organisation for Economic Co-operation and Development (OECD). Digital Services Trade Restrictiveness Index.

_____. 2019. *Handbook on Measuring Digital Trade.* World Trade Organization and International Monetary Fund. 2019. Paris: OECD Publishing.

_____.2021a. *Development Co-operation Report 2021: Shaping a Just Digital Transformation.* Paris: OECD Publishing .

_____.2021b. Lowering APEC Trade Costs Through Services Domestic Regulation Reform. *OECD Trade Policy Brief.* Paris: OECD Publishing

_____.2022a. Services Trade Restrictiveness Index: Policy Trends Up to 2022. Paris.

_____.2022b. *International Trade during the COVID-19 Pandemic: Big Shifts and Uncertainty.* Paris.

_____.2022c. Aid-for-Trade Statistical Queries. oecd.org/dac/aft/aid-for-tradestatisticalqueries.htm.

Shingal, A., and P. Agarwal. 2021. Increased Digital Connectivity and Implications for Services Trade. Manuscript.

Solis, M. 2021. *China Moves to Join the CPTPP, But Don't Expect a Fast Pass.* Brookings Institution, Washington, DC: Center for Strategic and International Studies.

Suominen, K. 2021. The CPTPP's Impacts on Digital Trade and the Path Forward. Washington, DC: Center for Strategic and International Studies.

Tham, S. Y. 2021. Digital Commitments in ASEAN's Free Trade Agreements. *Perspective.* Issue: 2021 No. 163. ISEAS Yusof Ishak Institute.

The Straits Times. 2021. Singapore, Vietnam to Work On Digital Economy Agreements. 22 June.

_____. 2021. Singapore, EU in Talks on Strengthening Bilateral Digital Trade, Forming Partnership. 8 December.

United Nations Conference on Trade and Development (UNCTAD). 2021. *Digital Economy Report*. Geneva.

_____. 2022. E-Commerce and the Digital Economy in LDCs: At Breaking Point in COVID Times. Geneva.

_____.2022. Summary of Adoption of E-Commerce Legislation Worldwide. Geneva.

United Nations Economic and Social Commission for Asia and the Pacific (ESCAP). 2021. *Digital and Sustainable Trade Facilitation in Asia and the Pacific 2021*. Bangkok.

White House. 2022. Indo-Pacific Strategy of the United States. Washington, DC.

van der Marel, E., H. Lee-Makiyama, and M. Bauer. 2014. The Costs of Data Localisation: A Friendly Fire on Economic Recovery. European Centre for International Political Economy. Brussels.

van der Marel, E. 2021. Digital-based Services Globalization and Multilateral Trade Cooperation. *Global Policy*. 12 (3). pp. 392–98.

World Economic Forum (WEF). 2020. Data Free Flow with Trust (DFFT): Paths towards Free and Trusted Data Flows. White paper. Geneva.

World Trade Organization (WTO). 2019a. *World Trade Report 2019: The Future of Services Trade*. Geneva: WTO

_____.2019b. Singapore. Text Proposal. INF/ECOM/25, 30 April 2019

_____.2019c. New Zealand and Singapore. Proposed texts: E-invoicing', INF/ECOM/33, 9 October 2019

_____.2021a. Reference Paper on Services Domestic Regulation. INF/SDR/1. Geneva.

_____.2021b. Joint Statement Initiative on E-Commerce, Statement by Ministers of Australia, Japan and Singapore. Geneva.

_____.2022. E-Commerce Negotiators Seek To Find Common Ground, Revisit Text Proposals. Geneva.

WTO and WEF. 2022. The Promise of TradeTech. *Policy Approaches to Harness Trade Digitalization*. 12 April 2022.

Wu, M. 2017. Digital Trade-Related Provisions in Regional Trade Agreements: Existing Models and Lessons for the Multilateral Trade System. RTA Exchange. Geneva: International Centre for Trade and Sustainable Development and the Inter-American Development Bank.

Zhuawu, C. 2021. PACER Plus Implementation: A Development Opportunity for Commonwealth Forum Island Countries. International Trade Working Paper 2021/12. Commonwealth Secretariat.

Agreements (legal texts)
ASEAN–Australia–New Zealand FTA 2009
ASEAN E-Commerce Agreement 2019
Comprehensive and Progressive Agreement for Trans-Pacific Partnership 2018
Digital Economy Partnership Agreement 2020
EU–UK Trade and Cooperation Agreement 2021
Regional Comprehensive Economic Partnership 2018
Singapore–Australia Digital Economy Agreement 2020
United Kingdom–Singapore Digital Economy Agreement 2022
United States–Mexico-Canada FTA 2018

5. Policy Recommendations

After several decades of rapid growth in Asia and the Pacific, the region faces at best sluggish growth or at worst a deep recession in the wake of the COVID-19 pandemic, which saw some exports fall steeply and supply chains disrupted, limiting output. Economic growth has rebounded in 2021 and 2022, boosted by increasing domestic demand and healthy exports.

In the last decade, the region has also pursued trade liberalization as an engine to accelerate growth. This includes negotiation of new bilateral and regional agreements, the inception of the Regional Comprehensive Economic Partnership (RCEP), and implementation of the Comprehensive and Progressive Agreement for Trans-Pacific Partnership (CPTPP). With the exception of food exports, most economies have rolled back protectionist measures taken during the pandemic. Digitalization of economic activity, meanwhile, has helped Asian economies remain robust during the pandemic, and this accelerated digital shift is likely to play a key role in future economic growth.

Yet, not all RTAs are created equal—some deliver substantial market liberalization and regulatory coherence and some less so. Some agreements may not provide countries with additional benefits beyond the market access afforded by their existing trade agreement networks. Developing countries, especially the least developed, after losing market access due to graduation or preference erosion,[42] are nonetheless looking to negotiate market liberalization. It is important that aid for trade (AfT) support efforts to generate more evidence-based analysis of RTAs to inform governments about best practices in market liberalization and regulatory convergence.

Aid for trade has a strategic role to play in helping countries, particularly LDCs and lower-middle-income, address graduation, inequality, and the emerging digital economy. The $16 billion in AfT deployed in the region is primarily spent on promoting economic infrastructure and building productive capacity. If the region is to emerge successfully from the pandemic, it needs to be selective about how it fosters its growth trajectory, particularly how it shapes its trade agreements and its digital economy policies. Aid for trade should help Asia and the Pacific become more competitive, better informed of best practices, and more able to make strategic decisions promoting regulatory convergence. The assistance can help if it finances research, capacity building, and information sharing to improve efficiency and effectiveness in trade policy making and negotiations.

Despite its importance, a mere $0.4 billion went to AfT for digital economy issues in 2017–19, only 0.4% of total AfT disbursements. Information and communication technology represents a small share of the "infrastructure" category in AfT relative to transport and storage (see section 1.1). Aid for trade needs updating. Developing economies particularly LDCs and low- and middle-income countries will

---

[42] Graduation refers to the exit of a country from the LDC list. Preference erosion can be the result of unilateral tariff reductions or of the signing of free trade agreements among trading partners of a given country. For more details, see sections 3.1.2 and 3.2.1 of this report.

need international support to focus on a range of digital economy challenges, infrastructure and digital connectivity, investment in and access to technologies, and digital literacy and skills (Mbise 2022, ADB 2022). AfT has an important role to play in meeting these challenges, but doing so will mean changing focus and ramping up its assistance for matters related to the digital economy and adjustments to it.

Traditionally, technical assistance and capacity building in trade policy and regulations have focused on (i) explaining agreements, (ii) showing how they work, and (iii) advising on implementation. Very little of that advice is based on quantifying the value of trade agreements or on their effectiveness. Without generating specific evidence of what is working and what is not, including addressing inequality, category 1 of the AfT agenda may fall short in meeting the challenges of the modern Asia and Pacific economy. The challenge of noninclusive liberalization is a big one, as is the emerging digital divide. With expert and research support focusing on the specifics of trade and digital agreements, a modernized approach to AfT should provide an evidence-based view of trade liberalization agreements in all their complexity. This includes digital areas, identifying best practices, ways to reduce inequality, and issues that promote failure, such as overly restrictive rules of origin or nontariff measures (NTMs), and that promote effective trade agreements.

In Asia and the Pacific, AfT should also focus on agreements that promote intraregional trade, particularly given overconcentration of exports to the US and the PRC markets. And more AfT is needed to help unscramble and liberalize the regulatory noodle bowl of digitalized services delivery and digitalized trade.

Trade liberalization has been helpful to economic growth and development. However, it has been also noted that trade and trade agreements have not addressed the growing problems of inequality and environmental sustainability in the region. If the benefits from trade liberalization are to be better distributed, the countries must be able to provide labor market skills training and skills upgrading for sectors hurt by liberalization. And policies and programs that promote inclusivity need to accompany trade liberalization. Aid for trade likewise needs to provide much more analysis of inequality and the means to overcome it, including adjustment assistance and workforce retraining and skills upgrading. Aid for trade has a key role to play in ensuring that sustainable and inclusive trade liberalization can benefit poorer economies, small businesses, women, youth, and marginalized workers while fostering economic diversification.

The chapter proposes that AfT initiatives be refocused in several ways, each in its own section. Section 5.1 looks at the technical tools and knowledge needed to support policy dialogue and raise awareness; section 5.2 looks at country-specific technical assistance and capacity building; section 5.3 discusses trade adjustment assistance; and section 5.4 proposes how to reorient aid for trade.

5.1 Building Technical Tools and Knowledge to Support Policy Dialogue and Awareness Raising

(i) Assessing the incremental value of regional trade agreements and digital agreements

Aid for trade activities should identify the costs and benefits of trade agreements, best practices, and lessons learned in existing and emerging trade agreements. The case is strong for a capacity building program based on policy-oriented research with extensive coverage of disciplines that creates an expert class of trade policy officials able to understand, apply and use research findings to negotiate, draft, and implement trade agreements. Aid for trade assistance would be required to develop an innovative research and capacity building program tailored to identification of methodologies to assess the incremental values in all these areas and provide lessons learned.

Aid for trade can support governments in the following ways:

  (a) designing effective and trade liberalizing RTAs that deliver on expected economic benefits;

  (b) assessing the liberalizing, regulatory, and economic benefits of existing RTAs and new trade opportunities of subsequent overlapping RTAs;

  (c) examining preference utilization rates to assess the effective market access of existing RTAs and the incremental value of new ones;

  (d) promoting the equitable emergence of the digital economy; and

  (e) diagnosing the type of adjustment assistance countries and populations require.

Such activities will require improvements in human and institutional capacity among government and trade officials. Aid for trade can help to build capabilities to assess export structures and reliance on market access, to develop trade negotiations expertise (such as in drafting alternative language) and trade policy strategies, and to address the challenges of LDC graduation and the challenge to smaller economies looking to further integrate into the regional and global economies.

(ii) Building mechanism for notification of utilization rates, database, and user-friendly rules of origin

Developing countries—particularly smaller, least-developed, and lower-middle-income—require far more clarity on specific aspects of trade liberalization. Accordingly, AfT programming could provide or support the following initiatives:

  (a) In close consultations with government officials and the private sector, leading international experts should explore rules of origin issues to determine which ones enable uptake of preferences and which are less effective. Evidence-based policy options built upon demonstrated best practices should suggest ways for policy makers to improve rules of origin and related certification requirements to avoid repeating past pitfalls and failures. Research supported by AfT could identify areas of significant convergence in product-specific rules of origin and options for simplification. It could also recommend better trade facilitation provisions and self-certification. These findings can form the basis for capacity building programs and for an intergovernmental mechanism aiming for convergence and simplification of rules of origin. The RCEP built-in agenda provides an opportunity to initiate this intergovernmental work in Asia and the Pacific.

  (b) As exists for tariffs, a database and user interface could be established to give the private sector accessible information on product-specific rules of origin and related certification procedures of existing and future RTAs, including micro, small and medium-sized enterprises.

  (c) In building an effective and conducive monitoring framework for assessing the incremental value of RTAs in the Asia and Pacific region, web-based tools can be created for the notification of utilization rates among parties to RTAs.[43]

  (d) The ASEAN and RCEP secretariats—as well as the Comprehensive and Progressive Agreement for Trans-Pacific Partnership parties and Asia-Pacific Economic Cooperation—could take the lead in this area with AfT assistance to build public knowledge. With availability of data and research, countries could measure the extent to which Asian economies have used existing

---

[43] Data should be made public using models that are already existing such as those provided by UNCTAD on the trade preferences granted by the QUAD countries, namely Canada, the European Union, Japan, and the United States, to the LDCs.

preferences available under overlapping RTAs. They could also measure utilization rates in trade with preference-giving arrangements such as Everything but Arms and the Generalized Scheme of Preferences. LDCs in particular would benefit from this knowledge.

(e) This database could also be expanded to include information on tariff line phase-out under RCEP, CPTPP, and other existing and future RTAs. This information, which should constantly be updated, should be publicly accessible online, facilitating the activities of the private sector and researchers alike.

(iii) Exploring new models and other key areas for regional trade agreements

Aid for trade can examine new models and areas of RTAs through the following activities:

(a) Aid for trade could promote innovative research on the feasibility of GVC-based RTAs. This research could be done in selected industrial sectors. It could support the move toward a "whole of supply chain approach" in which all policies bearing on tariff and nontariff barriers at different stages of GVCs are treated together (Hoekman 2014). For example, a pilot scheme could develop a test of the effectiveness of future trade agreements or agreements under negotiation on a specific supply chain of major interest to LDCs and low- and middle-income countries, such as textiles and clothing. In such a scheme, cooperation with the private sector would be essential for collecting information on factors affecting GVC operations. The research would focus on key barriers along the entire supply chain.

(b) Efforts can be direct toward developing model RTA provisions to facilitate trade during a pandemic. A recent handbook[44] (United Nations 2021) put forward such model provisions for ensuring resilient trade during a pandemic. These provisions could be discussed, developed, and tested for current Asia and Pacific RTAs, in cooperation with international stakeholders. The template would cover areas such as definitions of a "public health emergency" or "shortage" of essential goods; classification of "essential" goods; and adoption of international standards for regulatory cooperation.

(c) Aid for trade programming could promote policy-aimed research, capacity building, and implementing mechanisms to reduce the adverse impact of nontariff measures (NTMs), especially those arising from sanitary and phytosanitary measures and technical barriers to trade. Nontariff measures in Asia are rising and major potential markets, such as the PRC, have imposed the largest number of such measures. More than 50% of total NTMs in the PRC and ASEAN are sanitary and phytosanitary measures. No clauses in RTAs provide WTO-plus disciplines that reduce the incidence of NTMs while their dismantling could generate wide benefits.[45]

(d) Aid for trade could help raise understanding about possible enforcement mechanisms and their implications for the implementation of trade agreements. Few dedicated studies assess the trend in use of trade remedies in the region, their impact, and the causes of and the increase in disputes brought to the WTO Dispute Settlement Understanding. Aid for trade could fill the gap by supporting dedicated studies on the use of trade remedies in the region, their impact, and their causes. It could support studies on the intensity of the use of trade remedies in regional integration, their trade, and economic consequences, and seek alternative options to dispute resolution, such as mediation.

---

[44] The United Nations Handbook on Provisions and Options for Trade in Times of Crisis and Pandemic is the outcome of a global initiative on model provisions for trade in times of crisis and pandemic in regional and other trade agreements (IMP) launched by ESCAP and UNCTAD, in collaboration with UN regional commissions, the WTO and other partner organizations.

[45] For example, in the proposed Transatlantic Trade and Investment Partnership between the US and the EU, the overall dismantling of NTMs in all sectors have been found far the most economically beneficial for both.

5.2 Country-Specific Technical Assistance and Capacity Building

The international community should develop and implement AfT capacity building programs to help countries adjust to and identify their options in the CPTPP and RCEP.

At the country level, AfT could enable the following:

(a) Assist countries in the design and drafting of RTA chapters dealing with behind-the-border measures, including building dialogue between trade negotiators and regulators of such policies.

(b) Help countries set up effective provisions regulating market access in a predictable and transparent fashion, so that the private sector could take advantage of them.

(c) Address areas such as trade in services, investment, environment, e-commerce, and digital services.

Aid for trade programming could build up negotiation and implementation capacity and seek to equalize the different levels of technical preparation among the delegations. It should enable smaller delegations to draft language based on substantive applied research, consultations, and expert advice. Beyond traditional activities such as studies, workshops, training, and specific advisory services, multilateral development banks and bilateral donors could fund activities for long-term engagements between international experts and staff to provide regular and continuous assistance to trade ministries.

In this context, AfT could specifically address these issues:

(a) **Implementation.** Implementation of the larger trade agreements, especially the RCEP.

(b) **Negotiations.** Negotiations related to the RCEP's built-in agenda and accession of LDCs and lower-middle-income countries to the RCEP and CPTPP, which is becoming increasingly attractive with forthcoming membership by the UK, despite its higher standards and deeper commitments.

(c) **Assistance to graduating LDCs.** Adjustment assistance could also help enable LDCs and displaced workers to meet the challenges of graduation.

(d) **Negotiations and implementation of digital agreements.** These agreements are proliferating and increasingly complex. The future economic growth of the region is closely connected with digitalization. The new generation of highly complex trade agreements dealing with the digital economy requires specific technical skills. Least-developed and some other developing countries may require capacity building in these skills.

The following are specific topics requiring priority attention.

(i) Trade policy making for graduating LDCs

A major challenge for graduating LDCs will be to develop and implement a credible trade policy strategy (Chapter 3). It is probable that LDCs will seek to negotiate RTAs with previous preference-giving countries and, as a second option only available to ASEAN LDCs, to participate in the negotiations of an eventual ASEAN-EU FTA. In both scenarios, a heavy dose of technical assistance would be required to ensure the outcome of these negotiations substantially meets LDCs' expectations.

Assessing the incremental value of RTAs or mega-regionals that LDCs may consider is a challenging task. An in-depth analysis of utilization rates of trade preferences under current and future RTAs would be needed, including identification of the best cumulation options. Governments in LDCs will also need to identify the complex and challenging issues surrounding regulatory concessions or proposals for concessions that may be elaborated in the context of RTA negotiations.

A cost-benefit analysis could also be undertaken for the coverage and ambitions of LDC accessions to RTAs. Even more challenging would be to build a framework and design mechanisms in RTAs for regulatory convergence on areas of special interest to LDCs. These are areas in which AfT can play a role.

Each LDC will need to elaborate its own trade policy responses to graduation, because loss of this status may also have negative implications for GVC market access, due to exclusion or changes in the cumulation criteria for the rules of origin.

(ii) A regional website targeted at small and medium-sized enterprise users

Parties to an agreement could develop websites targeted at small and medium-sized enterprise (SME) users to provide easily accessible information on the agreement concerned and how SMEs can take advantage. Financial and technical assistance should be made available to LDCs in this endeavor. In line with the RCEP's specific provisions, SMEs in developing countries, especially LDCs, could be assisted in the following priority areas: (i) promoting the use of electronic commerce; (ii) promoting awareness, understanding, and effective use of the intellectual property system; and (iii) sharing best practices on enhancing the capability and competitiveness of SMEs.

(iii) Digital trade policy

Work can be done to examine new approaches to digital provisions in trade agreements or as standalone digital agreements. Aid for trade should assist countries in navigating the complexities of digitalization and digital trade agreements, which are multiplying throughout the region (see Chapter 4). It could also assist countries in managing digital regulation, negotiating, implementing and enforcing[46] digital agreements, particularly in DEPA areas for promoting end-to-end digital trade, enabling trusted data flows, building trust in digital systems, and facilitating opportunities for participation in the digital economy.

The region is rapidly creating access to digitally delivered services, and even domestically focused businesses are more resilient to external shocks if they are digitalized. Both the RCEP and the CPTPP have chapters on e-commerce, while the US-Japan Agreement is very similar to Chapter 19 of the United States–Mexico–Canada Agreement (2019). The RCEP calls for members to work together on improving the electronic, commercial, and legal frameworks for MSMEs and on a dialogue in electronic commerce. Aid for trade should build on this momentum and to support digital trade policy making, while considering inequality: 4.1 billion adults in Asia have a mobile phone, but 1 billion have no access to financial services, and only 1.7 billion have internet access.

The RCEP recommends "targeted cooperation which will help Parties to implement or enhance their electronic commerce legal framework, such as research and training activities, capacity building, and the provision of technical assistance" (RCEP Article 12.4)). Similarly, in the ASEAN E-Commerce Agreement, cooperation is proposed on a range of important elements of digital trade and the digital economy,

---

[46]   New approaches and solutions to enforce digital provisions need to be developed. For example, RCEP e-commerce chapter is at present not subject to dispute settlement.

including information and communication technology infrastructure, digital skills development, online consumer protection, trade facilitation, e-payments, logistics for e-commerce, intellectual property rights, competition policy, and cybersecurity (Tham 2021).

Aid for trade interventions could be extremely useful in the RCEP's Dialogue on Electronic Commerce. This forum could help:

(i) forge a common position for RCEP members within the WTO's Joint Statement Initiative on e-commerce;

(ii) build convergence on social issues (inclusion, SMEs, access to internet, safe online environment) and the most advanced topics in digital innovation, such as artificial intelligence and financial technology;

(iii) implement CPTPP commitments and accession of new members to the CPTPP; and

(iv) gain accession of low- and middle-income countries to digital economy agreements.

The Government of Australia's regional approach to AfT and the digital economy is a useful example (Box 5.1).

(iv) Domestic regulatory settings for the digital economy

Boosting AfT for the digital economy will require meeting several related challenges. Countries need to ensure that domestic and trade-related regulatory and policy settings are transparent, enabling, trusted, and responsive to tackle challenges raised as economies transform digitally. Cross-border regulatory divergences, opaque regulatory approaches, and a lack of interoperability at the technical and legal or regulatory level can add to transactions costs and may even prevent service suppliers from exporting. Domestic reforms for services regulation along the lines of the Reference Paper for Services Domestic Regulation (WTO 2021) constitutes a first step. The development of good regulatory practices for the broader digital economy will also be key.

An important starting point is a national digital economy strategy to develop a coherent approach that addresses the regulation of core elements, including electronic transactions, data protection, privacy, cybersecurity, and consumer protection. It can also include important policy areas such as innovation and entrepreneurship, competition, infrastructure, connectivity, taxation, and digital skills development. It will be critical for future integration into regional and global digital governance that domestic regulation is as compatible with international standards and best practices as possible (ADB 2022).

Digital services trade holds substantial promise for developing Asia and the Pacific. Countries with better digital connectivity have greater trade openness and sell more products to more markets. In short, more digitalization means more trade (López-González and Ferencz 2018). Digitally deliverable services trade is also more robust and resilient. This is valuable as a strategy for long-term economic development and in the short term to support pandemic recovery.

Box 5.1: Australian Aid for Trade Supporting Digital Economy, Digital Trade, and an e-Commerce Enabling Environment in the Indo-Pacific Region

The Pacific Digital Economy Programme, which began in April 2021, supports activities to enhance the inclusive digital economy in the region. The program is jointly implemented by the United Nations Capital Development Fund, the United Nations Development Programme, and the United Nations Conference on Trade and Development. It aims to achieve the following:

- **Enable policy and regulation:** With (a) online training for the production of statistics on the digital economy to build capacity in national statistical offices, and (b) an inclusive digital economy scorecard, a policy tool developed by the Capital Development Fund to support countries in better understanding and monitoring the status of their digital transformation, to make it more inclusive.
- **Open Digital Payment Ecosystems:** Through (a) a regional "e-commerce" request for proposal submissions from Fiji, Solomon Islands, Tonga, and Vanuatu to support the development and/or expansion of digital payment solutions for micro and small enterprises using mobile-based platforms such as smartphones and computer tablets; and (b) a regional "ecosystem development" request for application calling for the deployment, expansion, and improvement of innovative agent models to expand use and access to digital financial services in Fiji, Vanuatu, Tonga, and Samoa. This targets marginalized segments such as rural dwellers, women, youth, and small enterprises.
- **Inclusive innovation:** With a regional network analysis and mapping of institutions supporting entrepreneurship to identify priority actions that will strengthen entrepreneurship and innovation in the region.
- **Empowered customers**: With the development of the digital and financial literacy survey questionnaire and study protocol. It is the first international questionnaire to be developed to focus on the combination of digital and financial skills. The survey protocol will facilitate collection and measurement of digital and financial literacy across the population and within specific groups.

The Government of Australia also supported the development of the Pacific Regional E-commerce Strategy and Roadmap, which is ensuring coordinated, cost-effective, and best practice approaches to address common challenges on e-commerce that directly benefit Pacific governments and the region's private sector. The road map, developed by the Pacific Islands Forum Secretariat, led to a strong partnership between member countries, donors, and development agencies to identify and pursue measures to improve the enabling environment for e-commerce. The aim is that all businesses and consumers are actively and increasingly engaged in domestic and cross-border digital trade—from tourism, fisheries and kava, to call centers. Endorsed by all Pacific trade ministers, the road map has mobilized donor funds for regional priority actions that are under implementation across seven policy areas: (a) national e-commerce readiness and strategy formulation, (b) information and communication technology infrastructure and services, (c) trade logistics and trade facilitation, (d) legal and institutional framework, (e) electronic payment solutions, (f) e-commerce skill development, and (g) access to finance for e-commerce.

The Government of Australia's A\$5.6 million E-Commerce AfT fund helped developing and least developed countries in the Pacific and Southeast Asia benefit from digital trade. Open to the private sector, governments, and other organizations across the Indo-Pacifica, the fund helped address priority barriers to e-commerce, build greater e-commerce capabilities, and leverage digital trade opportunities, including through COVID-19. Over 850 micro, small, and medium-sized enterprises have developed specialized e-commerce skills with support from the fund. Project examples include:

- Building the capacity of online businesses to implement response plans around cybersecurity issues in Indonesia.
- New draft e-commerce laws in Tonga, Tuvalu, and Vanuatu under consideration for online buyer protection, securing data privacy and cybercrime—if adopted will bring the three countries into line with international regulatory standards on e-commerce.
- One stop national digital tourism booking platform in Vanuatu.
- A mobile app that promotes compliance with regulations and requirements for production and export in Viet Nam allowing producers, exporters and consumers to access key information about products such as coffee, pepper, mango, ceramics, and natural fibers.

ᵃ The Indo-Pacific is a term used by Australia to refer to the region ranging from the eastern Indian Ocean to the Pacific Ocean connected by Southeast Asia, including India, North Asia, and the United States.
Source: Australia Department of Foreign Affairs and Trade.

The legislative coverage of digital economy issues is uneven across countries in Asia and the Pacific. Aid for trade programming could do the following:

(a) Investigate the range of important challenges around infrastructure and digital connectivity, investment in and access to technologies, and digital literacy and skills.

(b) Explore cross-border regulatory divergences, opaque regulatory approaches, and a lack of interoperability at the technical and legal or regulatory level and advise on the development of good regulatory practices for the broader digital economy.

(c) Advise countries in developing trade-related regulatory and policy settings that are transparent, enabling, trusted, and sufficiently responsive to tackle new challenges raised by ongoing digital transformation.

(v) Capacity building in other trade-related matters

Trade agreements go beyond market access issues to include trade-related matters such as customs procedures, competition, and procurement. The coverage of basic domestic regulatory structures is uneven at best in Asia and the Pacific. In the recent WTO AfT Survey, one question asked survey respondents whether they had a national strategy, policy, or plan for digital connectivity, including for the digital economy and e-commerce. Over 70% of partner-countries and just over 50% of donors responded positively—but it is also clear that, for many, this remains a work in progress. Countries will also need assistance in implementing new regulatory frameworks effectively, and in adapting existing legislation to new digital realities.

(a) Customs procedures

Regional and multilateral technical cooperation and capacity building as well as financial assistance could be instrumental in helping developing countries and especially LDCs implement commitments under mega-regional and other RTAs. Inefficient customs procedures lengthen lead times and raise trade costs. AfT in this area will help enhance competitiveness in recipient countries and strengthen GVCs.

(b) Competition

Technical assistance, including capacity-building activities, can play an important role in the implementation phase of the RCEP, and particularly of the CPTPP, which devotes an entire separate chapter to state-owned enterprises, and provisions are much deeper, involving obligations in other critical areas such as procedural fairness in competition law enforcement and transparency.

(c) Procurement

Aid for trade could assist developing countries in complying with the commitments embodied in CPTPP. Although RCEP LDCs are exempt from virtually all current obligations, they could still benefit from the proposed initiative, in the context of future negotiations under RCEP's built-in agenda.

5.3 Trade-Related Adjustment Assistance

(i) Financial assistance to graduating LDCs

In addition to technical assistance and capacity building, financial support to graduating LDCs, especially Bangladesh and Cambodia, could help them deal with the costs of loss of trade preferences. Well-targeted financial assistance, including budgetary support, could accelerate the medium and long-term process of strengthening LDCs' supply-side capacity, diversifying their export structure in products and destinations and improving their competitiveness.

(ii) Assistance to developing countries suffering from trade diversion

Developing countries that are not members of RTAs, especially mega-regionals, may experience adverse effects as a result of trade diversion (section 3.1.1). Financial and technical assistance could be instrumental in supporting the affected countries' efforts to adjust their economies to worsening trade patterns.

5.4 Reorienting Aid for Trade

This chapter suggests new directions for AfT programming and a possible new initiative to focus on custom-made research and capacity-building tailored to countries' specific needs. It would:

 (i)   develop applied research on trade liberalization agreements and their impact,

 (ii) become a key source of lessons and best practices,

 (iii) provide tailored trade policy guidance for governments to support them in developing policy and negotiating positions, and

 (iv) identify areas for and models of adjustment assistance programming.

Aid for trade needs the work of trade policy experts, economists, and statisticians able to quantify trade agreements and trade policy issues across a broad spectrum of disciplines—economics, labor, trade, and development. A new initiative could coordinate research and output with other expert trade policy organizations. In particular, new approaches to AfT could be designed to ensure close consultation with the private sector, labor organizations, universities, and specialist trade policy organizations from around Asia and the Pacific.

The new AfT initiative could have four broad product lines:

 • evidence-based studies, research on RTAs and relevant trade policy issues, such as digitalization;

 • databases that track the specific performance of trade agreements;

 • country-specific technical assistance and capacity-building; and

 • trade adjustment assistance.

The Joint Integrated Trade Assistance Programme format may serve as one reference model, with the necessary adjustments and updates (Box 3.4). The program worked to create synergies among agencies in delivering joint capacity-building activities. Under the program, agencies developed and refined instruments and methodologies to act together to the benefit of recipient countries. Each agency simultaneously delivered the best of its expertise to the beneficiary countries, enabling comparisons and cross fertilization.

However, the new AfT would differ from existing initiatives in that its research and advice could be forward-looking based on investigating proposed or new agreements to study their impact and effectiveness and provide country and/or region-specific advice to governments.

To implement the proposed aid for trade initiative, a multilateral trust fund could be established at the WTO or other trade-centric body with a clear mandate to design and carry out a tailored work program. The resources available will be shared at the outset among relevant institutions, based on the agreed work program, and used to develop synergies and complementarities among them while exploiting their comparative advantage.

This report highlighted the importance of AfT for development in Asia and the Pacific. By supporting trade and investment, AfT could reduce vulnerability, strengthen resilience, foster economic growth, and help developing Asia meet the Sustainable Development Goals. However, to achieve these long-term objectives, a refocusing and modernization of the AfT dating back to 2005 is needed to reflect new economic and trade realities. For this purpose, multilateral, regional, and bilateral cooperation is needed among donors and recipient countries thus ensuring sustainable and inclusive development for all.

Bibliography

ADB. 2022. *Asian Economic Integration Report: Advancing Digital Services Trade in Asia and the Pacific.* Manila.

Hoekman, B. 2014. Supply Chains, Mega-Regionals and Multilateralism: A Road Map for the WTO. CEPR Press. https://voxeu.org/content/supply-chains-mega-regionals-and-multilateralism-road-map-wto.

Mbise, T. 2022. *Aid for Trade Monitoring and Evaluation—Preliminary Insights.* Aid for Trade Unit, WTO Secretariat.

United Nations. 2021. Handbook on Provisions and Options for Trade in Times of Crisis and Pandemic. https://www.unescap.org/sites/default/d8files/knowledge-products/Handbook%20FINAL%20 4Nov2021(edited).pdf.

World Trade Organization (WTO). 2021. Reference Paper on Services Domestic Regulation. INF/SDR/1. Geneva.

www.ingramcontent.com/pod-product-compliance
Lightning Source LLC
Chambersburg PA
CBHW050044220326
41599CB00045B/7277